THE STABILITY OF SHAKESPEARE'S TEXT

THE STABILITY
of
SHAKESPEARE'S TEXT

by

E. A. J. HONIGMANN

*Lecturer in English in
the University of Glasgow*

UNIVERSITY OF NEBRASKA PRESS

LINCOLN

PRINTED IN GREAT BRITAIN BY
ROBERT CUNNINGHAM & SONS LTD
ALVA, SCOTLAND

Preface

A BOOK on Shakespeare will be casually picked up by a great many potential readers, and swiftly put down again by almost as many lost readers. The title perhaps holds out a false promise, or the author's argument seems so specialised that the general reader modestly owns his incompetence and abandons the contest to those more heroically inclined.

A study of Shakespeare's text need not intimidate the general reader —on the contrary, the subject positively invites the common sense of readers uncorrupted with prejudices who, in the words of Dr Johnson, 'after all the refinements of subtilty and the dogmatism of learning', must decide the fate of every new edition. Now more than ever this general responsibility for the text of Shakespeare should be publicly asserted, since editors are taking liberties with the text that deserve the most careful scrutiny. In the following chapters I have therefore kept in mind Shakespeare's enormous reading public: anyone acquainted with the plays will, I hope, find my argument intelligible. Where further documentation seemed desirable, for the benefit of specialists, I have resorted to end-of-chapter Notes and Appendices.

★   ★   ★

For permission to cite extracts from manuscripts in their possession I am most grateful to the Trustees of the British Museum (Burns, *The Cotter's Saturday Night*; Heywood, *The Escapes of Jupiter*; Keats, *The Eve of St. Mark, Hyperion, Lines on the Mermaid Tavern*); the Director of Harvard College Library (Keats, *The Eve of St. Agnes, Lines on the Mermaid Tavern, Ode to Psyche, On Fame I, Staffa, To Autumn* (two copies)); the Librarian of the Henry E. Huntington Library and Art Gallery (Middleton, *A Game at Chesse*); the Irvine Burns Club (Burns, *Address to the Deil, The Cotter's Saturday Night, The Twa Dogs*); Keats Memorial House and the Public Libraries Committee of the Hampstead Borough Council (Keats, *On Sitting Down To Read King Lear Once Again*); the Kilmarnock Burns Monument Library (Burns, *Address to the Deil, The Cotter's Saturday Night, Tam o' Shanter, The Twa Dogs, Winter*); the Trustees of the National Library of Scotland (Burns,

v

Lament for James, Earl of Glencairn, Lament of Mary Queen of Scots, Tam o' Shanter, To Robert Graham of Fintry (two copies); Keats, *On Sitting Down To Read King Lear Once Again*); the Director of the Pierpont Morgan Library (Keats, *Ode to Psyche, Staffa*); the Master and Fellows of Trinity College, Cambridge (Middleton, *A Game at Chesse*).

   Miss Mabel A. E. Steele, Curator of the Keats Collection, Harvard College Library, kindly checked some of my transcripts, taken from microfilms and photostats, with the originals. Mr Philip Drew helped me, most carefully, as a proof reader: and I am also deeply grateful to other friends and colleagues who read all or part of this book in manuscript and suggested various improvements: Professor Peter Alexander, Mr J. C. Bryce, Professor R. A. Foakes, Mr Bernard Harris and Professor Kenneth Muir.

Contents

Plate

Thomas Middleton's Autographs:
A Game at Chesse v. 3. 155-63.
facing page 61.

Abbreviations

THE customary abbreviations are employed for Shakespeare's plays, and for periodicals (*S.B.* = *Studies in Bibliography*, Papers of the Bibliographical Society of the University of Virginia; *Sh. Survey* = *Shakespeare Survey*, etc.). F=Folio, Q=Quarto, Q1=First Quarto, etc. Works frequently referred to are quoted by short titles only: their full titles will be found in the list below.

ALBRIGHT, *Publication*. Dramatic Publication in England, 1580–1640. By Evelyn May Albright. New York, D. C. Heath; Oxford, University Press, 1927.

ASPECTS. Aspects of Shakespeare. Being British Academy Lectures by L. Abercrombie, etc. Oxford, Clarendon Press, 1933.

BALD, *A Game at Chesse*. A Game at Chesse. By Thomas Middleton. Edited by R. C. Bald. Cambridge, University Press, 1929.

BOWERS, *Editing*. On Editing Shakespeare and the Elizabethan Dramatists. By Fredson Bowers. University of Pennsylvania Library, 1955.

CHAMBERS, *Eliz. Stage*. The Elizabethan Stage. By E. K. Chambers. Four volumes. Oxford, Clarendon Press, 1923.

CHAMBERS, *W. Sh.* William Shakespeare. By E. K. Chambers. Two volumes. Oxford, Clarendon Press, 1930.

DEKKER. The Dramatic Works of Thomas Dekker. Edited by Fredson Bowers. Four volumes. Cambridge, University Press, 1953 etc.

GREG, *Bibliography*. A Bibliography of the English Printed Drama to the Restoration. By W. W. Greg. Four volumes. The Bibliographical Society, 1939 etc.

GREG, *Documents*. Dramatic Documents from the Elizabethan Playhouses. By W. W. Greg. Two volumes. Oxford, Clarendon Press, 1931.

GREG, *Ed. Problem*. The Editorial Problem in Shakespeare. By W. W. Greg. Oxford, Clarendon Press, 1942. Third edition, 1954.

GREG, *F.F.* The Shakespeare First Folio. By W. W. Greg. Oxford, Clarendon Press, 1955.

GREG, *Henslowe's Diary*. Henslowe's Diary. Edited by Walter W. Greg. Two volumes. London, A. H. Bullen, 1904, 1908.

GREG, *Henslowe Papers*. Henslowe Papers, being documents supplementary to Henslowe's Diary. Edited by Walter W. Greg. London, A. H. Bullen, 1907.

JONSON. Ben Jonson. Edited by C. H. Herford, and Percy and Evelyn Simpson. Eleven volumes. Oxford, Clarendon Press, 1925 etc.

KEATS, *Letters*. The Letters of John Keats. Edited by Maurice Buxton Forman. Oxford, University Press, 1931. Second edition, 1935.

KIRSCHBAUM, *Stationers*. Shakespeare and the Stationers. By Leo Kirschbaum. Columbus, Ohio State University Press, 1955.

NASHE. The Works of Thomas Nashe. Edited by Ronald B. McKerrow. Five volumes. London, A. H. Bullen, 1904 etc.

O.E.D. The Oxford English Dictionary. Edited by James A. H. Murray, etc. Thirteen volumes. Oxford, Clarendon Press, 1933.

POLLARD, *Foundations*. The Foundations of Shakespeare's Text. By Alfred W. Pollard. British Academy Shakespeare Lecture, 1923. Reprinted in *Aspects*.

POLLARD, *Richard II*. A New Shakespeare Quarto. The Tragedy of King Richard II. With an introduction by Alfred W. Pollard. London, Bernard Quaritch, 1916.

RIDLEY, *Othello*. Othello. By William Shakespeare. Edited by M. R. Ridley (the New Arden Shakespeare). London, Methuen, 1958.

SISSON, *New Readings*. New Readings in Shakespeare. By C. J. Sisson. Two volumes. Cambridge, University Press, 1956.

S.R. The Stationers' Registers. (*Cited from* A Transcript of the Registers of the Company of Stationers of London; A.D. 1554–1640. Edited by Edward Arber. Five volumes. London, privately printed, 1875 etc.)

WALKER, *Othello*. Othello. By William Shakespeare. Edited by Alice Walker and John Dover Wilson (the New Cambridge Shakespeare). Cambridge, University Press, 1957.

WALKER, *Problems*. Textual Problems of the First Folio. By Alice Walker. Cambridge, University Press, 1953.

WALKER, *Troilus and Cressida*. Troilus and Cressida. By William Shakespeare. Edited by Alice Walker (the New Cambridge Shakespeare). Cambridge, University Press, 1957.

WILSON, *Retrospect*. Shakespeare and the 'New Bibliography'. By F. P. Wilson (*In* The Bibliographical Society 1892–1942. Studies in Retrospect. London, Printed for the Bibliographical Society, 1945).

WILSON, *The Manuscript of Sh.'s Hamlet.* The Manuscript of Shakespeare's 'Hamlet' and the Problems of its Transmission. By J. Dover Wilson. Two volumes. Cambridge, University Press, 1934.

Modernised quotations from Shakespeare, and line-references to the plays, are taken from Peter Alexander's *William Shakespeare, The Complete Works* (the Tudor edition, Collins, 1951), unless I state the contrary.[1]

In quotations from Shakespeare's quartos and Folio I change italicised proper nouns in the dialogue to roman, to avoid confusion with italics indicating variants.

In quotations from manuscripts I transcribe deletions in square brackets [ ], interlineations in half-brackets ⌐ ⌐, and barely legible letters in pointed brackets ⟨ ⟩.

---

[1] As this edition follows the line-numbering of the old Cambridge editors some prose passages are not numbered precisely, and therefore some of my references may be a line or two out.

I

The New Bibliography and the Stability of Shakespeare's Text

*

ONE reason for the astonishing successes of the New Bibliography has been its emphasis on checking inferences about printed books by comparison with collateral manuscripts of the same period. Such 'dramatic documents' as survive from Elizabethan-Jacobean times unfortunately total far fewer, and cover a smaller range of types, than Shakespeare's editors require, and as a result even the most cautious textual critics not infrequently indulge in what can only be called hopeful guessing, when manuscript parallels fail to turn up. In particular the editors have never given serious attention to the vagaries of authors in copying out their own work—because not many Jacobean dramatic manuscripts survive to throw light upon the matter. Yet abundant evidence may be gathered from later writers to make good the deficiency, wherever two or more autograph drafts of the same work can be compared: and a re-examination of the thousands of variants in Shakespeare after such a comparison will necessitate, I am convinced, a fundamental rethinking of our textual criticism.

Editorial procedure in so far as Shakespeare is concerned often traces back to the eighteenth century: and when it does the New Bibliography almost as often finds occasion for doubt, and for a fresh beginning. In the eighteenth century it was natural for the editors of Shakespeare to model themselves upon the slightly more experienced editors of the classics, and perhaps this accounts for the now scarcely questioned assumption that where two substantive readings differ one or both must be corrupt. An editorial tradition that disposes so easily of what could well become an embarrassment of riches inevitably recommends itself before the alternative that both readings may be correct, that is, may be the author's. But an editorial convenience must give way at last when new facts appear: and the many excellent studies of literary manuscripts brought out of late have circulated new facts and make desirable a close scrutiny of a very insecure tradition.

Sir Walter Greg received no thanks from one brilliant textual critic when at the end of his distinguished career he moved in the direction that I shall follow. He diagnosed in *Othello* abandoned 'first thoughts' and also the possibility of a second layer of authoritative, revised readings. 'If this is correct, chaos is indeed come again' countered Miss Walker.[1] 'Chaos' is too pessimistic a word, though my argument will not make an editor's lot more agreeable. In the long run, however, if I add another unknown quantity to his calculations, the editor will be able to take a firmer stand, simply because he will have retreated from a position of unjustified confidence: whatever his added burdens, the editor will see more clearly towards the frontiers of knowledge.

According to Sir Edmund Chambers' polemical masterpiece, 'the disintegration of Shakespeare is an open career for talent'.[2] Though, like Greg,[3] I subscribe wholeheartedly to Chambers' scepticism about literary revision and at the same time canvass for another form of textual instability, I keep to the windward of the disintegrators: to submit that Shakespeare introduced verbal changes in copying out a play is not to assert large-scale revision. My argument turns in effect on the concept of a 'finalised text'—though I take a rather different view from R. B. McKerrow's:

> It is very doubtful whether, especially in the case of the earlier plays, there ever existed any written 'final form'. Shakespeare as an active member of a theatrical company would, at any rate in his younger days, have been concerned with producing, not plays for the study, but material for his company to perform on the stage, and there can be little doubt that his lines would be subject to modification in the light of actual performance . . .[4]

While the main concern of the disintegrators has been to detect tampering with the text after its completion, I shall investigate the possibilities of authorial 'second thoughts' *before* its delivery to the actors. I envisage, in short, two copies of a play, each in the author's hand, disagreeing in both substantive and indifferent readings: the play being regarded as 'finished' by Shakespeare in each version though not therefore beyond the reach of afterthoughts. Manuscript copies of their own works by at least one contemporary of Shakespeare and by many later writers

---

[1] A. Walker, *Othello*, 1957, p. 125; Greg, *F.F.*, p. 369.
[2] *The Disintegration of Shakespeare* (*Aspects*, p. 31).
[3] *F.F.*, p. 345, n. 18.
[4] *Prolegomena for the Oxford Shakespeare*, 1939, p. 6; cf. Bowers, *Editing*, p. 127.

reveal precisely the textual instability which I postulate, especially when written out shortly after their original composition (as, one imagines, Shakespeare's 'fair copies' would be too). In rejecting the notion of a finalised text I picture, then, not so much a fastidious author's determined attempts to improve passages that fail to satisfy as an author so unconceited with himself and so fluent that little verbal changes, not necessarily always for the better, ran quite freely from his pen when the process of copying refired his mind.

Despite Sir Edmund Chambers' British Academy Lecture, research into Shakespeare's 'second thoughts' continued. A glance at some of the many tentatives upon the subject by so cautious a critic as Sir Walter Greg will give a taste of the dangers to be encountered, and may serve in lieu of a tedious general introduction.

In his *Principles of Emendation in Shakespeare*, 1928, Greg urged that some readings of *Hamlet* Q2, inferior to those of F and Q1, 'cannot be regarded as errors of the compositor, but must be supposed to have stood in the autograph'. He concluded that the better readings found in F and Q1 must 'have been the author's, or at least authorized, corrections, introduced into the prompt-book previous to the preparation of the actors' parts'. A second group of variants (Q1 and Q2 *versus* F) seemed to Greg to reveal 'deliberate alterations made in the prompt-book while in use, but subsequent to the preparation of the actors' parts'.[1] Dover Wilson, however, was able to show, from coincidental spellings and misprints in Q1 and Q2, that where Q1 and Q2 agree *versus* F the printers of Q2 consulted Q1, and that where Q1 and F agree *versus* Q2 'graphical similarity stares one in the face' (that is, misreading accounts for the variants).[2] This seemed to settle the question. Greg recanted, and in a holier-than-thou mood even declared that, after giving up his own theory of 'first shots' he felt 'little disposed to admit the one instance in which Professor Wilson is inclined to fall back on it'.[3] Nonetheless, he once more raised the possibility of first and second shots in other plays in *The Editorial Problem in Shakespeare*, 1942, though only with the utmost diffidence, thereafter to return to it with unexpected boldness in *The Shakespeare First Folio*, 1955.[4] In this

---

[1] Reprinted in *Aspects*, pp. 149 ff., 183 ff.

[2] J. Dover Wilson, *The Manuscript of Sh.'s 'Hamlet'*, I, 152–65. For another view of 'graphical similarity' cf. below, p. 67.

[3] Cf. Greg in *M.L.R.*, 1935, XXX, 84–6.

[4] See Greg's treatment of *Troilus and Cressida* and *Othello*, and compare with the discussions of the same plays in *Ed. Problem*.

last book he repeated that Dover Wilson had 'exploded' the theory of first shots and second thoughts in *Hamlet*, but also pointed out 'a double false start' in Q2 corrected in F.[1] One is moved to ask: What is the difference between a first shot and a false start? As evidence of textual stratification they are equally valuable, they both indicate that one version belongs to an earlier state.

Greg's special interest in *The Shakespeare First Folio* in the 'textual stability' of the canon emerges in a number of ways. He devoted a great deal of space to 'false starts'; he held that revision was possible in the course of preparing the prompt-book; and, the clearest sign of the times, he denied again and again that plays underwent revision *after* their first performance, submitting instead that textual differences and dislocations 'are best regarded as part of the original composition'.[2]

Though a few textual critics of note beside Greg have looked with sympathy upon the thesis of 'first shots', the new, advanced techniques of bibliography encouraged others in the belief that variants are witnesses of corruption and that texts convicted as frequent offenders will not turn out to be, in isolated cruxes, innocent.

> Probability for probability, which is the more reasonable; that out of a sea of 1300 variants a select handful are to be explained by Shakespearian revision which left the remainder untouched; or that the handful in question are simply part of the general corruption of these texts and to be explained, as I have shown they can be, by the same causes that produced that general corruption?[3]

The stand taken by Dover Wilson on *Hamlet* may recommend itself as a general principle—to the purpose that any argument for 'second thoughts' in a corrupt text should be stoutly resisted. Miss Walker seems to go to this extreme in some of her books,[4] and I therefore use these from time to time to point my moral. Such a principle is all very well as long as we are certain that our author did not copy out his own text and thus create a second arch-text, for, if he did, though one of the substantive texts is as corrupt as may be, on occasion it could speak true. Unfortunately we can make no sweeping claims about Shakespeare's arch-texts; and, far worse, no one has so far demonstrated the extraordinary similarities between authorial substitutions and the familiar

---

[1] *F.F.*, pp. 315, 314.
[2] See Greg, *op. cit.*, pp. 178, 204, 222, 242, 250 n. 9, 279, 289, etc. For Greg's comments on 'false starts' cf. his index.
[3] J. Dover Wilson, *op. cit.*, I, 165.
[4] Cf. p. 85.

types of textual corruption,[1] and therefore no one has faced the dilemma that in one and the same text these two sets of almost indistinguishable phenomena may join forces in a masquerade. A too confident identification of the disguised parties provoked a smile, in a slightly different argument, from A. W. Pollard.

> In most of the plays, if we look closely enough into them, we shall find enough discrepancies, enough evidence of what seems imperfect revision, enough diversity of style, to tempt us to believe that Shakespeare wrote all his plays in the years of his dramatic apprenticeship and spent the rest of his working life in constantly rewriting them. That theory is not much more untenable than its opposite which envisages each play as the result of a continuous effort throughout so many weeks and then finished and done with.[2]

Some say that Shakespeare rewrote his plays many times, and behind each inconsistency they detect a botched revision: others say that he wrote his plays only once, and behind each variant there lurks an incompetent scribe or a drunken compositor. But perhaps it is not so simple: perhaps corruptions and 'revisions' exist side by side. Dover Wilson feels he has won his case by whittling down the supposed first shots to a 'handful'. Neither he nor Miss Walker recognised that to allow, as they both do,[3] a single instance of 'revision' in a text is to supply the fixed point with which we may move the world. There might be only a single obvious one, but it is as good as a pledge that others lie concealed amongst the so-called corruptions. Once a single second thought is granted the 'sea of 1300 variants' cannot, I submit, wash away the likelihood of more second thoughts in the same text or group of texts: on the contrary, as Shakespeare knew, a single foreign body may put a new complexion on the most multitudinous seas. While some very able textual critics, such as Miss Walker, still

---

[1] In C. T. Prouty's *'The Contention' and Shakespeare's '2 Henry VI'*, 1954, an attempt was made to underline the resemblances between authorial revision and substitutions in pirated texts: my concern here is to compare authorial changes with non-authorial ones in good texts. M. R. Ridley, in his New Arden edition of *Othello*, 1958, used the text of Keats to explain editorial problems in Shakespeare (p. xxxii ff.), but relied on transcripts (which could be corrupt) in tracing authorial changes—whereas I prefer the evidence of two or more autograph copies of the same work.

[2] *Foundations (Aspects,* p. 15).

[3] Cf. Miss Walker, *Problems*, p. 74; Dover Wilson, *op. cit.*, I, 166–9. Greg swiftly pounced on the illogicality of the 'single exception', in his review of Dover Wilson (cf. p. 3), but seems to make the same mistake in allowing a 'false start' (cf. pp. 3–4, above).

strenuously oppose the notion of 'second thoughts', preferring to fall back always in the first instance on the hypothesis of corruption, a reaction to this overemphasis upon the compositor has already gathered force. Not only Greg's monumental *The Shakespeare First Folio* but also a transatlantic study of the first importance of the same year, 1955, showed how far the new bibliography has pushed beyond its immediate past. 'Few authors can resist the opportunity to revise during the course of copying', warned Fredson Bowers; and—'I am not so convinced as some critics that the perfection of Shakespeare's plays was achieved in only a single act of composition.'[1]

Ignorance of printing-house practices has led some modern scholars to represent 'the errors of compositors . . . as the milk of the word'[2]: Miss Walker's sarcasm landed very near the mark, but the pendulum has now swung the other way. We must now take care not to throw Shakespeare's words out of the canon through over-confidence regarding printing-house practices—which, I believe, has happened in some recent editions.

[1] Bowers, *Editing*, pp. 19, 107.   [2] *Problems*, p. 162.

II

The Transmission of Dramatic Manuscripts

★

BEFORE I turn to individual plays a survey of recent work on textual transmission will be essential. I shall take for granted the reader's familiarity with basic terms: they are mostly self-explanatory, except that 'foul papers' can be variously defined.[1] And I shall say nothing, for the moment, about such texts as lie outside the framework of my argument (e.g. plots, private transcripts). Four theories then deserve pondering.

1. *A. W. Pollard*. First in the field, Pollard proposed the simplest explanation, which must almost certainly be modified.

> In the case of some plays by other playwrights we find that it was the author's autograph manuscript which was first submitted to the censor and then used as a prompt copy and equipped with the notes and stage-directions necessary for this purpose. From the notes and stage-directions which occur in some of the printed quartos, there is a high probability that these were printed from prompt copies, and if what happened with other plays by other playwrights is any guide to what happened to Shakespeare's, some of these prompt copies were probably in his autograph. Some of them, also, were probably *not* . . . as a ready means of persuading the wardens of the Stationers' Company that a play might be printed without special 'authority' being obtained for it, the production of the manuscript on which the censor's licence was inscribed, as the copy sent to the printer, would carry all before it.[2]

2. *R. B. McKerrow*. Against Pollard's thesis that foul papers employed as the prompt-book (one text) would normally become the printer's copy, McKerrow contended that both foul papers and prompt-book (two texts) would be available to the players, so that the natural course for them to take would be to surrender the foul papers when they agreed to publish. If the printer smudged his copy, as sometimes

---

[1] Cf. Note A, p. 17.
[2] Pollard, *Foundations* (*Aspects*, pp. 6–7). See Greg's criticisms, *F.F.*, p. 88 ff.

happened, the prompt-book, if used, would be less serviceable when returned—and, since it contained production-notes and the official 'licence', it would be senseless to risk its loss.[1]

As a starting-point McKerrow demanded why Elizabethan-Jacobean plays are often so badly printed that they 'cannot possibly represent with any approach to accuracy what their authors wrote'. Were their printers 'an utterly careless and incompetent crew of rascals'?[2] Certainly not when they brought out non-dramatic books, which, as McKerrow showed, were printed 'with reasonable accuracy'. Fair copies would lie behind such cleanly printed texts, one assumes, and the obvious inference follows that the quality of the printers' workmanship fell away when they tackled dramatic manuscripts because their copy proved to be not fair but 'foul'. My summary gives only the bare bones of an argument to which R. C. Bald has paid the highest tribute,[3] though he added the caution that 'alongside a scientific hypothesis it [McKerrow's] has one grave disadvantage: it cannot be proved'.

3. *Fredson Bowers.* McKerrow's comparatively straightforward account of textual transmission, endorsed by Greg[4] and many more, has come under fire from Bowers,[5] who conjectured that more texts than the two postulated (foul papers; fair copy later used as prompt-book) must have existed in the early history of a play. 'Fouler papers' might precede the foul papers[6]; and an intermediate fair copy, not necessarily without some deletions and afterthoughts, intervened, in his opinion, between the foul papers and the second fair copy that would become

---

[1] Pollard saw that 'the owners of the play would not be likely to let such a precious thing as a prompt copy out of their hands', but felt that if a printed copy reached the players within three or four weeks 'this objection is greatly weakened' (*Aspects*, p. 7).

[2] McKerrow, 'The Elizabethan Printer and Dramatic Manuscripts' (in *The Library*, Fourth Series, 1932, XII, 253–4). Only 'good' texts are referred to, of course, not piracies corrupted before their arrival in the printing-house. McKerrow's article condenses, with some interesting changes, his unpublished Sandars Lectures of 1928, which can be seen in typescript in the British Museum ('The Relationship of English Printed Books to Authors' Manuscripts in the Sixteenth and Seventeenth Centuries', Add. MS. 41, 998).

[3] 'A brilliant and illuminating hypothesis, and the more likely to win acceptance from its simplicity!'—'It is a paper which can legitimately be compared to the one in which Darwin first formulated the theory of evolution . . .' (R. C. Bald, 'Evidence and Inference in Bibliography' in *English Institute Annual 1941*, Columbia University 1942).

[4] *F.F.*, pp. 96–7.

[5] *Editing*, Lecture I: 'The Texts and Their Manuscripts'.

[6] *Ibid.*, p. 13. So Greg, *F.F.*, p. 106.

the prompt-book. Reviewing Bowers, Greg recalled Occam's razor but raised no serious objections—even though the argument runs counter to his own expressed views. One reason for assenting to Bowers's thesis as perhaps valid in some cases (Miss Walker has argued along the same lines with regard to isolated plays[1]) is the survival of a number of texts that bear the marks of fair copies but could not have been prompt-books.[2] In the upshot Bowers swung round against McKerrow's belief that *normally* the players would hand foul papers to the printers:

> I am concerned . . . to point out that the evidence may not be so strong for foul-papers printer's copy as has been thought . . .

> I am not concerned to argue that the theatre never received an author's foul papers, but only that, in more cases than we have customarily thought, it is very probable fair copy was submitted instead . . .[3]

4. *Leo Kirschbaum.* Still another type of printer's copy has been suggested in a book which, again, appeared in 1955, Kirschbaum's *Shakespeare and the Stationers.* After arguing that the King's Men withstood the attentions of publishers anxious to print their plays less successfully than was once propounded, Kirschbaum looked at some of Shakespeare's 'good quartos' and declared 'that there is no evidence . . . to rule out the possibility of surreptitious publication from a transcript'.[4] One might reply that there is even less evidence to rule it in, apart from the admittedly 'conjectural history' of the feud between the players and the stationers. Indeed, the inclusion of *Love's Labour's Lost*, 1598, *Romeo and Juliet*, 1599, and *Hamlet*, 1604–5, among the possibly surreptitious editions (pp. 162–5) should surely have worried Kirschbaum when later in the same book (p. 206) he conceded that the combined evidence of printer's blurb ('Newly corrected . . .' etc.) and foul paper signs

> does point to the actors' supplying the publisher who owned the copyright with a good version to take the place of a preceding printed version that was maimed and deformed.

The actors will hardly have supplied a surreptitious transcript! In other cases (*Merchant of Venice, Much Ado, 2 Henry IV*) one may think

---

[1] Walker, *Problems*, p. 109 ff.   [2] See Note B, p. 19.
[3] *Editing*, pp. 111 ff., 18 ff.; cf. Greg, *Documents*, pp. 197–8.
[4] *Stationers*, p. 168.

Kirschbaum's hypothesis equally unnecessary, though he is perfectly right to stress that the established 'tests' for foul papers will sometimes fail to differentiate foul papers from transcripts (p. 158 ff.). Kirschbaum's scepticism here coincides with other recent work,[1] but without something more tangible to fasten on to than the purely negative 'there is no evidence . . . to rule out the possibility of surreptitious publication', criticism must continue, I fear, to cling to its old assumptions—unless we are to ascribe the responsibility for unauthorised publication in some instances to the dramatists.[2] In what follows I by-pass Kirschbaum's suggestion because it remains unproved. He himself allows that textual oddities usually taken as signs of foul paper provenance (divergent speech prefixes, false starts) do 'bring us close to the author'.[3] There the matter must rest, while we wait for more positive arguments, if possible from within the texts.

The proposition which I shall urge, that in *some* of Shakespeare's plays *some* of the verbal variation between substantive texts reflects consecutive authorial drafts, cannot stand without a theory of textual transmission. Pollard's is the only one of the first three irreconcilable, as I see it, with the notion of more than a single draft by Shakespeare, since he envisaged one manuscript with three lives, figuring as foul papers, then as prompt-book, then as printer's copy. Even in its earlier form, however, Pollard's theory allowed for a fair copy to replace the foul papers when too untidy: while, after reading McKerrow's paper, Pollard veered and dropped his hostility to the 'fair copy' (which did not affect his chief contention that Shakespeare's holographs might reach the printer).[4] If, on both occasions, Pollard assumed as a matter of course that the preparation of the fair copy would fall to the 'play-house scrivener' and not to the author, this was because in the pioneer phase of enquiry the alternatives and their consequences were not yet sharply focused.

Greater concern for the identity of the copyist was displayed by McKerrow, though he could offer no clear-cut solution.

---

[1] Cf. Bowers: 'In great part the customary evidence used to distinguish foul-papers copy does no such thing and would be as generally applicable to authorial fair copy as to foul papers' (*Editing*, p. 109).

[2] Cf. Appendix A.   [3] *Op. cit.*, p. 159.

[4] 'Shakespeare's Text' in *A Companion to Shakespeare Studies*, ed. H. Granville-Barker and G. B. Harrison (Cambridge 1934), pp. 271, 279. Pollard wrote earlier: 'when there was a risk of piracy it would be foolish to increase that risk by making a single needless transcript' (*Aspects* p. 7).

It would be interesting if we could determine to what extent it was customary for an author to get his work professionally copied for the licenser and the printer . . . the probability is that there was no . . . rule in the matter . . .[1]

At the same time McKerrow observed that even if a scrivener did the copying the author would probably correct the manuscript, especially if he occupied Shakespeare's position in the company.[2] Both Shakespeare's foul papers and fair copy, or his foul papers and a scribal transcript corrected by him, could thus come into the possession of the players, and both, or descendants of both, might ultimately find their way to the printers—so that the Quarto and Folio of one play could easily record variants stemming from Shakespeare.

Thirty years ago the inspired simplicity of McKerrow's hypothesis created a deep impression. In Bowers's rival hypothesis no one acquainted with the closer study of texts, superintended with such vigour and distinction by Bowers himself, will look for simplicity, not, at least, after encountering his list of thirteen major classes of copy.[3] Despite his commitment to the view that normally just a single authorial draft (a fair copy) would reach the theatre and therefore the printers, enough qualifications punctuate his lecture to allow for the arrival in the printing-house of a second authorial draft (foul papers) in some cases. Shakespeare might 'sometimes have contented himself, as an important shareholder, with submitting something like foul papers', the scribal fair copy being revised by him. He may have re-worked his own fair copy, as did Daborne. And—

we cannot be certain that both foul papers and intermediate transcript would not be preserved and in some cases the foul papers given to the printer, even though the transcript would have been the superior copy.[4]

[1] McKerrow, *op. cit.*, pp. 260–1. F. P. Wilson summed up the probabilities as follows: 'The evidence is too slight to decide whether in Shakespeare's life-time it was customary for prompt-books to be autograph. There may have been some difference in practice between company and company, and in the fifteen–nineties prompt-books may have been more often autograph than in the sixteen-tens and later. Shakespeare's company is more likely to have employed a scrivener in his later years when the dramatist was famous, his company's financial position established, the drama taken more seriously, and the danger of piracy remote' (*Retrospect*, p. 102).

[2] Authors' corrections are found in some scribal transcripts of the period, Berkeley's *Lost Lady*, Glapthorne's *Lady Mother*, Middleton's *Game at Chesse*, and of course in printed books as well (e.g. Massinger's).

[3] Bowers, *Editing*, p. 11.   [4] *Editing*, pp. 20 and 111; 15–16; 22–3; 117.

If, as Bowers insists, dramatists did not surrender their foul papers to the actors, and if not only Jonson but also Webster, Marston, Dekker and others could retain or reacquire their right to print,[1] we must in addition ask whether Shakespeare could not have done so too, and himself have delivered some quarto texts for publication: for if Shakespeare gave the foul papers to the printers and the company later gave the prompt-book or a derivative for the Folio collection, two arch-texts would again survive.

Several reasons have in the past cut short further pursuit of this exciting possibility. It was assumed that dramatists surrendered all their texts and all their rights in their texts in selling to the actors. The first of these two assumptions has been shaken, but not, perhaps, demolished, by Bowers, the second I examine at some length in Appendix A. Again, it seemed incredible that slipshod texts such as the second quartos of *Romeo* and *Hamlet* should have been sent forth by the greatest of all poets, and the critics have therefore very willingly thrown the responsibility upon the players. Before we accept this evasion let us be clear that it implies that Shakespeare, supposing he resented the publication of untidy texts, was a man to be ignored. There is, however, ample evidence that the creator of Hamlet could assert himself, and, even if there were none, it is surely common sense to admit that publication by his own company signifies to all intents the same as publication by Shakespeare. The good quartos could not have been sneaked into the world again and again without his knowledge, and the replacement of bad quartos by good ones points to the author's concern for his reputation rather than to the players' for theirs (as Shakespeare's fellows admitted *via* the Lord Chamberlain's letters to the stationers)[2]. If Shakespeare did not hand in his foul papers to the players he could have retained the right to publish and sent even *Romeo* and *Hamlet* to the printer himself, or his fellows could have requested him to give his spare 'copy' to the printer to save them the trouble of making another.[3]

Both McKerrow and Bowers allow that two authorial versions of a

---

[1] Cf. Appendix A.

[2] 'There can be no reasonable doubt that the players were behind it' wrote Greg (*F.F.*, p. 16) of the Lord Chamberlain's letter to the stationers of 1619. The 1637 letter, apparently a recapitulation of the earlier one, complained of losses to the players if their 'books' were published without their consent—and of 'the iniury and disgrace of the Authors' when these books were corrupt (cf. Greg, *F.F.*, p. 24).

[3] For Shakespeare's indifference to the textual tidiness of his quartos cf. also p. 191.

play could come into being, and their arguments will bear development. What concrete evidence is there, however, for authorial as distinct from scribal fair copies? Greg in 1955 expressed scepticism regarding fair copies in Shakespeare's hand, but his discussion is less coherent than any other part of his excellent book and invites some comment.

Before approaching Shakespeare we may consider the dramatists of the period as a body. How many wrote out their own fair copies? Greg claimed that 'of fifteen manuscripts that can reasonably be regarded as prompt-books not more than five (including *Believe as you List* and *The Launching of the Mary*) seem likely to be autograph'.[1] Yet we need not restrict the search to prompt-books: any autograph copy of a play not obviously foul papers qualifies as evidence that dramatists might sometimes prepare a fair text, the anonymous *Dick of Devonshire*, Middleton's *Game at Chesse*, or Munday's *Sir Thomas More*.[2] And here we ought to remember Greg's warning that 'among the waifs and strays of theatrical manuscripts that have come down to us, there is not much that we can confidently claim as foul papers'[3]: for he himself shut his eyes to the danger-signals in putting such a text as Heywood's *The Captives* in this class. Anyone who moves on from *The Captives* to genuine first drafts by poets and even prose writers notorious for their fertility or facility—to the manuscripts of Shelley, Keats, Dickens or Oscar Wilde—will find it hard to conceive of Heywood's play, almost word-perfect page after page, as anything but a copy. Indeed, some typical 'copyists' errors' occur in *The Captives* and, though they can be explained in more ways than one, give strong support to the impression made by Heywood's remarkably clean text.[4] We shall do well, therefore, to ponder Bowers's words that 'there is no evidence whatever . . . in Henslowe that an author ever submitted for payment anything but

[1] *F.F.*, p. 104.
[2] Of this last Greg wrote: 'it is only an accident that the scribe who prepared it was himself part author' (*F.F.*, p. 94). Recurring accidents, however, call for investigation—and Greg apparently did not check how many fair copies other than prompt-books were written out by the author or a part-author.
[3] *F.F.*, p. 108. McKerrow observed that, apart from *More*, the extant dramatic manuscripts of the period are free from the 'manifest errors' which are so extraordinary a feature of some of Shakespeare's good quartos: this corroborates that very few of the extant manuscripts will be foul papers, for Shakespeare's hand was by no means the most illegible among the dramatists (McKerrow, *op. cit.*, p. 263).
[4] Cf. Appendix C, p. 200. Bowers recognised that some texts, including *The Captives*, have been labelled foul papers too hastily (*Editing*, pp. 14, 115). For Greg's opinion of the play cf. *Documents*, p. 203: and cf. p. 15, below, for Greg's optimism regarding Shakespeare's foul papers.

a fair copy'.[1] Daborne, we know, sent in 'fair copy', and the leading dramatists of the age, in so far as we can check, copied out their own plays at least sometimes, Munday, Middleton, Massinger, Fletcher, Dekker,[2] and, I think, Heywood—and why not Shakespeare?

We owe it to Bowers that resistance to the idea of fair copies in Shakespeare's hand is now crumbling. Bowers rightly pointed to Greg as the leading spokesman of the other side[3]:

> a number of texts [of Shakespeare] do not appear to derive from a prompt book, yet they are markedly cleaner and more uniform than the group taken as manifestly printed from foul papers. Sometimes, as with *Julius Caesar*, the comparative lack of authorial characteristics is noticeable. That in some of these cases Shakespeare might have broken his rule and submitted fair copies is admitted, as possibly for *King John* and more probably for *Julius Caesar*. But in each of these cases, despite the strong evidence he presents against a prompt-book origin, Greg feels it necessary to conjecture that the Shakespeare fair copy was utilized as the prompt. With some possible strain, *Antony and Cleopatra*, though described by Chambers as 'very carefully written copy prepared by the author for the stage with directions respecting the means of production', is assumed to be printed from foul papers, or original drafts. It seems evident that Greg felt these decisions to be required because he distrusted any intermediate manuscript, whether authorial or scribal, filling the gap between foul papers and the preparation of prompt copy.[4]

Perhaps the clearest example of the difficulties Greg exposed himself to comes, according to Bowers, in the first quarto of *The Merchant of Venice*:

> The text suggests to Greg an author's fair copy, but he takes it that such a fair copy would necessarily become the prompt book, and since the quarto for various reasons offers too many difficulties for

---

[1] P. 15.

[2] For Fletcher cf. Bowers, pp. 16–17; for Dekker's fair copy of a play he wrote in collaboration, G. R. Price in *The Library* (Fifth Series), 1956, XI, 180–6.

[3] Others of course have taken the same line as Greg. Richard Flatter wrote in 1952: 'We cannot assume that Shakespeare was capable, and still less that he was willing, to sit down for several days and make a fair copy of his own original script, writing out 60 or 70 pages' (' "The True Originall Copies" of Shakespeare's Plays' in *Proceedings of the Leeds Philosophical and Literary Society* (Literary and Historical Section), 1952–5, vii, 34). Greg's, however, is the most closely argued statement of the case known to me.

[4] Bowers, *op. cit.*, pp. 30–1.

belief in a prompt origin, he is reluctantly forced back on foul papers. When we compare the *Merchant* text with that found in the ordinarily assigned foul-papers group, it might perhaps seem that the most reasonable explanation for the *Merchant* is that Shakespeare submitted something like a fair copy . . .[1]

To Bowers's argument, that Greg disregarded his own findings in order to disallow the 'intermediate manuscript', I would add another inconsistency. It was an article of faith with Greg that 'an experienced dramatist would doubtless be able to produce at once a sufficiently coherent text', and that 'Shakespeare doubtless composed fluently and seldom went back over what he had written'.[2] This, largely on the strength of Heminge and Condell's remarks about Shakespeare's 'unblotted papers',[3] does not square with Greg's conjectures about some of the foul papers used by Shakespeare's printers and copyists: 'a rather heavily corrected manuscript' (*Othello*), 'foul papers, with sundry alterations and corrections' (*Troilus*), 'foul papers that had been left in a rather rough state' (*Measure for Measure*), etc.[4] 'Seldom' may seem to cover these exceptions—until we wonder whether, at least in the profounder plays, correction could not have been the rule, the appearances being against it simply because the evidence has vanished. Why, otherwise, should *Troilus* and *Othello* and a few more stand out as exceptions? Greg conceded, as Bowers observed, that *some* of Shakespeare's plays were printed from autograph fair copies[5]: if *Othello*, *Troilus* and

[1] P. 31.

[2] *F.F.*, pp. 106, 92 n. 2. Greg's optimism about the experienced dramatist's fluency derives, apparently, from such texts as the 'Shakespearian pages in *Sir Thomas More* and Heywood's *Captives*' (*F.F.*, p. 109): I take the latter to be a copy and not foul papers (cf. p. 200), and the former as unrepresentative of Shakespeare's writing habits (cf. p. 28).

[3] *F.F.*, p. 92: cf. my next chapter.

[4] *F.F.*, pp. 370-1, 347, 356.

[5] In *F.F.*, the writing of which overlapped with Bowers's book, Greg returned to the subject of Shakespearian fair copies. The entries in his index are not quite complete and I therefore subjoin references to some plays which Greg in 1955 regarded as printed from fair copy in Shakespeare's hand: pp. 183, 187 (*Henry VI*, Parts I, II, III); p. 291 (*Julius Caesar*); p. 342 (*Troilus*, Q); p. 407 (*Coriolanus*). The quarto of *The Merchant of Venice*, he thought, was based on foul papers rather than fair copy, 'but it is not possible to pronounce with any confidence' (p. 258); he apparently agreed with Chambers that behind *Antony and Cleopatra* there lies 'a very carefully written copy, elaborately prepared by the author for the stage' (p. 398), only to decide later (pp. 402-3) that the copy was foul papers; and he felt that it 'is, perhaps, not impossible' that Sh.'s 'much-altered fair copy [of *L.L.L.*] was used as a prompt-book' (p. 222, n. 10). Cf. also p. 364. In his 'Summary' Greg, however, classed *Coriolanus* as 'from foul papers' (p. 427).

Measure for Measure were not exceptions we can understand that there might arise a need for autograph fair copies, and that more might have existed than Greg reluctantly allowed.

It is worth noting, too, that Greg resisted the idea of autograph fair copies partly because he thought that Shakespeare 'might leave occasional tangles and loose ends to be dealt with by the book-keeper or settled in rehearsal'.[1] I believe that he had two principal reasons for this conjecture. (*a*) For a long time he held that in the most heavily deleted lines in *Sir Thomas More* Shakespeare 'seems to have lost patience and given up all attempt to reduce the passage to order'.[2] Later, in a 'Final Note on Certain Readings' appended to Alexander's *Shakespeare*, 1951, which is easily missed, Greg abandoned this view, though an integral part of his argument: 'The whole passage is clumsy but I no longer think, as I was once inclined to do, that the author was conscious of having left it in confusion.'[3] Four years thereafter, in *The Shakespeare First Folio*, 1955, he reiterated, with slight changes, the conclusion of *Editorial Problem*—through an oversight, I suspect, since Greg here and there fell back upon the first book in writing the second.[4] (*b*) The textual tangles found in some of Shakespeare's printed plays must be Greg's second principal reason: but, as I explain elsewhere (p. 33), it seems more reasonable that Shakespeare, knowing that he himself would copy out the play again, left some lines 'unfinalised' and wrote on, because he preferred not to risk losing his poetic impetus—than that he abdicated his responsibilities in favour of a book-keeper.

Between Greg's generalisation that 'Shakespeare doubtless composed fluently and seldom went back over what he had written', and his diagnosis of a particular case, that it represents 'a rather heavily corrected manuscript', there lies a gap well worth exploring. With what degree of accuracy can we describe the 'unblotted papers'? May we believe Heminge and Condell's blurb? These questions must be answered before we can speak of 'textual instability' with any assurance.

[1] *F.F.*, p. 107.   [2] *Ed. Problem*, p. 104 and note.
[3] P. 1351.   [4] *F.F.*, p. 111 and note 2.

Note A (page 7)

FOUL PAPERS

Some experts call foul papers the author's 'original drafts', but Bowers defines them as 'the author's last complete draft in a shape satisfactory to him for transfer to fair copy' (Bowers, *Editing*, pp. 107–8; 13; cf. Wilson, *Retrospect*, p. 101). Greg agreed with Bowers since behind the 'foul papers' there may have been rougher drafts (*Sh. Q.*, 1956, VII, 102).

Bowers's definition seems to be dictated by editorial convenience ['I prefer to define . . .' (*Editing*, p. 108)] rather than by any strict examination of the usage of the time. Everyone knows that Knight found the foul papers of *Bonduca*, and that Daborne sent Henslowe 'the foule sheet' of a play in 1613— but is this enough to prove Bowers's view that 'the author's last complete draft' was 'known at the time and subsequently as his "foul papers"' (*Editing*, p. 13)? I believe, on the contrary, that all manuscripts preceding the first fair copy would be referred to as foul papers—and that this term and its congeners (foul sheet, draft, etc.) do not signify an exclusive type of theatrical manuscript but any rough draft throughout the world of letters. Here are some examples:

(i) 'TO the Reader . . . thou hast heard much talke of one captain *Ward* . . . If thou hast a minde to heare more of him, spend thy time on a fewe foule papers following, and thou shalt know as much as I know.' (*Newes from Sea, Of two notorious Pyrats Ward . . . and . . . Danseker*, 1609, (anon.) Epistle.)

(ii) '*Acquaintance*. Is the first draught of a friend, whom we must lay downe oft thus, as the foule coppy, before we can write him perfit, and true' (Earle, *Microcosmographie*, 1628).

(iii) The publisher to the reader in the 1653 edition of Henry Killigrew's *Conspiracy*, concerning the first edition of 1638: '[the author] was so farre from consenting to the printing of his Book at that time, that he had not then Corrected [it] . . . the former Impression is no better than a *Corrupted Fragment*, or *Foul Draught*, of what this Play was intended, and differing so much from what it now is, that if the Corrections, Expungings, and Additions, be consider'd, it is almost the one half otherwise'.

(iv) A Dr Petty was accused in the House of Commons in 1659 of not surrendering the originals of certain documents: 'he had only returned transcripts of them, and keeps the originals himself, in his own hands'. '*Dr. Petty* informed the House that the particulars in his hands were foul books and papers, out of which those he had returned were extracted' (*Diary of Thomas Burton*, ed. 1828, IV, 470).[1]

'The earliest form of the play that would have any normal chance of serving as printer's copy will be the author's last complete draft', Bowers submits (*Editing*, p. 13). At this point he calls this last complete draft the foul papers: later in his book (p. 127) Bowers suggests that the 'final form of a play' handed to the players, the 'authorial fair copy expressing final intention',

---

[1] My second and fourth examples were supplied by O.E.D. (foul, 3).

17

could 'still have included the vague assignment of speeches among minor characters and permissive stage directions'. Is this 'final form' then so very different from 'the author's last complete draft'? Presumably it would contain fewer deletions, would be less 'foul': it will be apparent, however, that even from the point of view of editorial convenience Bowers does not distinguish as rigorously between the two types of text as would be desirable,[1] while historically his definition seems to me unproven. His 'foul papers' are already, in part at least, a fair copy, and he denies the name to those rougher drafts which may more properly claim it. Seventeenth-century usage, in fact, gives no backing to the opinion that 'foul papers' must be a complete draft. The reason why Bowers prefers to call the author's last complete draft the 'foul papers' is, I believe, that he regards earlier jottings as, for editorial purposes, unimportant.

> Fouler papers might in part lie behind this complete version [viz. the 'foul papers'], such as we may perhaps see in Shakespeare's *Timon of Athens*, but there is no point in attempting such distinctions in relation to printer's copy.[2]

The conjecture that Shakespeare wrote his plays on loose sheets of paper, with the corollary that some sheets would be first drafts and some transcripts in the first completed manuscript,[3] leads to a different conclusion. Once compositor studies of such texts as *Hamlet* Q2 have reached a measure of finality the editor may be able to tell which parts of the copy were clean (and therefore perhaps transcripts) and which were foul—and this will interest him. Again, to pin the same label on the texts of *Timon* and *Hamlet* Q2 will cause confusion: whether or not contemporaries called both foul papers, the modern editor must nevertheless (*pace* Bowers) attempt to distinguish their 'copies'. The definition of terms will one day require more thought: for the time being, however, no great harm will be done if we use 'foul papers' to denote any kind of draft preceding the first fair copy and define more circumspectly as the need arises.

---

[1] J. C. Maxwell noted in his review of Bowers's book that 'to some extent, the controversy is a verbal one' (*R.E.S.*, 1957, VIII, 294).
[2] *Editing*, p. 13.   [3] Cf. pp. 144, 150.

Note B (page 8)

INTERMEDIATE FAIR COPIES

Bowers's case for an 'intermediate' fair copy rests upon three main arguments:
(1) some of the extant texts, both manuscript and printed, do not appear to represent either foul papers or prompt-copy (*Editing*, pp. 21 ff., 29 ff., 114); (2) Bowers urges that the actors' parts would be made out before the prompt-book, and this would require legible copy (p. 111 ff.); (3) 'There is no evidence whatever ... in Henslowe that an author ever submitted for payment anything but a fair copy' (pp. 15, 23). I subjoin some comments.
(1) We do not at present know enough about printing-house procedures to be able to ascribe differences between good quartos to 'the state of the copy'. Some printers could have cleaned up their texts more than others. Regarding Folio texts printed from fair copy Bowers writes

> Dr Williams is now able to conjecture on bibliographical evidence that *Coriolanus* is definitely from a scribal copy ... I may suggest that if, as seems likely, his full investigations materially reduce the number of Folio plays which can be thought of as set from autograph, more weight in the future will need to be given to the question of the intermediate transcript
>
> (p. 114)

If the 'definite conjecture' about scribal copies for the Folio is right, it does not follow, however, that these would be the sort of 'intermediate copy' under discussion (viz. intermediate between foul papers and prompt-book). Almost certainly some scribal copies were made for the Folio by Crane, yet 'there is no reason to suppose that he was ever officially connected with the company' (Greg, *F.F.*, p. 100): 'clean' texts in the Folio not showing the obvious signs of Crane's penmanship could therefore have been commissioned from other scriveners at this late date. Similarly quartos (e.g. *The Merchant of Venice*) could be set up from *ad hoc* fair copies prepared for the printer.
(2) Cf. Greg, *Documents*, p. 198, footnote. Bowers and Greg have missed some of the evidence. Daborne wrote to Henslowe on 8 May, 1613 'of this new play they ar now studijnge', though the play was not finished a week later ('I am vnwilling to read to ye generall company till all be finisht'). 'Studying' seems to mean 'learning'. Compare a memorandum made by Herbert, Master of the Revels, dealing with current practices that he wished to reform: 'The players ought not to study their parts till I have allowed of the booke'.[1] At the same time Herbert wrote to the book-keeper of the King's Men, stating that he has altered a prompt-book and ordering him to incorporate the changes in the players parts: 'Purge ther parts, as I have the booke' (*ibid.*). Here Herbert refers to an old play, Fletcher's *The Woman's Prize*, yet his memorandum has a more general ring: it suggests, however, that the Master would not have sanctioned the study of parts before he had 'allowed of the booke', and only occasionally heard of this abuse. McManaway's *caveat*, 'is it likely that players' parts would be copied out and the cast required

[1] Cf. *The Dramatic Records of Sir Henry Herbert*, ed. J. Q. Adams, 1917, p. 21.

19

to memorise them before the prompt-book was ready and *licensed*?' (*Sh. Survey 9*, 1956, 149–50), also raises doubts. To memorise a play which the Master might suppress or cut drastically would be folly. Again, if many alterations were introduced during rehearsal, which I cannot believe likely with experienced dramatists, the re-writing of badly 'blotted' leaves or sheets rather than of whole manuscripts would recommend itself in the first instance. In the absence of more comprehensive information I think it safer to follow Greg ('The preparation of Parts, therefore, sometimes began before the Book was complete . . .') rather than Bowers ('My own opinion is that the preparation of the parts would normally precede the prompt-copy transcription.').

(3) Here too Greg anticipated Bowers: 'if we may generalize from the . . . correspondence with Daborne, it would seem that what the author delivered was a fair copy, so that he retained his rough draft for reference' (*Henslowe's Diary*, II, 123; cf. *Documents*, pp. 197–8, F.F., p. 467). But Bowers's generalisation goes beyond Henslowe and his circle: he assures us that 'we have not the slightest scrap of evidence' that the actors

> required a dramatist to turn over his original foul sheets along with the fair copy. That this last was ever required is sheer guesswork on our part without a shred of substantiating evidence.[1]

Yet the words of Heminge and Condell in the First Folio ('wee haue scarse receiued from him a blot in his papers') most probably refer, despite all Bowers's efforts to the contrary, to foul papers, and *receiued* suggests 'manuscripts still in their possession rather than . . . ephemeral papers that had once passed through their hands'.[2] Other scraps and shreds also cause trouble. The late resurfacing of the foul papers of *Bonduca* is no isolated incident: some of Shakespeare's Folio texts are likewise based on foul papers (*Troilus, Timon*). Still, a lot more can be said on Bowers's side. The author of the anonymous *Defence of Cony-catching* (1592) alleged that Greene sold his play *Orlando Furioso* to the Queen's men and, when they were out of the way touring, sold it to the Admiral's men for a second profit. Whether or not this was a joke (cf. Greg, F.F., pp. 164–5), it testifies that to one informed contemporary a dramatist's retention of the foul papers, or of a copy, of his play seemed feasible: and Heywood's attack on dramatists who sold their work to the actors and later to the printers (*Rape of Lucrece*, 1608, 'To the Reader') comes from another expert witness. Again, the widely held belief that the printing of some plays in the 1623 Folio was delayed because no text lay at hand suggests that not more than one text was available: and the exclusion of *Pericles* from the collection has been explained on similar grounds (Greg, F.F., p. 98). In the Beaumont and Fletcher Folio of 1647 Humphrey Moseley likewise wrote as if under the impression that the players possessed only one text of a play:

> One only Play . . . hath beene long lost, and I feare irrecoverable; for a

---

[1] *Editing*, pp. 15–16, 23.
[2] In this sentence I follow Greg's review of Bowers (cf. p. 23 n. 1), and F.F., p. 108, n. 1.

Person of Quality borrowed it from the *Actours* many yeares since, and (by the negligence of a Servant) it was never return'd; therefore now I put up this *Si quis*, that whosoever hereafter happily meetes with it, shall be thankfully satisfied if he please to send it home.[1]

In Appendix A I suggest that more dramatists than has been suspected took their own plays to the printers: this would be possible only if the dramatist was not required to hand in his foul papers at the theatre. Since the scraps of evidence that contradict Bowers centre on the King's Men it may be that authors closely connected with one company (Shakespeare, Fletcher) sometimes handed over their foul papers not because compelled to but because, in an age when lodgings could be searched and papers removed (e.g. Kyd's), and when 'pirates' tried to steal plays, the theatre was the best place for safe deposit; or it may be, too, that the players contacted Shakespeare's and Fletcher's representatives and obtained foul papers from them after the dramatists had died.

Whether or not an intermediate fair copy existed normally, and a second fair copy would be made (later to become the prompt-book), we cannot in the present state of ignorance decide. Minor alterations determined during rehearsal, such as Bowers envisaged (p. III ff.), could be introduced in the original fair copy—while the existence of some autograph prompt-books (cf. Bowers, p. 16) suggests that sometimes only one fair copy was necessary, for few authors would wish to write out an intermediate version and the prompt-book as well. All Bowers's arguments remain open to dispute. An impartial judge will nevertheless agree that the 'intermediate manuscript' probably existed in some cases, if not in all: and this verdict I try to reinforce in Appendix C.

---

[1] Moseley refers to *The Wild-Goose Chase*. The play was found, and published in 1652 from what looks like a private transcript rather than a prompt-book, though it has one interesting direction on sig. I₂ᵇ: 'Enter Leverduce des Lugier, Mr. Illiard.' According to the *dramatis personae* list Lugier was 'Acted by Mr. Hilliard Swanston'.

III

The Unblotted Papers

*

His mind and hand went together: And what he thought, he vttered
with that easinesse, that wee haue scarse receiued from him a blot in
his papers.

FROM his own day to ours Shakespeare's fluency has been taken for
granted. To Pollard, for example, Heminge and Condell's words in the
Folio appeared meaningless if the papers referred to were not original
drafts. Bowers, on the other hand, deploying his argument for various
drafts and revisions by Shakespeare, felt it necessary to explain away
Heminge and Condell, but, unfortunately, gives instead the impression
of hustling a couple of embarrassing witnesses. He submitted that
Pollard pressed the remark of Shakespeare's fellows 'far beyond its
evidential value, and into the realm of pure speculation'—for Pollard
omitted to consider 'the fossil revisions in *Romeo and Juliet* and *Love's
Labour's Lost* which might represent serious blots'. And, concluded
Bowers,

> Pollard's theory requires us to take with absolute literalness and far-
> reaching significance as external evidence a statement that had its
> origin as a pious literary compliment . . . the compliment seems to
> have been a part of literary tradition, as evidenced by the fact that
> Moseley, the publisher of the Beaumont and Fletcher Folio, appropri-
> ated it for his authors.[1]

To which Greg retorted:

> We may suspect that what we are told of the unblotted condition of
> Shakespeare's papers is exaggerated—'scarcely' is an elastic term—

[1] Bowers, *Editing*, p. 25 ff. For an earlier discussion of the 'unblotted papers'
see R. C. Rhodes, *Shakespeare's First Folio* (Oxford 1923), chap. IV. Moseley
wrote of Fletcher in 1647: 'What ever I have seene of Mr. *Fletchers* owne hand, is
free from interlining; and his friends affirme he never writ any one thing twice: it
seemes he had that rare felicity to prepare and perfect all first in his owne braine . . .
before he committed one word to writing, and never touched pen till all was to
stand as firme and immutable as if ingraven in Brasse or Marble.' For different
views of Fletcher's papers cf. p. 27.

and we may allow that they were probably not all of a kind; but unless a substantial proportion of those papers showed manifest signs of free composition, such as careful fair copies would not, to appeal to them as proving the author's ease of utterance would be absurd. This is what Pollard saw and what Professor Bowers apparently does not. Moreover, we have Ben Jonson's word for it that this was no casual flower of speech but an habitual boast of the players. And unless Professor Bowers can point to earlier examples of the like claim, what business has he to assert that in making it Heminge and Condell were merely following a fashion, rather than setting one that Moseley followed a quarter of a century later?[1]

With the best will in the world it is impossible, even for those who sympathise with Bowers's general thesis, to brush aside Heminge and Condell as not over-scrupulous. Yet Greg erred too, I believe, when he countered that Heminge and Condell in their boast about Shakespeare's facility set a fashion rather than followed one that was well established. Long before Shakespeare's birth the study of poetry went hand in hand with the study of rhetoric, in England as earlier in Rome, and according to some teachers the 'art of poetry' could be mastered as easily as the art of Cicero: facility in poetry came to be regarded as an accomplishment as admirable as the orator's eloquence, and thus the boast and the fashion originated.[2] Boys would be taught by their Holofernes to 'affect the letter, for it argues facility', and this spurious facility, 'begot in the ventricle of memory, nourish'd in the womb of pia mater', would be 'delivered upon the mellowing of occasion'. Suetonius wrote flatteringly of Nero, 'Itaque ad poeticam pronus, carmina libenter ac sine labore composuit', and of Titus, 'Latine Graeceque vel in orando vel in fingendis poematibus promptus et facilis ad extemporalitatem usque'.[3] And Ovid of himself:

---

[1] *Sh. Quarterly*, 1956, VII, 103. Greg perhaps placed too much weight on 'Ben Jonson's word', for Jonson was careless in his opening sentence: '*I remember*, the Players have often mentioned . . . that . . . hee never blotted out line.' 'Never' goes much further than 'scarse' (as in the Folio), and 'often' may be an exaggeration as well, or could refer back to the Folio and to discussions arising from the Folio compliment, in which case Heminge and Condell would naturally maintain their earlier assertion. Here and throughout I deal with the Folio address 'To the great Variety of Readers' as Heminge and Condell's, for, if they did not compose what they signed, the address 'may be confidently taken to express the views of those who signed' (Greg, *F.F.*, p. 17 ff.).

[2] See J. F. D'Alton, *Roman Literary Theory and Criticism*, 1931, p. 450. I am indebted to chap. VII ('The Supremacy of Rhetoric') of D'Alton's book in this paragraph.   [3] *Caes*. Nero 52, Titus 3.

> sponte sua carmen numeros veniebat ad aptos;
> quicquid temptabam dicere, versus erat.[1]

—lines quoted approvingly in some English books on rhetoric. With the University Wits the fetish of fluency came once more into its own, growing into a popular superstition in Shakespeare's lifetime. Nashe may speak for the generality:

> giue me the man whose extemporall veine in any humour will excell our greatest Art-maisters deliberate thoughts; whose inuentions, quicker then his eye, will challenge the prowdest Rhetoritian to the contention of like perfection with like expedition.[2]

Dilating upon Heminge and Condell's words Jonson also compared the poet Shakespeare quite instinctively with Haterius, an orator.[3] Slow writing fell into disrepute, and some of the great dramatists were actually taunted because of the care they lavished on their work.[4] All in all one may claim that, when dramatists spawned plays at the almost unconscionable rate of Heywood and Lope de Vega, the age encouraged free composition as the fashion long before 1623.

By good fortune we can track the First Folio into the field of force of this once potent fashion. It has long been known that four of the men behind the Folio were connected in other literary ventures—Edward Blount, the publisher, Ben Jonson, author of two sets of verses, and Leonard Digges and James Mabbe who supplied complimentary poems for the Folio printed together on one page and apparently both handed in late. Because of the fascinations of the 'Pavier' Shakespeare of 1619, and of Jaggard's compositors, recent studies of the Folio have tended to underestimate the influence of Blount and his three associates—but a characteristically exciting series of discoveries by Leslie Hotson has confirmed that Blount and the rest can be regarded almost as a team, perhaps as *the* team as far as the Folio is concerned.[5] One of the four,

---

[1] *Tristia*, IV.10.25–6.   [2] *Nashe*, III, 312.

[3] *Timber*, 'De Shakespeare nostrati'.

[4] Webster by Henry Fitzjeffrey in *Certain Elegies*, 1617; and cf. *Jonson*, IX, 584. The slow writers hit back, of course, as in Webster's pungent counterblast in *The White Devil*. Jonson spoke up in the Apologetical Dialogue appended to *Poetaster*, and indirectly through those of his fools who boast of facility: Matheo will 'write you your half score or your dozen of sonnets at a sitting' (*E.M. in his H.*, II.3), Crispinus thinks no one 'could pen more verses in a day, or with more facility, than I' (*Poetaster*, Act III). But in the Prologue to *Volpone* Jonson is proud that 'five weeks fully penn'd it'.

[5] Cf. Note A, p. 34.

Mabbe, translated in a mere matter of 'a few weekes' Aleman's huge novel, *The Rogue*, 1622, so that one friend praised him as an author 'whose Quill both writes and flyes/With equall speed' (A_4a); and the same volume, printed for Blount and graced with complimentary verses by Leonard Digges and Ben Jonson, contains a description of Aleman's 'quicknes of wit', his facility in composition which, we are told, 'may almost be counted a miracle'. I quote this at some length for I believe that it proves beyond reasonable doubt that the First Folio circle had heard of the wonders of free composition just before the Folio preliminaries were drafted.

> putting his papers from hand to hand to the Presse, and wanting matter for that dayes worke, I knew for certaine, that ouer-night he composed so much stuffe, as did serue to keepe the Presse going all the next day following: for he was troubled at that time with diuers other businesses, which did necessarily require his help and assistance. And in those short houres of the night, he was seene to imploy him-selfe with a great deale of diligence, as well in the affayres of his other businesses, as in the ordering and sorting of papers to send them to the Printers, as also, in the composing of more matter for the Presse, besides his attendance vpon other things, importing his owne person and house. Euery one of which would haue well required a whole man, free from all other incumbrances.[1]

The chief emphasis in Heminge and Condell's praise of Shakespeare's papers falls on his ease of utterance and therefore reflects rather than sets a fashion. And the assertion that they 'scarse receiued from him a blot in his papers', though not quite so commonplace, also reflects the cult of 'quicknes of wit'. One of Drayton's sonnets, first published in 1619 by John Smethwick, another member of the First Folio syndicate, bracketed 'quicke Invention' and 'unblotted papers' quite naturally.

> A WITLESSE Gallant, a young Wench that woo'd,
> (Yet his dull Spirit her not one jot could move)
> Intreated me, as e'r I wish'd his good,
> To write him but one Sonnet to his Love:
> When I, as fast as e'r my Penne could trot,
> Powr'd out what first from quicke Invention came;
> Nor never stood one word thereof to blot, . . .

Placed in its historical context, Heminge and Condell's boast loses some of its respectability. It loses more when we check up on the

---

[1] *The Rogue*, 1622, Part II, sig. XX_5.

fashionable formulae employed elsewhere in the Folio preliminary matter. True, not many opportunities existed for an original dedication or epistle—but, nevertheless, one must reluctantly admit that the two documents signed by Heminge and Condell echo all the most familiar claptrap. Both make much of the flourish traditionally prefixed to printed plays ('these Playes haue had their triall alreadie, and stood out all Appeales': they have been applauded by all the best wits in the kingdom, etc.[1]), and the dedication ends with a cannonade of clichés:

> But, there we must also craue our abilities to be considerd, my Lords. We cannot go beyond our owne powers. Country hands reach foorth milke, creame, fruites, or what they haue: and many Nations (we haue heard) that had not gummes & incense, obtained their requests with a leauened Cake. It was no fault to approch their Gods, by what meanes they could: And the most, though meanest, of things are made more precious, when they are dedicated to Temples.[2]

Even the complaint that bad texts ('maimed, and deformed') of the plays had come abroad followed an established ritual. In the 1604 edition of his *Passions of the Mind* Thomas Wright stigmatised an earlier, surreptitious print as 'maymed and corrupted' (epistle), and, as Kirschbaum observed, the second quarto of *Philaster*, 1622, classed the first as 'mained and deformed', the very words of Heminge and Condell.[3] Indeed, this particular line in sales-talk became so popular that A. W. Pollard's useful distinction between 'good' and 'bad' quartos really finds justification only in the state of the texts and not in the words of Shakespeare's fellows, for allegedly 'surreptitious' books could be brought out with perfectly sound texts.[4] Their *penchant* for traditional phrases and compliments does not, of course, rule out Heminge and

---

[1] Cf. *Tamburlaine*, 1590; *Sejanus*, ed. 1616; *The Family of Love*, 1608; *The Golden Age*, 1611; *Greene's Tu Quoque*, 1614, etc.

[2] Cf. Greene's *Morando*, 1587, *Pandosto*, 1588, etc. Malone recognised that here we have to do with 'the common-places of dedication in Shakespeare's age' (*Shakespeare*, 1821, II, 661).

[3] Cf. Kirschbaum, *Stationers*, pp. 244, 372. 'Main' and 'maim' were interchangeable in 1622 (cf. *O.E.D.*).

[4] Thus in Aleman's *The Rogue* (cf. p. 25, above) the author claimed that he was 'robbed, and defrauded' because he had 'beene too prodigall in communicating my papers' (Pt. II, sig. XX₂ᵃ). The unoriginality of dedications can also be illustrated from W. Jaggard's in Favyn's *Theater of Honour and Knight-hood*, 1623, which comes at times very close to that in *The Decameron*, 1620 (printed by I. Jaggard).

Condell's praise of the unblotted papers as empty verbiage, but, on the other hand, we shall do well to remember that prefatory compliments rarely amount to much more than a solemn game. To adapt Dr Johnson: in dedicatory inscriptions a man is not upon oath.

Greg believed in the unblotted papers, though he pictured the *Othello* draft as 'a rather heavily corrected manuscript': the inconsistency did not bother him. Moseley's compliment to Fletcher brings up another awkward fact to which Greg gave some attention—without modifying his general account of Shakespeare's papers.[1] By 1647, Greg recognised, 'the unblotted papers became a literary tradition': yet he held (and those who think that the 'tradition' goes back beyond 1623 must agree) that Moseley's words 'may have been true to much the same extent as what Heminge and Condell said of Shakespeare'. At the same time he allowed that the foul papers of *Bonduca* probably 'contained a considerable amount of not very clear alteration'.

Fletcher, when he began writing *Bonduca*, was uncertain even of the number and relationship of some of his principal characters: in the first scene he gave the British queen a son and a daughter; later he introduced a second daughter and turned the son into a nephew. And at the end of the play he left one strand of the plot in the air, to be tucked in perhaps by a different hand.[2]

An informed contemporary corroborates that Fletcher's 'firm and immutable' writings were in fact 'blotted':

> . . . *Beaumont* was faine
> To bid thee be more dull, that's write againe,
> And bate some of thy fire, which from thee came
> In a cleare, bright, full, but too large a flame . . .
> Added his sober spunge, and did contract
> Thy plenty to lesse wit to make 't exact . . .[3]

If we are to bracket Shakespeare's papers and Fletcher's, as even Greg recommends, Heminge and Condell's 'scarse', in 'wee haue scarse

---

[1] Cf. p. 22, n. 1, for Moseley on Fletcher.
[2] Cf. Greg, *F.F.*, pp. 109–11.
[3] W. Cartwright to Fletcher in the 1647 Folio. Moseley could not foresee that Beaumont's correction of Fletcher would become famous (cf. Pope, *Imitations of Horace*, II.i), as Heminge and Condell could not that their aside about the unblotted papers would be echoed and garbled down the centuries (by Jonson, Aubrey, Pope, etc.).

receiued from him a blot in his papers', must be stretched to breaking point.

Conjectures about Shakespeare's manuscripts can be tested by comparison with the Shakespearian parts of *Sir Thomas More*, though I am not as sure as Greg that these are truly representative.

> The Shakespearian pages in *Sir Thomas More* and Heywood's *Captives* alike prove that an author's foul papers may be reasonably free from alteration.

> What Shakespeare could produce as a draft we may, I believe, see in the famous three pages of *More*, and I imagine that it was something of this sort that he often handed to the company.[1]

I find it difficult to believe that Shakespeare would take as seriously the patching of someone else's play of little more than average quality, upon which a team of rescue-workers had already descended, as the writing of a *Hamlet* or a *Lear*, 'the precious life-blood of a master spirit, embalmed and treasured up on purpose to a life beyond life'. The three pages of *Sir Thomas More*, which at their best rise to rhetorical commonplaces rather than to the finest poetry, show what Shakespeare could do 'with the remaining ink of a pen otherwise employed'. That they exhibit very little blotting supports Heminge and Condell up to a point. But let us not forget that Sir Edmund Chambers and other cautious critics believed that Addition III could well be Shakespeare's, although Hand C wrote it out[2]: here, in soliloquy, we come nearer to the precious life-blood of poetry and, it seems, the first draft was not clean enough and had to be copied.

It should be emphasised, too, that some of the 'additions' to the play cannot qualify as 'free composition' in that they fall back upon long stretches of dialogue transcribed from the original text.[3] The addition in Hand D fills in a scene missing from the original before Folio 10, and it is therefore quite possible that Shakespeare, like his colleagues, *copied* rather than *composed* some of the cleaner parts in his 147 lines

---

[1] See Greg, *F.F.*, p. 109, and in *Sh. Q.*, 1956, VII, 102. I agree with Greg (*F.F.*, p. 99) that the case for Shakespeare's authorship of the three pages of *More* 'is likely to be held conclusive by anyone capable of judging evidence'.

[2] Chambers, *W. Sh.*, I, 514–15; cf. R. C. Bald, '*The Booke of Sir Thomas More* and its problems' (*Sh. Survey 2*, 1949), p. 59.

[3] Cf. scene IV and Addition II, scene VIII *a* and Addition IV in Greg's Malone Society Reprint.

(supposing the original was his or partly his), or leaned heavily upon the work of his predecessor.

Another contemporary close to Shakespeare deserves to be heard before a summing-up. With characteristic bluntness Jonson condemned Shakespeare in *Timber* for not blotting more, and at first glance this seems to confirm Heminge and Condell's words. Yet the note 'De Shakespeare nostrati' was actually written as an attack on the players' 'ignorance', and if not torn from its setting points the other way.

Some entries in *Timber* run in series, and that on Shakespeare connects so neatly with its predecessor, 'Censura de Poetis', and more particularly with the last paragraph of the section, that we isolate it at our peril. Before his passage on Shakespeare Jonson compared the opinions of 'the multitude' and of the enlightened critic:

> the unskilfull are naturally deceiv'd, and judging wholly by the bulke, thinke rude things greater then polish'd; and scatter'd more numerous, then compos'd: Nor thinke this only to be true in the sordid multitude, but the neater sort of our *Gallants*: for all are the multitude; only they differ in cloaths, not in judgement or understanding.[1]

Jonson then went on at once to take as an example of the 'unskilfull' who 'thinke rude things greater then polish'd' the 'players' who, in praising Shakespeare's unblotted papers, 'choose that circumstance to commend their friend by, wherein he most faulted', viz. his facility. Now the whole drift of the note, lavishly praising not only Shakespeare the man but also the artist, makes it impossible that Jonson thought of the other's works generally as 'rude things': on the contrary, Shakespeare's plays provide him with examples of 'rude things' *and* 'polish'd', and with more of the latter than the former since there 'was ever more

---

[1] *Jonson*, VIII, p. 583. Since there is some dispute about the correct order of Jonson's notes in *Timber* it should be observed that in his conversations with Drummond Jonson's judgment 'That Shaksperr wanted Arte' comes *in* the section 'His Censure of the English poets', as here 'De Shakespeare nostrati' follows straight *after* 'Censura de Poetis'. A note in the Oxford *Jonson* (XI, 230) warns us that the passage I have quoted is reproduced, in part verbally, from the address 'To the Reader' prefixed to the 1612 Quarto of *The Alchemist*: in the address Jonson's target was faulty poetry 'especially in plays'—which helps to show how in *Timber* his mind switched to Shakespeare. There can be little doubt that *The Alchemist* attack was directed partly, and perhaps mainly, against Shakespeare, for its very words are picked up again in the undisguised gibes of *Bartholomew Fair* (cf. *Jonson*, X, 51 ff.).

in him to be praysed, then to be pardoned'. Defending what had been called a malevolent speech Jonson naturally dwelt upon Shakespeare's 'fault', but admitted it was only occasional ('*sometime* it was necessary he should be stop'd'), implying that the players failed to observe the real 'polish' in Shakespeare.

Drummond, it will be objected, records Jonson's opinion 'That Shaksperr wanted Arte'. In attempting to pierce beneath this terse summary of what may have been a lengthy disquisition we must again beware of neglecting the context. Jonson evidently let off steam in his comments on the poets: those who might be regarded as threats to his own pre-eminence he spoke of comparatively, taking himself as the standard of excellence, as in 'That *next himself* only Fletcher and Chapman could make a Mask'. Now I cannot believe that Jonson, who 'would not flatter though he saw death', would contradict himself as blatantly as he seems to do if we accept at face value the judgment of Shakespeare confided to Drummond and place it beside the lines in the First Folio published five years later:

> Yet must I not giue Nature all: Thy Art,
> My gentle *Shakespeare*, must enioy a part.
> For though the *Poets* matter, Nature be,
> His Art doth giue the fashion.

Jonson was not the man to say one thing in private and another in public, and indeed the subject of Shakespeare's 'art' could have been touched upon less directly in the commendatory verses. How, then, explain the inconsistency? The Drummond note, I suggest, must be treated as another comparative judgment—'That [*next himself*] Shaksperr wanted Arte.' Such a reading is forced upon us by the two pronouncements from Jonson's own pen, which must be given precedence over the condensed, second-hand report that reaches us filtered through Drummond's four words.[1]

The lines quoted above from Jonson's First Folio verses start off a train of thought which becomes nothing less than a flat contradiction of Heminge and Condell's assurances about the unblotted papers. Jonson continued:

---

[1] In *Timber* Jonson's attitude to Shakespeare differs profoundly from his contempt for those poets who 'wanted art' completely and who, 'if a man should goe about, to examine, and correct them, hee must make all they have done, but one blot. Their good is so intangled with their bad, as forcibly one must draw on the others death with it' (*Censura de Poetis, Jonson*, VIII, 582).

And, that he,
Who casts to write a liuing line, must sweat,
   (such as thine are) and strike the second heat
Vpon the *Muses* anuile: turne the same,
   (And himselfe with it) that he thinkes to frame;
Or for the lawrell, he may gaine a scorne,
   For a good *Poet's* made, as well as borne.
And such wert thou. Looke how the fathers face
   Liues in his issue, euen so, the race
Of *Shakespeares* minde, and manners brightly shines
   In his well torned, and true-filed lines:

'True-filed lines' directs us to Horace's 'limae labor' (*A.P.*, 291), and this gives the clue to a longer passage, also from the *Ars Poetica*, which puts beyond doubt the meaning of Jonson's 'second heat'. I quote from Jonson's own translation of Horace:

If to *Quintilius*, you recited ought:
Hee'd say, Mend this, good friend, and this; 'tis naught.
If you denied, you had no better straine,
And twice, or thrice had 'ssayd it, still in vaine:
Hee'd bid, blot all: and to the anvile bring
Those ill-torn'd Verses, to new hammering.[1]

Quite deliberately Jonson selected for Shakespeare the critical jargon used by Horace in describing the *Musarum sacerdos*—one who, according to Horace, revised ten times over if necessary (*A.P.*, 294). Is this then another 'pious literary compliment'?[2] Or an *apologia pro vita sua*, since the cap fits the speaker in various respects? I think not. The considered language, the solemn occasion, and above all the double emphasis that what he says is in fact true of Shakespeare ('such as thine are', 'And such wert thou') cannot be lightly brushed aside. Jonson was convinced that Shakespeare not infrequently struck 'the second heat', that is, corrected with second thoughts like Horace's poet.

To conclude: Shakespeare's free composition is vouched for by his fellows, but there are good reasons for moderate scepticism. Some of his own texts seem to tell a different story; the evidence adduced from

---

[1] *A.P.*, 438–41; Jonson, 623–8 (VIII, 332–3). 'Torned' comes from *tornare*, to turn in a lathe, to round off.

[2] That Jonson falls back upon the words and images of Horace in no sense invalidates his tribute to Shakespeare, for he habitually echoed the classics when they conveniently expressed his own views: cf. R. F. Patterson, *Ben Jonson's Conversations*, ed. 1924, pp. xxxv–xxxvi.

manuscripts of the time in support of the fluent writing of the dramatists is either open to question (*The Captives, Sir Thomas More*), or contradicts the 'unblotted papers' (*Bonduca*). The fashionable admiration
of free writing must have influenced Heminge and Condell, who prove
themselves plastic to clichés in their other First Folio preliminaries: if
their words are only 'true to much the same extent' as Moseley's of
Fletcher (Greg's estimate), we may without injustice subjoin that they
are *untrue* to much the same extent. In excuse of their boast on their
friend's behalf one need only recall that many *authors*, let alone author's
friends, have taken pride in their own facility and have not hesitated to
broadcast the fact with exaggerations.[1]

One way remains of more or less reconciling all this conflicting evidence. Both Heminge and Condell *and* Jonson are right if Shakespeare
introduced 'second thoughts' in his fair copy without deleting (or
blotting) the original phrasing in his foul papers: both versions would
look clean, and either would corroborate the myth of the unblotted
papers even though Shakespeare had in fact changed his mind. This
solution, for which I shall argue with the help of the texts, enables us,
among other things, to steer round one of the rocks towards which
Pollard and Greg allowed their argument to carry them. Shakespeare's
dialogue, thought Pollard, sometimes came to his mind as fast as he
could write it down—so that 'some passages he could hardly have
troubled himself to read over'. 'Shakespeare', Greg echoed, 'doubtless
composed fluently and seldom went back over what he had written.'[2]
Of how many other authors would one dare to speak so damagingly?
Of how many supreme artists, especially such as had pronounced upon
the necessary 'labour' of 'a wise man's art'? Greg's judgment was deeply
influenced, let us remember, by his view that Shakespeare expected the
book-keeper to tidy and even to correct his contribution to *Sir Thomas
More*. Yet Shakespeare was only a minor collaborator in *More* and
would recognise the need for some tidying once the half-dozen co-

---

[1] Dr Johnson, for example, 'told Dr. Burney that he never wrote any of his
works that were printed, twice over' (Boswell's *Johnson*, ed. Hill and Powell,
1934, I, 71, n. 3). Sending a leaf of the manuscript of *Oliver Twist* to a correspondent
Dickens wrote: 'it is a portion of the original and only draught.—I never copy.'
(Cf. John Butt and Kathleen Tillotson, *Dickens at Work*, 1957, p. 20, ftn. The
authors show that Dickens did sometimes copy.) In the *Epistle to Arbuthnot* Pope
boasts that in his earliest writings 'I lisp'd in numbers, for the numbers came': but,
adds Robert H. Taylor, 'they soon ceased to come readily', as extant manuscripts
of Pope's later poems prove (*Authors at Work*, 1957, p. 15).

[2] Pollard, *Richard II*, p. 98, quoted Greg, *F.F.*, p. 111; and Greg, p. 92, n. 2.

authors had handed in their papers—a complicated situation not arising in his own plays; and, as I have said (p. 16), Greg dropped the view that Shakespeare actually left tangles in *More* for correction.

The impression made by some of Shakespeare's texts, that he did not bother to go back over what he had written, may nevertheless be a sound one: if Shakespeare intended to go forward to a fair copy in his own hand he might justifiably put off his final decision about some minor tangles while engaged on the foul papers. When, two or more years later, the foul papers were passed on to the printers, their occasional deviation from the acted version could easily escape notice. In a sense, therefore, the comparative untidiness of some texts gives us a hint that there may have been a later recension—a hint amply borne out by the variants in some two-text plays.[1]

[1] Greg (*F.F.*, p. 106) admitted the possibility of authorial improvements in the fair copy ('If the author was going to prepare the fair copy himself . . . he might leave some details to be determined in the process'): but, not having much faith in Shakespearian fair copies, he did not pursue the matter to its logical conclusion.

Note A (page 24)

BLOUNT, JONSON, DIGGES AND MABBE

For the Blount circle cf. Sidney Lee's article in *Bibliographica*, 1895, vol. I, and Arthur W. Secord's 'I.M. of the First Folio Shakespeare and other Mabbe Problems' (*J.E.G.P.*, 1948, XLVII, 374–81). Even in Secord's admirably detailed discussion some of the facts do not find a place: there is no reference to Leslie Hotson's work on Digges and Mabbe and on Digges and Blount (cf. *I, William Shakespeare*, 1937, pp. 238–50, 255), and none to Blount's entry in the S.R. of Jonson's translation of Barclay's *Argenis* in October 1623.

Greg thought that Blount 'seems to have become associated with the First Folio only after a considerable portion of the volume was already printed' (*F.F.*, pp. 18, 3–4), admitting, however, that his evidence (the absence of Blount's name from the First Folio advertisement of 1622) was tenuous. Even if Greg is right, which I doubt, since Blount may have been an agent of the players as far back as 1608 (when he entered *Pericles* and *Antony* in the S.R.),[1] this does not affect my argument that the Blount circle could have inspired parts of the First Folio dedication and epistle, for the preliminaries were printed last.

Jonson's authorship of the Folio epistle was not accepted by Percy Simpson (*Jonson*, XI. 140–4), but Greg pressed it once more in *F.F.*, pp. 18–21. There are various difficulties: I think we can get round these by regarding the epistle—and, perhaps, the dedication—as a composite work, to which several interested parties contributed. Jonson, Heminge and Condell, Blount and Jaggard may all have examined the preliminary matter, and may all have had the opportunity to rephrase the epistle and dedication.

Acquaintance with the fetish of fast writing emerges not only from Blount's *The Rogue*, 1622, but also from his *Don-Quixote* of 1620, in which he brought out again the translator's original dedication of 1612:

> MIne Honourable Lord; hauing Translated some fiue or sixe yeares agoe, the Historie of *Don Quixote* . . . in the space of forty daies: being thervnto more then halfe enforced, through the importunitie of a very deere friend . . . After I had giuen him once a view thereof, I cast it aside, where it lay long time neglected in a corner, and so little regarded by me as I neuer once set hand to reuiew or correct the same . . .

Shelton, the translator, pretends to be disgusted that a labour which occupied him a mere forty days and was never corrected should reach the public, but quite clearly he was proud of his facility.

It is worth noting that there survive unpublished letters from Blount, scattered through the invaluable Trumbull manuscripts, now deposited at Reading, from which one obtains an impression of his character far more vivid than any hitherto available. Among other things they confirm Blount's intimacy with Mabbe in the year 1623. By courtesy of the Marquess of Downshire and the Berkshire Record Office I was permitted to inspect the relevant papers. At the end of an amusing letter from London (8 November, 1622) to Trum-

[1] Cf. also p. 119 n. 3.

bull in Brussels, Blount added in a postscript that Trumbull's son is well, and a great proficient in the Spanish tongue by the means of Mr James Mabbe, of Magdalen College, who takes as much delight in reading to him and other gentlemen of that house as they take in that their desire (*Miscellaneous Correspondence*, vol. XIV, No. 152). In a letter of 30 May, 1623, Blount wrote to Trumbull that his good friend Mr Mabbe laid a strict charge upon him to send an (unspecified) enclosure, and continued that yesternight Mabbe remembered Trumbull's health in a glass of canary, in which he was joined by Dr Fox, Mr Rob. Dallington and Blount himself; that Mabbe hath made half a promise to see Brussels this summer, if his gout will give him leave, and hath prevailed with himself (Blount) to keep him company in that journey (*M.C.*, XV, 46). Elsewhere Blount tried to retrieve a manuscript which he had lent to Trumbull, having promised two or three other friends the reading, suggesting that Trumbull either reads it quickly or copies it (15 June, 1621; *M.C.*, XII, 116), and had to write a second time for the same purpose (6 July, 1621; *M.C.*, XIII, 11)—which may have a bearing on First Folio 'copy', and on First Folio texts that arrived late in the printing-house. Blount also commented sometimes on the best books of the term, which he selected for Trumbull (3 May, 1623, *M.C.*, XV, 46; 9 May, 1623, *M.C.*, XV, 55), but, unfortunately, no letter remains dated November 1623 or so with Blount's views on the only book of worth come forth this term (as he described Eadmer's *Historia* earlier that year).

All in all these letters give a picture of a man of independent mind and taste, a correspondent both witty and judicious who manifestly enjoyed writing. Blount felt perfectly at his ease in the company of scholars and in addressing distinguished men of affairs such as Trumbull: his interest in Lyly, Marlowe and Shakespeare, one concludes, was very much in character.

IV

Shakespeare's 'Instability': Some Examples

★

In order to obtain a clearer picture of Shakespeare's 'unblotted papers' and writing habits I turn next from the statements of his fellows to the evidence of the printed texts. I shall try to show that despite the over-all perfection of Shakespeare's dramatic poetry he wavered about many details in his work, and changed his plotting, the names and functions of his characters, leaving loose ends simply because he concentrated on essentials and knew that his audience would do the same. For if it can be established that Shakespeare changed his plans impenitently in the course of writing, so much the more likely that he would change in the re-writing, or transcribing, what could still be improved, the language in particular.

Until quite recently every so-called inconsistency in Shakespeare was pounced on by the disintegrators as a clue for revision-theories: it is a sign of the times that in *The Shakespeare First Folio* Greg insisted repeatedly that such clues need point to no more than alterations made during composition.[1] My argument, obviously, will rehearse some familiar facts, though several examples are, I believe, new: tedious as the method will be, and as all documentation must be, it supplies the proof that Heminge and Condell were wide of the mark when they said that Shakespeare's 'mind and hand went together'. Shakespeare's mind covered a great deal of ground in preparing a play, his hand reported only what could be compressed into 'the two hours' traffic of our stage': not surprisingly, he sometimes abandoned his first intentions.

At an early date Shakespeare's 'instability' in plotting provoked interest.

Shakespear show'd the best of his skill in his *Mercutio*, and he said himself, that he was forc'd to kill him in the third Act, to prevent being kill'd by him. But, for my part, I cannot find he was so dangerous a person: I see nothing in him but what was so exceeding

---

[1] Cf. above, p. 4, n. 2.

harmless, that he might have liv'd to the end of the Play, and dy'd in his bed, without offence to any man.[1]

Whether or not Dryden sank beneath himself in claiming to know best, there can be no dispute that it is far easier to allege than to prove authorial afterthoughts. A highly plausible and much-admired allegation by Sir Walter Raleigh may serve as a caution.

Some of Shakespeare's characters, thought Raleigh, 'incommode him by their vitality, and even refuse the duties for which they were created'.

> Barnardine, in *Measure for Measure*, is one of these rebels . . . Barnardine, a mere detail of the machinery, comes alive, and so endears himself to his maker, that his execution is felt to be impossible . . . A way out must be found; the disguised Duke suggests that Barnardine is unfit to die, and the Provost comes in with the timely news that a pirate called Ragozine, who exactly resembles Claudio, has just died in the prison of a fever. So Barnardine, who was born to be hanged, is left useless in his cell . . . [He] is a wonderful portrait of the gentleman vagabond, and is presented by Shakespeare to his audience, a perfect gratuity.[2]

Is Shakespeare so transparent? If we remember that throughout the play the Duke's elaborately prepared schemes misfire (his disguise is pulled off by Lucio, despite his contempt for 'the dribbling dart of love' (I.3.2) he submits to it at last, Angelo does not reform the state, the substitution of Mariana for Isabella fails to win Claudio's pardon), the drawn-out plot to deliver Barnardine's head instead of Claudio's seems to fit into a pattern. Gently but persistently Shakespeare ridicules his hero's simple faith in last-minute readjustments, whether of the state laws or of private dilemmas, to explain which we need look no further than the Duke's dramatic character and may safely drop the idea, in this instance, of *authorial* second thoughts.

But by no means in every instance, for just such a change as Dryden and Raleigh imagined can be proved, often enough, from textual evidence. I confine myself to a single example, a quite fascinating one—the 'governorship' of Montano in *Othello*.

At Montano's first appearance, Q directs '*Enter* Montanio, *Gouernor of* Cypres, *with two other Gentlemen*' (II.1; F: '*Enter Montano, and two*

---

[1] Dryden, quoted Chambers, *W. Sh.*, II, 251.
[2] Walter Raleigh, *Shakespeare*, ed. 1950, pp. 148–9.

SST D

Gentlemen'). A *dramatis personae* list at the end of the F text also mentions Montano's office ('The Names of the Actors . . . Montano, *Gouernour of Cyprus'*) but the dialogue never directly refers to it. Yet Montano's governorship, vouched for by both of the substantive texts,[1] remains a point of stress in the structure of the play which, provided the lines giving the necessary information were not unaccountably lost,[2] Shakespeare forgot to make absolutely clear or decided to modify in the course of writing. In Act I Shakespeare probably envisaged Montano as governor, for a messenger tells the Duke and Senators of Venice—

> Signior Montano,
> Your trusty and most valiant servitor,
> With his free duty recommends you thus,
> And prays you to believe him.
>
> (I.3.39–42)

If we may accept Clark's ingenious emendation *relieve* (for the weak *believe*), the man who asks for relief for himself must be the governor: yet no audience will recall 360 lines later, on first meeting with Montano, who or what he is—because, although he gives orders and is obeyed, the dialogue does not reveal his name. Moreover, neither Cassio nor Othello on stepping ashore in Cyprus greet Montano distinctly, as one would expect were he the governor—though Othello knows after the briefest interval that Montano 'is of great fame in Cyprus,/And great affinity' (III.1.45). On the other hand it can be no accident that, when the news arrives that Othello 'is in full commission here for Cyprus' (II.1.29), it is Montano who exclaims, 'I am glad on't; 'tis a worthy governor'—and adds, spontaneously, after a moment:

> I have serv'd him, and the man commands
> Like a full soldier.

If the 'governor of Cyprus' has been replaced his reaction, open and gentlemanly and quite without rancour, provides a contrast of the most telling sort to Iago's when passed over for the lieutenancy (I.1). Such a contrast between characters became almost a standard feature of Shakespeare's dramatic exposition, linking the first scene with the second, or

---

[1] Cf. Note A, p. 44.

[2] Unlikely, since Shakespeare never reverts to Montano's position later in the play, which confirms, I think, that he decided to drop the 'governor of Cyprus' side-issue while writing Act II.

the opening of the first and second movements, with the help of a common factor—the melancholy of Antonio and Portia in the first two scenes of *The Merchant*, the attitudes of Viola and Olivia to the death of their brothers in *Twelfth Night*, the fortitude of Hamlet and Laertes when visited by paternal advice, and so on.[1] It seems, then, that somewhere in Act II Shakespeare abandoned his plans for Montano, the build-up for which he had already commenced.

So characteristic is Shakespeare's change of plans with Montano that anyone not acquainted with this side of his genius can study it in a number of excellent books.[2] Where was Hamlet at the time of his father's death? How many children had Lady Macbeth? Such questions, the vigorous tail if not the backbone of A. C. Bradley's method, attacked as critically misguided by some gifted moderns, will continue to exercise all those who believe, with Aristotle, that a play is made of parts, of a fable no less than of diction, and that all the parts deserve our attention whether inept Victorians have queered the pitch or not.[3] For we can learn a great deal from the double time-scheme of *Othello*, the double location of *The Tempest* and from Bradley's admirable Notes: we learn, among other things, that when caught up in his subject Shakespeare did not hesitate to modify and even to abandon his plot, to improvise as he went along. If his attitude to a play's different parts was all of a piece we may take it that whenever he chanced to transcribe his own foul papers he would not hesitate, any more than Burns or Keats, to touch up the diction as earlier he did the fable.

'Ghost' characters, who figure in stage directions but thereafter speak

---

[1] Cf. Ernst Th. Sehrt, *Der dramatische Auftakt in der elisabethanischen Tragödie* (Göttingen 1960), pp. 160–1, 172; Hereward T. Price, *Construction in Shakespeare* (Michigan 1951), p. 28.

[2] See Bradley's Notes at the end of *Shakespearean Tragedy*, 1904, G. F. Bradby's *The Problems of Hamlet*, 1928, Harold Jenkins' *The Structural Problem in Sh.'s Henry 4*, 1956. J. I. M. Stewart explained Shakespeare's attitude to inconsistencies in *Character and Motive in Sh.*, 1949 (p. 66: 'The neglect of minor consistencies . . . is simply a function of concentration upon a whole').

[3] Textual critics may be expected to agree with L. C. Knights that the words come first in a play and that we must treat Shakespeare 'primarily as a poet' (*How Many Children Had Lady Macbeth?* 1933 etc.). Yet surely Sh. invites us to take an equal interest in character, plot, even in 'moral canons', and generations of play-goers can hardly have been as mistaken about their appetite as Knights supposes. To put forward a Sh. who is 'primarily a poet' is to return to the chicken and the egg, the body and the soul. I record this controversy because those who believe that Bradley has been 'dislodged' may feel that whatever Sh.'s changes in plotting he would never have changed his (more important) words—a form of bardolatry in which Knights, of course, does not indulge.

no lines, point unequivocally to the author's changed plans, provided that we may discount the possibility of abridgement. So many survive in the texts of Shakespeare that we can be sure that he left a good deal in his plotting to the last moment, adjusting details as the need arose.[1]

Another indication of Shakespeare's 'instability' as a writer is provided by his spelling. According to Greg, the case for Shakespeare's authorship of Addition D in *Sir Thomas More* is 'likely to be held conclusive by anyone capable of judging evidence'.[2] The 147 lines of Hand D yield five different spellings for 'sheriff' in five consecutive lines (Shreiff, shreef, shreeve, Shreiue, Shreue), three of 'More' in one line (moor, more, moore),[3] three of 'country' in two lines (Countrie, Country, Countrey), as well as many less striking examples often, again, in neighbouring lines (masters-maisters, Comaund-comand, lyft-lift, scilens-sylenc(t), etc.) Shakespeare's printed texts tell the same tale, though their irregular spellings will be to some extent scribal or compositorial.[4]

We come very close to Shakespeare's dialogue—which I am approaching circuitously—when we reach the character-names in stage directions and speech prefixes. From the printed texts, as from *Sir Thomas More*, it emerges that he could not resist varying these names—even when his final choice had been made. His foul paper texts, at any rate, are riddled with multiple names for single parts some of which serve a purely *ad hoc* purpose; in *Richard II*, for example, Bolingbroke figures also as 'Hereford' and as 'King', Mowbray as 'Norfolk', and in *Love's Labour's Lost* Ferdinand is also 'Navarre' and 'King', Moth is 'Page' and 'Boy', Dull is 'Constable' and 'Anthony', and so on. Sometimes Shakespeare even resorted to the actor's name instead of the dramatic character's, knowing in advance as he did for which actor each part was designed: in the hurry of composition he evidently jotted down the first adequate or nearly adequate speech prefix that sprang to mind, aware that the text would require some tidying.

Variations in Shakespeare's names may be due to his failure to fix on a final form before he began writing: Dogberry and Verges appear as

---

[1] Cf. Greg's index in *F.F.* for ghosts and mutes, and also *F.F.*, pp. 166, 230, 296, 420.   [2] *F.F.*, p. 99.

[3] Cf. John Crow, 'Editing and Emending' (*Essays and Studies*, 1955), p. 16.

[4] Unusual spellings of the author survive quite often in printed texts, and we may take it that many in the quartos and Folio are Shakespeare's: cf. Greg, *F.F.*, 147-8, H. T. Price in *Papers of the Bibliographical Society of America*, 1959, LIII, 160-87, and also below, p. 79 n. 5.

such in *Much Ado* III.3, but in some later scenes they are simply 'the Constables', or 'Kemp' and 'Cowley' (actor names), and Dogberry also bobs up as 'Andrew' (i.e. clown). It is possible that III.3 was composed out of order, *after* some of the following scenes (cf. chap. XI). Yet in many plays Shakespeare took over the names of his sources and still stood out against uniformity, and then variation can mean only one thing, indifference: so in *Richard II*, and in *Romeo*, where Lady Capulet is the most 'varied' example ('Lady of the house', 'Old Lady', 'Lady', 'Wife', 'Mother').[1]

Quite often Shakespeare did not pause to check up on his character-names, or perhaps scribbled a section of a play when away from his papers and author-plot and sources: in such circumstances errors could multiply. One extraordinary manifestation of his genius for muddling names, 'Nell', causes trouble in three plays. In *2 Henry VI*, III.2, Queen Margaret is addressed by the king as Nell (l. 26), and later speaks of herself as Elianor (l. 79 etc.); in *Comedy of Errors* the servant Luce, whose name is dwelt on in III.1 ('If thy name be called *Luce*, *Luce* thou hast answer'd him well') becomes 'Nell' in III.2, and in *Henry V*, V.1.75, Pistol complains 'my *Doll* is dead i' th Spittle of a malady of France', though Nell (Mrs Quickly) and not Doll is his wife. Without wishing to blow up this threefold error into a matter of esoteric significance we may, I think, insist that it gives a fair picture of Shakespeare's careless-ness: nor should it be forgotten that in each of these three plays there are other similar confusions.[2]

Evidently Shakespeare dithered not only about names and spellings but also about the spelling of names. In *Macbeth* Banquo figures first as 'Banquoh' (I.2.34), though later he is 'Banquo': as Holinshed called him 'Banquho' the form with 'h' must be Shakespeare's, and the name was too unusual to allow us to regard 'Banquo' as a compositor's cor-rection. (The *Macbeth* compositors retained 'Menteth' and 'Cathnes', spellings originating in Holinshed, and apparently took Shakespeare's Scottish names on trust.) Apemantus in *Timon* appears as such and as 'Apermantus', the latter odd spelling being also found in Lodge's *Wits Miserie*, 1596, and, though here some compositorial or scribal regulari-sation must be assumed as between one section of text and another, both

---

[1] The variation in *Romeo* may be partly the result of the use of 'heterogeneous copy' viz. the first half of the play fair copy and the second half (from III.5) foul papers: cf. Fredson Bowers, *Textual & Literary Criticism* (Cambridge 1959), p. 89, and also p. 149, below.

[2] Cf. Greg, *F.F.*, pp. 178, 201, 287–8.

forms may go back to Shakespeare since they go back further. Titus Lartius in *Coriolanus* appears as such and as 'Titus Latius', which looks like Shakespeare's oversight again, for the 1595 edition of Plutarch's *Lives* (p. 238) gives side by side 'Titus Latius' (in the text) and 'Titus Lartius' (in the marginal gloss): the Folio error will hardly be independent of Plutarch's.[1] The switch in 1 *Henry VI* from 'Puzel' (Act I) to 'Pucell' (Act III), once regarded as evidence of heterogeneous copy, also traces back to Shakespeare's sources and may signify nothing more out of the way than his carelessness.[2] When Shakespeare's texts duplicate the variant names of his sources we must ascribe this to the author rather than to the random mutations of compositors, especially when one form appears to perpetuate a misprint.

As with names, so with titles. Ferdinand is both 'King' and 'Duke', the Princess is also called 'Queen', in *Love's Labour's Lost*; after succeeding to the empire Saturnine in *Titus* is 'King' as well as 'Emperor'; and the King in the play within the play in *Hamlet* is also referred to as a duke. I would be reluctant to regard these discrepancies as signs of revision, as even Greg does in one case, and am heartened by the refusal of our most ingenious advocate of Shakespearian revision to capitalise the bleeding captain-sergeant variation in *Macbeth*.[3]

The jingling couplets, and prophecies, taken over almost verbatim from his sources in a number of plays may also, perhaps, illustrate Shakespeare's weakness for tinkering with more or less finished material. I quote the source first and then Shakespeare; the italics are mine.

(a)   Heere lyes a wretched corse, of wretched soule bereft,
        Seeke not my name: a plague consume you wicked
                                                    wretches left.

---

[1] For Banquo and Titus Lartius cf. Greg, *F.F.*, pp. 147, 407. The 1579 Plutarch reads 'Lartius', the 1603 edition 'Latius' in text and margin but 'Lartius' in the Index. The Lartius–Latius variation therefore gives some support to the not wholly conclusive evidence that Shakespeare generally used the 1595 text. For 'Apemantus' cf. Honigmann, 'Timon of Athens', *Sh. Q.*, 1961, XII, 13, 18 ff. Cf. also p. 146.

[2] Cf. p. 150.

[3] Greg thought that the variant titles in *L.L.L.* 'may conceivably have survived from an earlier play' (*F.F.*, p. 224): cf. my note on Monsieur Marcadé, p. 45. For Dover Wilson on the 'bleeding captain' cf. his *Macbeth*, 1947, p. 96. The confusion of duke and king in *Hamlet* may just possibly originate in the consultation of Q1 by the Q2 compositor, supposing his MS. was torn or illegible: we know that Q1 was used in this way, and both texts have the key words 'the Dukes name, his wife *Baptista*' (III.2.234).

Heere lies a wretched Coarse, of wretched Soule bereft,
Seek not my name: A Plague consume you, wicked
                                    Caitifs left[1]:

(*b*)   *Iacke* of Norffolke be not *too* bold,
        For Dikon thy maister is bought and sold.
        Iockey of Norfolke, be not *so* bold,
        For Dickon thy maister is bought and sold.[2]

(*c*)   *Who so* will France win, *must* with Scotland first begin.
        If that you will France win, *then* with Scotland
                                            first begin.[3]

It might be urged that where the plays deviate from their sources the plays are corrupt. But this is unlikely in (*a*) at least, since a minor source of *Timon*, Painter's *Palace of Pleasure*, in a different rendering of Timon's epitaph uses the word 'catife'[4]: and I do not see why it should be any more true in the other cases. It seems, then, that Shakespeare accepted the words of the source and yet, probably at the last moment, could not resist alterations, some of them perfectly superficial—just as, I suggest, though satisfied with his foul papers, he might still introduce new readings in a fair copy.

*   *   *

The different types of authorial 'instability' outlined in this chapter lead one to expect another, variation in Shakespeare's dialogue. Especially if one has studied the holographs of Shakespeare's peers, or of writers of any standing, the suspicion is hard to resist that the variants in some of his plays call for a more thoughtful editorial policy than they have so far received. What precisely we can learn from other holographs I try to describe in the next chapter: thereafter I return to my central theme, the variants in Shakespeare.

[1] North's Plutarch, ed. 1595, 'Marcus Antonius', and *Timon*, V.4.70–1.
[2] Holinshed's *Chronicles*, 1587, 'Richard III', and *Richard III*, V.3.304–5(F).
[3] Holinshed, *op. cit.*, 'Henry V', and *Henry V*, I.2.167–8.
[4] See H. J. Oliver, *Timon of Athens*, 1959, p. xxxiii.

Note A *(page 38)*

'DRAMATIS PERSONAE' LISTS AND 'OTHELLO'

It has been suggested that the reading 'Montano, *Gouernour of Cyprus*' in the *dramatis personae* list of the Folio *Othello* derives from Q (II.1, s.d.: '*Enter* Montanio, *Gouernor of* Cypres . . .'), 'and may have no authority' (A. Walker, *Othello*, pp. 138–9). The authority of the F list does not materially affect my case concerning Montano, of course, since Q betrays Shakespeare's probable plans in II.1: but these lists have a general interest and deserve more attention than they have received.

Miss Walker submitted that only seven Folio plays give a *dramatis personae* list, of which two 'in the Histories and Tragedies, following *2 Henry IV* and *Timon of Athens*, were clearly inserted to provide matter for what would otherwise have been a blank space . . . Hence, we must infer that they were drawn up in the printing house.' There is a flaw in this argument. The epilogue of *2 Henry IV*, and the prologue of *Troilus*, were also 'clearly inserted to provide matter for what would otherwise have been a blank space',[1] yet no one will contend that they were therefore 'drawn up in the printing house'. And if old epilogues could be found, at a pinch, why not *dramatis personae* lists? I fancy that the real reason for Miss Walker's decision springs from the fairly widespread view that 'dramatis personae and scene-locations are purely literary features virtually unknown in theatrical manuscripts' (Greg, *F.F.*, p. 121; cf. p. 355, n. 3). But, as R. Crompton Rhodes observed, the Folio *dramatis personae* lists are in each case 'printed not as in modern editions at the front of the play: they follow at the end, which scarcely argues any special consideration for readers' (*Shakespeare's First Folio*, p. 116). (Printing at the end was not a literary convention, by the way, as with the continental *Table des Matières*, for quartos almost invariably printed the lists at the beginning: this confirms the 'stop-gap' theory for the Folio lists (but cf. Greg, *F.F.*, p. 418), but not their printing-house origin.) Quite a few manuscript plays do in fact contain such lists—*The Launching of the Mary*, *The Two Noble Ladies*, *Dick of Devonshire*, *The Soddered Citizen*, *The Welsh Embassador*, *The Witch*, *Juno's Pastoral* (some autograph, some scribal, and perhaps rather more than Greg implied)—though more do not.

Like Crompton Rhodes I believe that these lists could and did exist in the theatres, if only sometimes—as their sporadic occurrence in dramatic manuscripts indicates.

> The only theatrical purpose that could be served by 'the actors' names' is that of a remembrancer for casting, or as a catalogue to a bundle of written parts.

So Crompton Rhodes (p. 118). The first of his alternatives would surely impress Elizabethan-Jacobean companies with their frequent revivals and

---

[1] Cf. C. Hinman, *The Printing and Proof-Reading of the First Folio of Shakespeare* (Oxford 1963, 2 vols.), I, 38.

their perpetually fluctuating personnel, for over the years a list of parts would save a great deal of time.

Quite as useful as for casting, such lists would also help the dramatist during composition, and would interest the prospective purchasers of his work: conceivably a Shakespearian list could derive from the author, as with *The Launching of the Mary* and *The Soddered Citizen*. This is worth stressing because a list may give us information not supplied by the text and may take us back much further than to the printing-house—to an early phase in the writing of the play. The list appended to *Measure for Measure* states that the Duke's name is Vincentio, a fact not revealed in the preceding text. Greg commented: 'Unless the scribe omitted this name from the direction at I.1.1 he apparently invented it for the list' (*F.F.*, p. 355, n. 2). A scribal fabrication seems highly improbable, for other leading characters in the Folio lists (e.g. the dukes in *Two Gentlemen* and *Othello*) and in contemporary plays (e.g. Beaumont and Fletcher's) remained nameless, and apart from Shakespeare himself no one seems to have felt any great need to 'individualise' characters with name-tags. On the other hand we know that Shakespeare did feel this need (witness his brilliant inventions, Shylock, Othello, Caliban, etc.), and not infrequently pinned down a character with a name in I.1. or I.2 which turned out to be superfluous, that is, was immediately dropped or never used in the dialogue ('Solinus' in *Errors*, I.1.1, 'Prince Eskales' in *Romeo*, 'Ferdinand' in *Love's Labour's Lost*, 'Lamprius, a Southsayer' in *Antony and Cleopatra*).[1] It seems likely, therefore, that Vincentio, like Solinus, Escalus and Ferdinand, belongs to the early, perhaps 'prehistoric', phase of its play—as it existed chiefly in Shakespeare's mind. (When he first planned these works it perhaps never occurred to him that no other character would be sufficiently important or would require to address a duke or king with his name.) And if the authenticity of 'Vincentio' is defensible, the 'Montano, *Gouernour of Cyprus*' of *Othello* could equally well trace back to Shakespeare, whether F was printed from Q or not—which would strengthen my interpretation of the Montano change.

The 'Argument' prefixed to *The Rape of Lucrece*, incidentally, does not tally exactly with the story as told in Shakespeare's poem (e.g. concerning the messengers despatched by Lucrece), and may transmit an early outline for the narrative superseded in some details in the actual poem—something like which seems to have happened in *Othello* as well.

I do not, of course, wish to suggest that the seven Folio *dramatis personae* lists transmit Shakespearian originals *verbatim et literatim*: some of them may be entirely the product of the printing-house, others were no doubt tidied up if authentic. The *Measure for Measure* list in particular deserves pondering, for its incompleteness as well as over-completeness discredits the notion of a scribal or printer's compilation.

At the end F adds one of its rare lists of personae. This gives 'Mistris Over-

---

[1] Because of Shakespeare's passion for naming his characters I would disagree with Greg's note on an unimportant part in *Love's Labour's Lost*, 'Monsieur Marcadé, who appears at V.2.723 in place of the usually anonymous messenger, must certainly have had an earlier history' (*F.F.*, p. 224), and with those who erect disintegration theories upon Shakespeare's abandoned names.

don, a Bawd', but only 'Clowne' for Pompey; it distinguishes Thomas and Peter as '2. Friers'; it omits the Justice and Varrius; but it gives the Duke's name as Vincentio, though it appears nowhere in the text. From this Wilson concludes that 'the F. list, whencesoever derived, relates to a form of the play different from that which has come down to us'. This is an attractive fancy, but for what purpose could such a list have been prepared?[1]

The purpose, I imagine, was to aid the author in his plotting: this does not mean that 'a form of the play different from that which has come down to us' ever existed, only that, as is to be expected, the complete play did not shape itself in Shakespeare's mind instantaneously. The label 'Lucio, a fantastique' may give some corroboration: 'fantastique' was an unusual substantive, first recorded in O.E.D. under 1598, more likely to occur to Shakespeare than to a scribe, and compares with some of Shakespeare's other neat one-word descriptions of newly-conceived or newly-introduced characters (e.g. 'Gremio a Pantelowne' in Shrew, I.1.46, 'Holofernes, the Pedant' in L.L.L., IV.2.1).

Why, if Shakespeare himself at times wrote out these lists, is there none in the quartos? It looks as if the 'copy' for the quartos could not have included them. While occasionally manuscript plays commence with 'The Names of the Actors', the most convenient place for the dramatist's list, if this was to facilitate plotting and lie at hand for reference, would be in the author-plot. Only one such plot survives from the period, and this, happily, starts off with just such a list of characters—a fairly full list but, apparently, not a finalised one, precisely what seems to lie behind Measure for Measure.[2] I suggest elsewhere (p. 21) that Shakespeare could have deposited his papers in the theatre for safe keeping, or that his fellows were given access to his 'literary remains' after his death: Heminge and Condell certainly managed to fish out the draft of one play, Timon, in a rather early state, not to mention prologues and epilogues with an 'occasional' ring and long out-of-date, so it seems quite feasible that they tracked down a few author-plots as well. The dramatis personae lists of such plays as Measure for Measure, Othello and Timon may therefore afford us a unique glimpse of 'Shakespeare at work'—even if an edited one.

---

[1] Greg, F.F., p. 355.
[2] See J. Q. Adams, 'The Author-Plot of an Early Seventeenth Century Play' (The Library, 1945–6, XXVI, pp. 17–27). The plot, reprinted by Adams, probably belongs to 1627 or a slightly later date, but, as Adams noted, the leaves of the MS. are the same size ($11\frac{3}{4}'' \times 7\frac{1}{2}''$) as Elizabethan prompt-books, and there is no reason for thinking it the exception rather than the rule. I regard the dramatis personae list in the plot as provisional because (a) some of its names differ from the forms given in the scene-summaries (e.g. Panascaeus—Panascrus); (b) some of its names, especially those in the right-hand column, do not recur in the scene-summaries (which, however, break off at the end of Act III and are therefore incomplete).

V

Other Authors and their 'Instability'

★

WHEN Lewis Theobald undertook the perusal of 'above 800 old English Plays' in order to equip himself for the editing of Shakespeare he started a new era in English studies. While Pope and Bentley botched many of the most perfect lines in Shakespeare and Milton simply because they felt that these authors would benefit from 'correction', Theobald defended difficult passages with the aid of a new method: 'I have constantly endeavoured to support my Corrections and Conjectures by parallel Passages.'[1] The method was established in other fields, as Theobald acknowledged, and, indeed, preached by Pope himself in *An Essay on Criticism*,

> Still with *It self compar'd*, his *Text* peruse,

but it had never been applied to the English classics. Theobald helped to indict the excessively 'corrective' editing then in vogue, the weakness of which was that it relied on the editor's superior judgment (as he thought) or whims (as his critics at once affirmed) rather than on a detailed knowledge of the author's language. Modern commentators still rely on mere whims, I fear, when they discuss authorial drafts and corrections, for no one has tried to test our everyday assumptions in textual criticism with a dedicated search through holographs of every type and period. Some of these assumptions have proved more pernicious than the wanton 'improvements' of Pope and Bentley: it is time, therefore, to follow Theobald's lead and to look about for eight hundred authorial manuscripts.

Fortunately we can proceed selectively. It will be useful to glance at manuscripts by all and sundry but, if one poet in particular is our quarry, we may expect to illustrate textual problems in his printed books most successfully from manuscripts by writers of the same authorial habits, or temperament.

Dr Johnson once said, 'Sir, of a thousand shavers, two do not shave

[1] See Theobald's Preface to his *Shakespeare*, 1733, I, xliii, lxviii.

47

so much alike as not to be distinguished.' One might echo that of a thousand writers two do not write alike. But with both types of artist some rough classification is possible: of the writers one might claim that they fall into various groups, fast and slow, tidy and untidy, those who copy and re-copy and those who train themselves to dispense with afterthoughts, those who leave gaps and those who refuse to, those who begin composition all over again on their proofs and those who toss aside their proofs unread, and so on. We may at any rate eliminate all those authors of note who, for one reason or another, have little in common with Shakespeare—admitting, naturally, that the 'unblotted papers' elude rigid definition. Thus we eliminate Firbank and his 'huge blue postcards', if any still exist, as also meticulous correctors, Tennyson, Yeats, Housman or Eliot, who are too far removed from the flowing vein to qualify. Nor can prose writers who learned to flow greatly assist us, even those who boasted 'I never copy' (Dr Johnson and Dickens) and 'I hate re-writing' (Scott), since the problems encountered in prose and verse composition differ, and dramatic prose demands a polish more usual in poetry than in criticism or the novel.

As far as possible we must concentrate on fast writers—yet by no means every fast writer will serve. Of Shelley, for example, it could not be said that he scarcely blotted a word, on the contrary his first drafts sometimes consist of little else than deletions, or amount to no more than rough notes for a poem—which he might re-work half-a-dozen times.

When my brain gets heated with thought it soon boils and throws off images and words faster than I can skim them off. In the morning, when cooled down, out of the rough sketch . . . I shall attempt a drawing.[1]

Ideally, dramatic texts would be the best ones to compare with Shakespeare's. Yet not many great dramatists carried on where Shakespeare left off, and of the few who did most wrote in prose, or wrote slowly or failed to preserve their drafts. In addition, 'textual stability' being my main concern, it is more useful to examine works of which two or

---

[1] Shelley, quoted by Trelawny, cited in Neville Rogers' *Shelley at Work*, 1956, p. 4. Mr Rogers describes a typical Shelley draft as follows: 'Impulse, which he never lacked, would run madly ahead leaving where he stumbled a blank, a hieroglyph or the indication of a rhyme or an idea; his difficulty at all times was to get a line or a stanza completed upon the page before its successors came crowding in . . .' (pp. 207-8).

more autograph manuscripts survive than to restrict the search to the dramatic *genre*. It so happens that two holographs of a play by a contemporary of Shakespeare, a dramatist of a high order, confirm my argument—but to prove it up to the hilt I must go further afield. I have gone as far as Burns and Keats, though neither wrote a successful play and both lived long after Shakespeare: they are in their different ways supreme poets, have much in common with Shakespeare, and, last but not least, we can still study large numbers of their manuscripts.

No one nowadays disputes that Keats, as a poet, proved almost the equal of Shakespeare—if only of the young Shakespeare. 'I think I shall be among the English poets after my death,' he said: and Arnold acknowledged it—'He is; he is with Shakespeare.' Even A. C. Bradley, no more lavish than Arnold in praising undeservers, paid tribute to the affinity of the two poets ('He was of Shakespeare's tribe')—a subject explored in a book by Middleton Murry. Miss Spurgeon repeated in 1928:

> we recognize now that Keats and Shakespeare had a very unusual, a very close, and subtle relationship. They were alike in certain qualities of mind and art, a fact of which Keats himself was fully aware, and in some of these qualities they are unique among English poets.[1]

Modelling himself upon the 'Chief Poet' and burning through his plays again and again in the most productive years of his life, Keats achieved a musicality in his verse and a richness of texture very similar to Shakespeare's, though not, to be sure, merely imitative.

According to a memorandum made by Woodhouse and first printed by Miss Lowell, Keats

> has repeatedly said in conversation that . . . He never corrects, unless perhaps a word here or there should occur to him as preferable to an expression he has already used—He is impatient of correcting and says he would rather burn the piece in question and write another or something else.[2]

Miss Lowell thought that Keats must have been 'pulling Woodhouse's leg', since extant manuscripts show that 'Keats corrected and corrected.

---

[1] Caroline F. E. Spurgeon, *Keats's Shakespeare*, 1928, p. 53. Cf. Matthew Arnold, *Essays in Criticism*, Second Series, 'John Keats'; Bradley, *Oxford Lectures on Poetry*, ed. 1950, p. 211.

[2] Amy Lowell, *John Keats* (2 vols.), n.d., I, 501 ff.

Not only at the moment of writing, but up to the last proof. All good poets correct . . .' By and large, however, Keats did not correct as ferociously as some contemporaries, Shelley and Byron for example, and the words 'perhaps a word here or there' accurately describe many of his manuscripts. He may have corrected more than Shakespeare, yet in this matter too he was essentially 'of Shakespeare's tribe'.

I do not claim quite the same general closeness between Burns and Shakespeare, though these two and Keats had much in common apart from being three of the greatest lyric poets of all time. They all came from the middle or lower classes of society in periods when not belonging to the gentry restricted the literary man: none of them enjoyed the benefits of 'higher education'. None could be called an intellectual, in spite of which they had intellects of the first quality. All of them relished the zest for life of a Mercutio or a Bastard Faulconbridge (witness Keats's letters and Burns's poems and letters), yet all suffered at times from acute depression. Much more than most poets they could not help warmly sympathising with every form of life: 'if a Sparrow come before my Window,' wrote Keats, 'I take part in its existence (*sic*) and pick about the Gravel'[1]; Burns felt similarly, whether for a mouse or a mountain daisy, and myriad-minded Shakespeare for 'poor Wat' or any other creature upon which he turned his mind. Each one could sparkle in conversation when he chose (I take it that there is some foundation for the many stories about Shakespeare's quickness in repartee)—and the same gift no doubt stood them in good stead as writers, for all of them could throw together verses with exceptional facility. Many of Burns' poems were composed in a few hours, behind the plough or walking through his fields,[2] while Keats managed to stick to his time-table of fifty lines a day for *Endymion* 'with as much regularity and apparently with as much ease as he wrote his letters'.[3] (If Shakespeare finished some of his plays in two months, like the speediest writers employed by Henslowe, this also works out at about fifty lines a day.) No doubt Keats's acknowledgment, 'I have for the most part dash'd off my lines in a hurry',[4] would have been equally true of Shakespeare and Burns. Finally, Burns and Keats spelt and punctuated as the mood of the moment dictated, and Shakespeare did the same, at least in

---

[1] Letter 31.

[2] For Burns' claims that some of his poems were almost extempore productions cf. *The Letters of Robert Burns*, ed. J. De Lancey Ferguson (Oxford 1931, 2 vols.), I, 42, 46, 123 etc. As is well known, even some of his most superb work was done at great speed.   [3] *Letters*, p. 38, ftn.   [4] *Letters*, p. 339.

Sir Thomas More; while they both—and, I think, Shakespeare—habitually introduced minor verbal changes in their fair copies, especially in those written shortly after a poem's first composition.

Of course, Shakespeare's 'closeness' to Keats and the rest often affects my argument only peripherally. I wish to bring into question certain negative propositions fashionable in present-day textual criticism, most of which urge: 'No poet would do such and such, therefore Shakespeare did not.' The reply takes the form: 'Burns and Keats and others did such and such, and did it often, therefore Shakespeare could have done the same.' Several of these negative propositions (cf. p. 64 ff., for example, *a*, *b*, *c*) can be discredited from the manuscripts of almost any author, a few (for example, *e*) from only a limited range; and most of them are of so general a nature that their validity can be tested as decisively in lyrics as in plays.

But, as I have said, some plays still survive in duplicate holographs and may properly claim the highest evidential value. My most exciting example of textual instability consists of the two final scenes of *A Game at Chesse* by Thomas Middleton, one of the major dramatists of Shakespeare's age. Thanks to R. C. Bald's helpful edition of the play a bare summary of the facts concerning texts and stage-history will suffice. Six manuscripts and three early printed quartos are now known, and exhibit innumerable variants. One of the manuscripts, that in Trinity College, Cambridge, is in Middleton's hand throughout, and another, that in the Huntington Library, California, has the last two scenes in holograph, the rest being the work of a scribe.[1] We can therefore collate two versions of the last two scenes in Middleton's own hand—two versions which differ as curiously as the Q and F texts of some of Shakespeare's plays. And since it is on record that the play 'was Acted nine days to gether at the Globe' in August 1624 and then suppressed, all the evidence points to the contemporaneity of the two authorial texts. Upon which R. C. Bald commented:

> If only the MSS. had survived it would be an even more baffling task than it is at present to explain why one MS. lacks certain passages

---

[1] All but one page, where Middleton filled in II.2.13–19, 48–60, 78, the scribe having left a blank for missing material which proved to be more than expected. In the circumstances Middleton had to condense and therefore his changes (there are several) cannot illustrate my argument as usefully as the last two scenes. For the fifth and sixth MSS. cf. Bald in *M.L.R.*, 1930, XXV, 474–8; 1943, XXXVIII, 177–80.

found in another, and *vice versa*. The known facts of the production and suppression of the play preclude any theories of alteration and revision for later performances such as critics tend to fall back upon to explain the differences between certain Shakespearian texts, such as the Second Quarto and Folio versions of *Hamlet*.[1]

If we bring into the discussion later texts in duplicate autographs the variation in the holographs of *A Game at Chesse* becomes less baffling, and Middleton's 'instability' then compels us to reinspect the assumptions that shore up the textual criticism of Shakespeare.

One word more, about the texts cited below. They will be found to differ frequently from the standard editions: the reason is that some of the standard editions are astonishingly inaccurate and others incomplete in their collation. The *Centenary Burns* (Edinburgh, 1896, edited by W. E. Henley and T. F. Henderson) still leads the field as regards textual apparatus but is quite unreliable. H. W. Garrod's *The Poetical Works of John Keats* (Oxford, 1939, 1958) makes fewer mistakes, but overlooks far too many variants and fails to record the very existence of some vital holographs[2]: though the second edition claims to be 'corrected' it is far from correct. R. C. Bald's *A Game at Chesse* (Cambridge, 1929) also omits to record many autograph variants. I quote Burns, Keats and Middleton either direct from their manuscripts, or from photostats, microfilms etc. of manuscripts, and always indicate the nature of the text and its location; and I italicise the more interesting variants. Only holographs have been used.

    I. Keats, *To Autumn*, lines 17-22. (*a*) Early draft; Harvard. (*b*) Letter 152, fair copy; Harvard.

(*a*)   Or on a half reap'd furrow sound asleep
      Dos'd with the fume of poppies while thy hook
      ⌜Spares the next swath and all its twined flowers⌝
      [Spares for ⟨ . . . ⟩ slumbrous minutes the next swath;]

---

[1] *A Game at Chesse*, ed. Bald, p. 36, n. 3. Later Bald admitted an element of revision, 'probably during the period between licensing and performance' (*M.L.R.*, 1943, xxxviii, 177–80). The two scenes from which I quote belong, however, to the later state of the play, and are identical in the two holographs except for purely verbal 'instability': and both, of course, contain stretches of dialogue without variation.

[2] In his *varia lectio* Garrod refers to no autograph of 'Spirit here that reignest' (p. 436: there is one at Keats House), to only one of 'Souls of Poets dead and gone' (p. 269: there is another in the British Museum), to only one of 'Old Meg she was a Gipsy' (p. 490: there is another in Letter 75). Here and throughout I quote from Garrod's second edition (1958).

And sometimes like a gleaner thost dost keep
   Steady thy laden head across *the* brook   [5]
   Or by a Cyder-press with patent look
Thou watchest the last *oozing* hours by hours

(*b*)   Or on a half reap'd furrow sound asleep,
      Dased with the fume of poppies, while thy hook
      Spares the next swath and all its twined flowers;
   And sometimes like a gleaner thou dost keep
      St ⟨ . ⟩ eady thy laden head across *a* brook;   [5]
      Or by a Cyder press, with patient look,
         Thou watchest the last *oozings* hours by hours.

In (*a*) the deleted line was written before the one above it, which was inserted between lines 2 and 3. *Dos'd* looks as though it might just possibly be *Das'd*, as in (*b*), but Keats tried out the word in a deleted passage just above ('Dosed with re[a]d poppies'), which clinches the matter. Neither *Dos'd* nor *Dased* satisfied him, however, for the reading *Drows'd* of the first printed edition (1820) must be his. Keats's pen stumbled over *gleaner, thost, patent* in (*a*), over *St⟨.⟩eady* in (*b*).

II. Keats, *Lines on the Mermaid Tavern.* (*a*) Fair copy; Harvard. (*b*) Fair copy; British Museum.

(*a*)   Souls of Poets dead and gone
        What Elysium have ye known,
        Happy field or mossy cavern
        Fairer than the Mermaid Tavern?
        Have ye tippled drink more fine   [5]
        Than mine Host's canary wine?
        Or are fruits of Paradise
        Sweeter than those dainty pies
        Of Venison. *Old generous* food
        Dress'd as though bold Robin Hood   [10]
        Would with his Maid Marian
        Sup, and *bowze* from Horn and Can.
        I have heard that on a day
        Mine Host's Signboard flew away
        Nobody knew whither till   [15]
        An Astrologer's old Quill
        To a Sheepskin gave the story;
        Says he saw y⟨o⟩u in your glory
        Underneath a *new-old* sign
        Lipping Beverage divine,   [20]

And pledging with contented smack
The Mermaid in the Zodiac!
    Souls of Poets dead and gone
Are the Winds a sweeter Home
Richer is uncellar'd Cavern   [25]
Than the merry Mermaid Tavern?

(*b*)   Souls of Poets, dead and gone,
What Elysium have ye known
Happy field or mossy cavern
Choicer than the mermaid tavern?
Have ye tippled drink more fine   [5]
Than mine Host's canary wine?
Or are fruits of Paradise
Richer than those dainty pies
Of venison? *delicious* food
Dress'd as though bold Robin Hood   [10]
Would with his maid Marian
Sup and *bouse* from horn and Can.
    I have heard that on a day
Mine Host's signboard flew away
Nobody know wither till   [15]
An astrologer's old quill
To a Sheepskin gave the story:—
Says he saw you, in your glory,
Underneath a *new old* sign
Sipping beverage divine   [20]
And pledging with contented smacᶦckᶦ
The mermaid in the Zodiac!
Souls of Poets dead and gone
What Elysium have ye known
Happy field or mossy cavern   [25]
Choicer than the mermaid Tavern?

The first printed text (1820) followed (*a*) in *Sweeter* (l. 8), and *new-old* (l. 19), and (*b*) in *Choicer* (l. 4), *Sipping* (l. 20), and in the last three lines. Two new readings also appeared: *Old generous food* ((*a*), l. 9) became *O generous food!*, and *Says* (l. 18) became *Said*.

III. Keats, *Ode to Psyche*, lines 24-35. (*a*) Early draft; Morgan Library.
   (*b*) Letter 123, fair copy; Harvard.

(*a*)   O *latest* born, and loveliest vision far
          Of all Olympus' faded Hierarchy!
          Fairer than [Night's wide full,] ⌜[orb'd] Phoebe's⌝
                                    sapphire-region'd, Star
          Or Vesper amorous glow worm of the sky;
          Fairer than these though Temple thou *hast* none,   [5]
          Nor Altar heap'd with flowers;
          Nor Virgin Choir to make *melodious* moan
          Upon the midnight hours;
          No[r] voice, *no*[r] lute, *no*[r] pipe, *no*[r] incense sweet
          From chain-swung Censor teeming,   [10]
          No[r] Shrine, *no*[r] grove, *no*[r] Oracle, *no*[r] heat
          Of pale-mouth'd Prophet dreaming.

(*b*)   O *lastest* born, and loveliest vision far
          Of all Olympus faded Hierarchy!
          Fairer than Phoebe's sapphire-region'd star,
          Or Vesper amorous glow worm of the sky;
          Fairer than these though Temple thou *hadst* none,   [5]
          Nor Altar heap'd with flowers;
          Nor virgin choir to make *delicious* moan
          Upon the midnight hours;
          No voice, *no* lute, *no* pipe *no* incense sweet
          From chain-swung Censer teeming   [10]
          No shrine, *no* grove, *no* oracle, *no* heat
          Of pale-mouth'd Prophet dreaming!

Lastest (l.1) is probably a slip, though it could just be a double superlative influenced by Shakespeare or some other early writer (cf. *Winter's Tale*, III.2.176: 'every word deserves/To taste of thy *most worst*').

IV. Keats, *On Visiting Staffa*, lines 32-44. (*a*) Letter 80, rough draft; Harvard. (*b*) Letter 156, fair copy; Morgan Library.

(*a*)   [Many a Mortal comes to see]   [1a]
                         [This Cathedrall of the S]   [1b]
                         Many *a Mortal* of these days
                         Dares to pass our sacred ways
                         Dares to *touch* audaciously
                         This Cathedral of the Sea—
                         I have been the Pontif priest   [5]
                         Where the Waters never rest

Where a fledgy sea bird choir
Soars for ever—holy fire
I have hid from Mortal Man
[Old] Proteus is my Sacristan.   [10]

(b)   Many *Mortals* of these days
Dare to pass our sacred ways,
Dare to *see* audaciously
This Cathedral of the Sea.
I have been the Pontif Priest   [5]
Where the waters never rest,
Where a fledgy sea-bird quire
Soars for ever; holy fire
Have I hid from mortal Man;
Proteus is my Sacristan—   [10]

V. Burns, *Winter*, stanza 1. (*a*) Fair copy, 1784; First Commonplace
Book[1] (*b*) Fair copy, 1785; Kilmarnock.[2]

(a)   The wintry West extends his blast
And hail & rain does blaw;
Or the stormy North sends driving forth
The blinding sleet & snaw:
And tumbling brown, the burn comes down,   [5]
And roars frae bank to brae;
And bird & beast in covert rest,
And pass the *weary* day.—

(b)   The wintry west extends his blast,
And hail and rain does blaw;
Or the stormy north sends driving forth
The blinding sleet and snaw;
[*While*] ⌜*Wild*⌝ tumbling, brown, the burn comes [5]
                                            [down,
And roars frae bank to brae;
While bird and beast in covert rest,
And pass the *heartless* day.—

The Kilmarnock edition, 1786, reads *While* (l. 5), *And* (l. 7), *heartless*
(l. 8).

[1] Available in facsimile in *Robert Burns's Commonplace Book* 1783–1785, ed. J. C.
Ewing and D. Cook (Glasgow, Gowans and Gray, 1938).
[2] Available in what claims to be a *verbatim et literatim* reproduction in *Burns
Holograph Manuscripts in the Kilmarnock Monument Museum*, ed. D. Sneddon
(Kilmarnock, D. Brown & Co., 1889). This is a sound enough work for its time,
but not completely accurate.

VI. Burns, *The Cotter's Saturday Night*, stanza 9. (*a*) Fair copy, 1785; Kilmarnock. (*b*) Fair copy; British Museum. (*c*) Fair copy (printer's copy), 1786; Irvine Burns Club.[1]

(*a*)   O happy love! where *suchen love* is found!
         O heart-felt raptures! bliss beyond compare!
       I've *paced long* this weary *mortal-round*,
         And sage Experience bids me this declare,
       If Heaven a *draught* of Heavenly pleasure spare, |5|
         One cordial in this melancholy vale,
       Tis when a youthful, loving, modest pair
         In other's arms breathe out the tender tale,   [gale.
       Beneath the milk-white thorn, that scents the ev'ning

(*b*)   O happy love, where *suchen love* is found!
         O heart-felt raptures! bliss beyond compare!
       I've *traced long* this weary, *mortal round*,
         And sage Experience bids me this declare,
       If Heaven a *drop* of Heavenly pleasure spare, |5|
         One cordial in this melancholy vale,
       'Tis when a youthful, loving, modest pair
         In other's arms breathe out the tender tale;   [gale!—
       Beneath the milk-white thorn that scents the ev'ning

Interesting variants in (*c*) include *love like this* (for *suchen love*, l. 1), *paced much* (for *paced long*, l. 3), *mortal round* (l. 3), *draught* (l. 5) and a deleted *balmy* (for *ev'ning*, l. 9, though *ev'ning* was later interlined. The Centenary edition, I, 364, gives *balmy* as the reading of the British Museum text. This is an error: the editors probably confused two manuscripts.)

VII. Burns, *Address to the Deil*, stanzas 10–13. (*a*) Fair copy, 1785; Kilmarnock. (*b*) Fair copy (printer's copy), 1786; Irvine Burns Club.

(*a*)   Thence, countra wives wi' toil an' pain
        May plunge, an' plunge the kirn in vain,
        For Och! the yellow treasure's ta'en
            By [cantraip] ⌈*wicket*⌉ skill
       An' *dautiet*, twal-pint Haukie's gane
            As yell's the bill.—   [6]

---

[1] The six Burns holographs in the possession of the Irvine Burns Club were apparently the 'copy' used by the printer of the Kilmarnock edition. I have not reproduced the various types of underscoring denoting capitals, italics, etc., in any of the quotations from Irvine texts.

Deleted stanza:

Thence, knots are coosten, spells contriv'd,
An' the brisk bridegroom, newly wiv'd
Just at the kittle point arriv'd,
  Fond, keen, an' croose,
Is by some spitefu' jad depriv'd
  O's warklum's use.—   [12]

Substituted stanza:

Thence mystic knots *breed* great abuse
To young guidmen, fond, keen & croose;
When the best warklum i' the house,
  By cantraip wit,
Is *made as useless as* a louse,
  Just at the bit.   [18]

When thowes dissolve the snawie hoord,
An' float the *jinglin,* icy boord,
Then Water-Kelpies [ply] ⌈haunt⌉ the foord
  By your direction,
An' *nightly* trav'llers are allur'd
  To their destruction.—   [24]

An' aft your moss-traversing Spunkies
Decoy the wight that late an' drunk is,
The *dancin,* curst, mischievous monkeys
  Delude his eyes,
Till in some miry slough he sunk is
  Ne'er mair to rise.—   [30]

Interesting variants in (*b*) include *witching* (for *wicket,* l. 4), *dawtet* (for *dautiet,* l. 5), [*breed*] ⌈*mak*⌉ (for *breed,* l. 13), *On* (for *To,* l. 14), *young guidmen* hyphened (l. 14), *instant made no worth* (for *made as useless as,* l. 17), *jinglan* (for *jinglin,* l. 20), *nig⌈h⌉ted* (for *nightly,* l. 23), *bleezan* (for *dancin,* l. 27).

VIII. Burns, *The Twa Dogs,* lines 117–36. (*a*) Fair copy, 1785; Kilmarnock. (*b*) Fair copy (printer's copy), 1786; Irvine Burns Club.

(*a*)   They lay aside their private cares
      An' mind the kirk an' state affairs,
      Foretell what new taxation's comin,
      An' *wonder* at the folk in Lon'on.
      As bleak-fac'd Hallowmas returns, [5]
      They get the jovial, *rantin* Kirns,

When rural-life, *in* ev'ry station,
Unites in common recreation;
Love blinks, Wit slaps, an' social Mirth
Forgets there's care *upon* the earth. [10]
That merry day the year begins,
They barr the the [*sic*] door on frosty win's;
The nappy reeks, wi' mantling ream,
An' sheds a heart-inspiring steam;
The *luntin* pipe, *the snishin* mill, [15]
Are handed round wi' right *good-will*;
The cantie auld *folk crackin* crouse,
The young anes *rantin* thro the house—

(*b*)   [They ⟨. . . . . .⟩ o' Patronage an' priests] [1a]
     [Wi' kindling fury ⟨.⟩] [1b]
     They lay aside their private cares,
     To mind the Kirk an' State affairs;
     They'll talk o' patronage an' priests, [3a]
     Wi' kindling fury i' their breasts, [3b]
     Or tell what new taxation's comin,
     An *ferlie* at the folk in Lon'on.

       As bleak-fac'd Hallowmass returns, [5]
     They get the jovial, *rantan* Kirns,
     When rural life, *of* ev'ry station,
     Unite in common recreation;
     Love blinks, Wit slaps, an' social Mirth
     Forgets there's care *upo'* the earth. [10]

       That merry day the year begins,
     They bar the door on frosty win's;
     The nappy reeks wi' mantling ream,
     An' sheds a heart-inspiring steam;
     The *luntan* pipe, *an' sneeshin* mill, [15]
     Are handed round wi' right *guid will*;
     The cantie, auld *folks, crackan* crouse,
     The young anes *rantan* thro' the house—

IX. Middleton, *A Game at Chesse*; extracts from Act V, scenes 2 and 3. (*a*) Fair copy; Trinity College, Cambridge. (*b*) Fair copy; Huntington.

(i) (*a*) Wh.Qs.P. strange of all *others hee should light* on him, to tye that holie knott that sought to undoo mee, were you requested to performe that *office*! Bl.Bs.P. I *name* you a sure Token

(b) Wh:Qs.P. strange! of all *men hee should first light* on ⌐him⌐
to tye that holie knot that sought to undoo mee,
were you requested to performe that *office* (*Sir*)
Bl.B⁸.P. I *namde* you a sure Token;

(V.2.51–4)

(ii) (a)   Enter Bl. Kts.p.
Yond's the White Bishops pawne, *haue at* his heart now,
Wh.Qs.P. Hold *Monster-Impudence*, wouldst *heape* a
murder, on thy first fowle *attempt*, tis time that
thou *wert* taken;
Bl.Kts.P. Death! proeuented!
Wh.Qs.P. for thy sake, and *yon'd* partner in thy shame,
Ile neuer knowe man farder then by name.

(b) Bl.Kts.P.   Enter Bl:Kts.P.
Yond's the White Bishop's pawne, *Ile playe at* his heart
now!
Wh.Qs.P. hold, *bloudie Villayne* wouldst *thou heape* a murder
on thy first fowle *offence*, tis time that thou *art* taken;
Bl.Kts.P. death! preuented!
Wh.Qs.P. for thy sake, and *that* partner in thy shame,
Ile neuer knowe man farder, then by name.

(V.2.128–34)

(iii) (a) did you but uiew the Vaults wthin our Monasteries
You'de *sweare* then, Plutus wch the Fiction calls
the Lord of Riches *were* entombd wthin 'em,
You cannot *walke* for Tuns
Wh.Kt. ist possible;
Wh.D. but how shall I bestowe the Vice I bring (*Sirs*)
you quite forgett mee, I shall bee *lockt* out
by youre strickt Key of Life;

(b) did you but View the Vaults wthin our Monasteryes,
youde *saye* then, Plutus, wch the Fiction calls
the Lord of Riches *is* entombd wthin 'em;
Bl.D. *you* cannot *passe* for Tuns?
Wh.Kt. ist possible?
Wh.D. but how shall I bestowe the Vice I bring (*Sir*)
you quite forgett mee, I shall bee *shut* out
by youre strickt Key of Life;

(V.3.125–32)

Thomas Middleton's Autographs, *see opposite page*: *A Game at Chesse*, v.3.155-63.
(i) Trinity College, Cambridge; (ii) Henry E. Huntington Library.

(iv) (a) Bl.Kt. ⟨I⟩s it so *uilde* there is no name ordaynde for't
Toades haue theire Titles, and Creation gaue
Serpents and Adders those names to bee knowne by
Wh.Kt. this of all others bear⟨e⟩s the *hiddest* Venom
the *smoothest* poyson,—*I am* an Arch-Dissembler S^r,
Bl.Kt. how!
Wh.Kt. tis my Natures Brand turne from mee, Sir,
the time is yet to come that ere I *spake*
what my heart mean't!

(b) Bl.Kt. is it so *uile* there is no name ordayn'd fort,
Toades haue theire Titles, and Creation gaue
Serpents and Adders those names to bee knowen by;
Wh.Kt. this of all others beares the *hiddenst* Venom
the *Secretst* poyson; *Im'e* an Archdissembler (Sir)
Bl.Kt. how?
Wh.Kt. tis my Natures brand, turne from mee (Sir)
the time is yet to come that e're I *spoke*
what my heart mean't!
(V.3.155–63)

(v) (a) aduancing theire perdition-branded foreheads
like Enuies *Issue*, or a Bed of Snakes:
Bl.B.sP. *see, alls* confounded, the Game's lost, Kings taken,
Fat.Bp. the Whitehouse h'as giuen us the Bag I thanke ⌈'em⌉
Iesting P. they had neede haue giuen you a whole Bagg
by youre selfe, *sfoote,* this Fat Bishop ha's so *squelcht*
and squeezde mee, so ouerlayde mee, I haue no Ver-
gis left in mee, you shall finde all my goodnes
and you looke fort, in the bottome of the Bagg;

(b) aduancing theire perdition-branded Foreheads
like Enuies *Issues*, or a Bed of Snakes
Bl.B^s.P. *all hopes* confounded, the Game's lost, kings taken,
Fat Bishop. the whitehouse ha's giuen us the Bagg I
                                                                [thanke em,
Iesting.P. they had neede haue giuen you a whole Bagg by
youre selfe, *slid* this Fat Bishop ha's so *ouerlayde mee,*
so squelcht and squeezde mee I haue no Veriuce
left in mee, you shall finde all my goodnes *if* you
looke for't, in the bottome of the Bagg,
(V.3.201–209)

One cannot always read Middleton's hand with assurance: his capitals,
exclamation and question marks, the precise place for his apostrophes,

often leave us guessing. I follow Bald in capitalising speech prefixes, though probably Middleton did not intend this in every case.

Since *A Game at Chesse* is in some ways my most crucial piece of evidence in the arguments that follow, it should be observed that the authorial variants in the two holographs have never been published in full. Of the twenty-five variants italicised in the five passages that I quote in duplicate $(3 + 6 + 6 + 5 + 5)$ Bald recorded only nine: only one out of five appears in his collation of the texts reproduced in my Plate (cf. p. 61).

X. Heywood, *The Escapes of Jupiter*. Here we possess only printed versions of the original plays (*The Golden Age, The Silver Age*), and Heywood's holograph of a single play drawn from the other two. Strictly speaking *The Escapes of Jupiter* qualifies as 'revision', but it is often so close to its predecessors that Heywood's minor changes resemble the 'instability' in examples I–IX. As one of the two texts is not autograph I include them only as a tailpiece interesting because, like *A Game at Chesse*, they are contemporary with Shakespeare, but base no arguments exclusively upon them. For further discussion of these Heywood texts cf. Appendix C, p. 200.

(*a*)   These sports, our Fawnes, our Satyrs and *ourselues*,
Make (faire *Calisto*) for your entertaine:
Pan the great God of Shepheards, *and* the Nymphes
Of Meades and *Fountaines*, that inhabite *here*,
All giue you welcome, with their Rurall sports,   [5]
Glad to behold a Princesse of your birth
A happy Citizen of these Meades and Groues.
These Satyrs are our neighbours, and liue here,
With whom we haue confirm'd a friendly league
And dwell in peace. Here is no City-craft.   [10]
Here's no Court-flattery: simplenesse and sooth
The harmelesse Chace, and strict Virginity
Is all our practise.
                    (*Golden Age*, D$_4$^{a})

(*b*)   These sports our Faunes our satyrs and *our selff*
make ffayre Calisto for your Enterteine.
Pan the greate god[s] off shepheards *wth* the nimphs
off Meades and *fforrests* that Inhabit *neere*,
shall giue you welcom wth theire rurall sports   [5]
gladd to beehould a princess off your byrthe,

to change court sollace for our solitude,
Heere is no flattry, heere no Citty pryde,
noe outrage, that beelongs vnto the Campe
the greatst ambition—at wch most wee ayme.
Is simple [soothe,] trothe and chast virgenity
(Escapes of Jupiter, F.76b)

After the sixth line Heywood began to re-write, yet his changes in the 'revised' part help us to decide whether verbal differences in the first six lines are the result of the faulty transmission of the printed text or of authorial afterthoughts (cf. p. 70).

*   *   *

Not all the manuscripts can be dated precisely, and even the genea-logical relationship of some fair copies remains doubtful.[1] Nevertheless, a few generalisations are possible. We may say, for example, that substitution seems to have occurred most frequently shortly after the writing of the first version, and that not even publication finalised a poem in the eyes of some poets. Burns continued to write out copies before publication with minor variations of every sort, and to change the printed texts. As far as Shakespeare is concerned, his fair copies would presumably come into being almost immediately after the com-pletion of the foul papers, therefore the highest possible 'instability' is to be expected.

Regarding the typicality of my quotations, I should acknowledge that I selected them to illustrate the weaknesses in our most widely-accepted assumptions in textual work. Some exhibit a little more varia-tion than is usually to be met with, but I have excluded texts which look like whole-sale revisions rather than transcripts graced here and there with casual afterthoughts. (The distinction, I admit, could easily cease to have meaning.) It will be observed that quite often trivial substitu-tions outnumber those with any real significance; less apparent, because my extracts are short, is the fact that one substitution often leads to another—if only because the author cannot stop tinkering. In some cases the concentration of variants per line rises to the same proportions as in *Hamlet* or *Othello*, which suggests that the high rate of variation in these plays should not be thought suspicious in itself. And that brings me to the first 'assumption'.

[1] I have not seen a fourth MS. of *Cotter's Saturday Night*, said to be earlier than the three quoted.

(*a*) Many editors of Shakespeare take for granted that 'indifferent' variants will not come from the pen that never blotted its papers. Even when they concede the presence of 'second thoughts' in a play they seem to think of these as limited to substantive variants—which is clearly implied in the following:

> Given the fair certainty that Shakespeare made some alterations in these [foul papers] *currente calamo*, their occasional illegibility and compositors' errors adequately explains why the dialogue of the two texts differs so frequently and yet, for the most part, in so very trivial a way.[1]

A perusal of the 'trivial' variants in the autographs of Middleton, Burns, Keats and others will warn us not to wave away those in Shakespeare without a hearing. As I shall argue (cf. p. 167), the mere possibility that some of the indifferent variants in Shakespeare are authorial has serious consequences for the editor.

(*b*) Similarly it is often affirmed that an author will not substitute equivalent words in a second draft, a view flagrantly at odds with the facts.

> I cannot reconcile with any reasonable conception of Shakespeare's methods of work a revision limited to the smoothing out of metre and the substitution of equivalent words, without any incorporation of any new structure or any new ideas.[2]

By using the word 'revision' Chambers blurred the issue: in an authorial transcript one does not expect a new structure or new ideas, while the substitution of single words, especially of synonyms, gives the author his best opportunity of introducing improvements without too much waste of time or effort. Single-word substitution is, indeed, a common phenomenon in nearly finalised texts. 'It is interesting to note that almost all of Browning's revisions are of single words only' observed R. H. Taylor of one manuscript[3]: the same is true of the British Museum fair copy of *The Ring and the Book*, and of many fair copies by other poets.

As with (*a*), even those willing to countenance some 'second thoughts' in a play disown substituted synonyms as post-authorial intruders.

The most striking features that emerge from a comparison of the

---

[1] Alice Walker, *Troilus and Cressida*, p. 128, following E. K. Chambers.
[2] E. K. Chambers, *W. Sh.*, I, 298; cf. G. I. Duthie, *King Lear* (C.U.P.), 1960, pp. 124–5. [3] *Authors at Work* (New York), 1957, of exhibit 29.

texts [of *Troilus*] are the frequent synonymous variants, differences in number and tense, and small alterations of word order. These suggest reporting, but other indications are absent . . . I can only conclude, as Chambers does, that the differences are to be set down to editing and to errors of transcription and printing.[1]

Though he went on at once to declare that 'Many of the variants must be deliberate' Greg evidently distrusted the synonymous ones. I differ from him in that I assume that synonym variants in texts showing deliberate alteration will also be deliberate in some, perhaps many, instances.

(*c*) The transposition of words and phrases is often taken as a sign of memorial corruption: yet few poets arrive at 'the best words in the best order' without some doubts about that order. Only two examples of transposition occur in my extracts (IV, l. 9; IX (v), l. 8), yet others are easy to find. *Tam o' Shanter* contains two famous ones: 'We think na on the lang Scots miles,/The *mosses, waters*, slaps & styles,' (l. 8, Kilmarnock; *waters, mosses* Glenriddell[2] and other MSS.); 'The landlady & Tam grew gracious,/Wi' *secret favors*, sweet & precious:' (l. 48, Kilmarnock; *favors, secret*, Glenriddell, Alloway).

That Shakespeare did not hesitate to try out his 'powerful rhyme' in a new word-order seems to be confirmed by some of his false starts. The 'fly' tangle in *Romeo* (III.3.41) gives as alternatives in Q2 four lines apart (one being usually ironed away in modernised texts): '*This may flyes do*, when I from this must flie' and '*Flies may do this*, but I from this must flie'.

(*d*) From the point of view of the editor a serious problem arises when it is asked whether the comparatively trivial variation described under (*a*), (*b*) and (*c*), indifferent and synonymous variants and transpositions, resulted from the author's carelessness or deliberate choice. Probably Greg spoke for the majority in explaining the variants in the second arch-text of *Troilus and Cressida*.

This copy Shakespeare wrote from the foul papers himself, observing of course his alterations, but making inevitably many small changes in the text. Whenever he was dissatisfied with an expression he doubtless altered it if on the spur of the moment he could devise a

---

[1] Greg, *Ed. Problem*, p. 112.

[2] The Glenriddell Manuscripts, now in the National Library of Scotland, Edinburgh, are available in facsimile in *The Glenriddell Manuscripts of Robert Burns* (privately printed, John Gribbel, Philadelphia, 2 vols., 1914).

better; *but most of the changes were probably unconscious,* and he may even have made occasional errors and omissions.[1]

Sometimes, of course, one of the variants repeats another word in the same line, and when this or a similar slip occurs in autograph manuscripts one readily agrees that the change was probably unconscious. But very often trivial variants can be proved to be conscious, as in the sestet of Keats's *On Sitting Down To Read King Lear Once Again.*

> [Chief! what a gloom thine old oak forest hath!]
> [O⟨.⟩] Chief Poet!
> [Chieftain]! and ye ⟨. . . .⟩ Clouds of Albion,
> > Begetters of this deep eternal theme!
> When through the old ok forest I am gone,   [5]
> > Let me not wander in a barren dream
> But when I am consumed in the fire,
> Give me new Phoenix wings to fly to my desire.[2]

An autograph fair copy preserved at Keats House, Hampstead, gives 'our' for 'this' (l. 4), and 'at' for 'to' (l. 8). These are definitely conscious substitutions because Keats first transcribed the passage as in the rough draft and then crossed out 'this' and 'to' and inserted his 'trivial' variants. In the rough draft Keats also made 'thine' out of 'thy' (l. 1), and corrections in his papers, especially 'double corrections' where he scores out a word only to return to it, amply demonstrate his interest in minutiae:

> > [will] still
> And the ripe plumb [still] wears its dim attire[3]

Early drafts by Burns reveal the same careful reconsideration of the least important words, and the same substitution of more or less 'indifferent' variants. And it is worth adding that there exist Burns and Keats duplicate holographs without any variation whatsoever, or with none in long stretches of verse: though both of them experimented on occasion in their spelling and punctuation, to which they attached little importance, we have no reason to suppose them unable to copy accurately when they tried.

I cannot accept Greg's view that 'most of the [indifferent] changes were probably unconscious' when Shakespeare wrote out a second

---

[1] *F.F.*, pp. 347-8. My italics.
[2] Rough draft, National Library of Scotland.
[3] *On Fame*, Letter 123 (Harvard).

arch-text. With Shakespeare, as with Burns and Keats, we simply cannot tell what proportion of his indifferent variants would be conscious, yet we must reckon with the possibility that many were.

(e) 'It is absurd to suppose that Shakespeare, when dissatisfied with a word in his text, commonly replaced it by another of generally similar appearance.' So Greg, echoing Dover Wilson[1]: and their assumption, one of the most dangerous in the textual criticism of Shakespeare in so far as it prejudices the believer against so many variants, has, I believe, never been challenged.

That an author will not 'commonly' substitute a graphically related word for another (e.g. hulkes for bulkes; Indian for Iudean) is more easily said than proved. I fancy that those who made this assertion have in mind such poetasters as are ridiculed in *Satiromastix* in the person of Horace, who composes mechanically—

> Immortall name, game, dame, tame, lame, lame, lame,
> Pux, ha it, shame, proclaime, oh—   (I.2)

From almost any poetical manuscript other than the cleanest fair copy we may learn, nonetheless, that not only indifferent versifiers but the very greatest poets often substituted words bearing a literal relationship to their first thoughts. In the Trinity MS. Milton had hardly begun *Comus* when, very much in the manner of the pseudo-Horace, he wrote 'aeternall roses grow, & hyacinth', deleted 'grow' and inserted and deleted the following alternatives: yeeld, blow, blosme.[2] The progress from 'grow' to 'blow' to 'blosme' has a literal inspiration which requires no further comment. Later in the same poem Milton changed 'garners' to 'granges' (l. 175), 'prospering' to 'prosperous' (l. 270), 'wearied' to 'wearie' (l. 280), 'wide' to 'wild' (l. 312), 'beads' to 'weeds' (l. 390), 'vast, & hideous wild' to 'wide surrounding wast' (l. 403), 'the lascivious' to 'lewd & lavish' (l. 465: 'lascivious' seems to have suggested 'lavish' literally: la . . . vi . . s), 'leapt' to 'slip't' (l. 498), 'garnish't' to 'garish' (to 'humid': l. 992), etc.[3]

---

[1] Greg, F.F., p. 315; Wilson, *The Manuscript of Sh.'s Hamlet*, I, 165; cf. Fredson Bowers: 'Of one thing we may be certain. When two words are so close in their shapes as *comart* and *covenant*, *lawless* and *landless*, or *jump* and *just*, one or other must be an error' ('What Shakespeare Wrote', in *Shakespeare Jahrbuch*, 1962, vol. 98, p. 44).

[2] The passage I quote from stands in the MS. between lines 4 & 5. Cf. *Facsimile of the Manuscript of Milton's Minor Poems*, ed. W. A. Wright (Cambridge 1899).

[3] Here, and throughout this section, I cite no words in rhyme positions, since such words would be 'literally related' for the rhyme's sake (e.g. 'shell' and 'cell' in *Comus*, l. 231).

Similar 'related' variants stand in innumerable manuscripts. The two main texts of *The Prelude* (neither in Wordsworth's hand, but both supported by versions very carefully checked by him) offer some excellent examples: '*cours'd* / Over the sandy fields' (I, 296, 1805 text; 1850: *scoured*); 'Back to the *Cavern* of the Willow tree' (I, 414; 1850: *covert*); 'Upon the top of that same *craggy* ridge' (I, 398, 1805 text; 1850: *craggy*; JJ text (autograph): *shaggy*); 'with Palaces and Domes / Of Pleasure *spangled* over' (VIII, 131; 1850: 'with domes / Of pleasure *sprinkled* over'); 'As Shakespeare in the Wood of Arden plac'd / *Where* Phoebe sigh'd for the false Ganymede' (VIII, 188; 1850: *Ere*).[1]

When we move on to poets probably more like Shakespeare in their writing habits we find, as one would expect, that those who composed swiftly tended quite often to substitute similar-looking words. Sometimes, in fact, authorial substitutions resemble the first shot so closely that editors have overlooked the one or the other, presumably because they thought the two words the same. Garrod in his *Keats* missed *Sipping—Lipping* in II, l. 20 (cf. p. 53), *bleak—black* in the two autographs of *Lines Written in the Highlands*, l. 46 ('Mountains *bleak* and bare'), and 'townwards' (for 'homewards') in one autograph of *The Eve of St. Mark*, l. 59:

> All was gloom, and silent all
> Save now and then the still footfall
> Of one returning townwards late—[2]

Keats's fair copy of *Hyperion* (in the British Museum) on its own supplies enough literally related variants to leave one very uneasy about the Greg-Wilson assumption—for a single fair copy will not reveal as much alteration as would two, or one together with a rough draft.

> and neighing Steeds were heard
> Not heard before by [either] Gods or ⌈wondring⌉ Men—
> [Sometimes] ⌈Also,⌉ when he would t[aste] ⌈[ake]⌉ ⌈taste⌉
>   the spicy wreaths
>
> the Porches wide
> [Were] opened upon the dusk d[omain] ⌈emesnes⌉ of night;

---

[1] *The Prelude* is quoted from de Selincourt's edition, revised by Helen Darbishire (Oxford 1959).

[2] Egerton 2780 (British Museum). As often, Keats did not cross his initial t, and therefore the two words are easily confused.

in thy face

I see astoni[sh'd] ⌈ed⌉ that severe content
Which comes of thought and musing. Give us help!

O ye whom wrath consumes who[m] passion [stings] stung
[Shut up your senses]
Writhe at defeat, and nurse your agonies

I stood upon a Shore, a pleasant shore
Where a sweet clime [came breathing from inland]
                          was breathed from a Land
Of Fragrance, Quietnesse, and trees and flowers

                          while I sang
And with poor skill let pass [unto] ⌈into⌉ the Breeze
The dull shell's echo;

                          when first thy infant hand
Pluck'd witless the [mead] ⌈weak⌉ flowers, till thine arm

In the extracts I have printed from duplicate holographs we find *Dos'd—Dased—(Drows'd)*[1] (I, 2), *Lipping—Sipping* (II, 20) and *Old* (—O) (II, 9), *While—Wild* (V, 5), *paced—traced* (VI, 3), *wicket— witching* (VII, 4), *Foretell—Or tell* (VIII, 3), and some debatable cases such as *melodious—delicious* (III, 7).

Many of the 'related' variants are, of course, cognates—and if we include these as well the list becomes much longer, especially if singular-plural changes and variant word-forms are added: *oozing—oozings* (I, 7), *Says—(Said)* (II, 18), *hast—hadst* (III, 5), *Nor—No* (III, 9 etc.), *Mortal—Mortals* (IV, 1), *Dares—Dare* (IV, 2), *nightly—nighted* (VII, 23), *rantin—rantan* (VIII, 6: and cf. other *-in* and *-an* endings in VIII), *Unites —Unite* (VIII, 8), *upon—upo'* (VIII, 10), *folk—folks* (VIII, 17), *name— namde* (IX, i), *wert—art* (IX, ii), *Sirs—Sir* (IX, iii), *uilde—uile, hiddest— hiddenst, spake—spoke* (IX, iv), *Issue—Issues* (IX, v).

I include cognates because they play such an important part in the text of Shakespeare. The opening of *Othello*, besides offering such teasing graphically related alternatives as *Oft capt—Off-capt* (l. 10), *Toged—Tongued* (l. 25), *Worships—Mooreships* (l. 33), gives us *has— hast* (l. 2), *chosen—chose* (l. 17), *Christian—Christen'd* (l. 30), and so on. Dare we say, after scanning similar variants in Keats, Burns, Middleton, not to mention Milton and many more, that 'it is absurd to suppose' that Shakespeare replaced *some* of these words by others of generally

---

[1] Variants in brackets come from printed texts.

similar appearance? Should we not consider more seriously the possi-bility of authorial afterthoughts in cases of variation where much can be said on both sides—as, perhaps, in *solid-sullied* (sallied) in 'O that this too too solid flesh would melt'?

The fact is that some poets were remarkably partial to this form of substitution. Burns, who made copies of many of his letters and of other prose, sometimes switched to graphically related variants in such tran-scripts as well. Considerable portions of his First Commonplace Book were copied into the Glenriddell Manuscripts: I have not collated these prose holographs but noticed some variants without looking far. One striking example: 'I have often *coveted* the acquaintance of that part of mankind commonly known by the ordinary phrase of of (*sic*) Black-guards' (*C.B.*, p. 7; *courted* in *Glenriddell MSS.* II, 37). There are, again, grounds for believing that the literally related alternatives in Heywood (No. X) derive from the conscious author and not from a 'copyist's' carelessness. Heywood certainly changed *soothe* to *trothe*, and *chast* in *chast virgenity* (X (b), l. 10) seems to have been suggested by *Chace* in the equivalent line, *The harmelesse Chace, and strict Virginity*: I am there-fore willing to accept *here—neere* (l. 3) and *All—shall* (l. 4) as first and second thoughts governed by the same mental process.

Shakespeare's weakness for assonance and alliteration makes it likely that he too, reputedly a fast writer, would sometimes substitute literally related words as second thoughts, since his first thoughts so often seem to follow from each other literally.

> And thus do we of wisdom and of reach,
> With windlasses and with assays of bias,
> By indirections find directions out;
> > (*Hamlet*, II.1.64 ff.)

These words are tied together literally in *wisdom . . . With . . . wind-lasses, windlasses . . . assays . . . bias, windlasses . . . indirections . . . find*, etc., windlasses acting as a sort of bonding agent. Or, to turn to *Othello*: 'to *slubber* the gloss of your new fortunes with this more *stubborn* and boisterous expedition' (I.3.227 ff.); 'will as *tenderly* be led by th'nose / As asses are. / I ha't—it is eng*ender*'d' (I.3.395 ff.); 'Let's teach ourselves that honourable *stop*, / Not to out*sport* discretion' (II.3.2 ff.), and so on.

(*f*) When the same two variants occur in two or more different plays of Shakespeare it is usually assumed that misreading explains the coincidence. This will be true in some cases, as in *denote—deuote*

(*Hamlet*, I.2.83; *Romeo*, III.3.110; *Othello*, II.3.308, III.3.433), but, since we have learnt from (*e*) that an author's unconscious associations may exert pressure when he substitutes variants it is worth pointing out that Keats and Burns on occasion switched mechanically, as it seems, from one word to the same alternative, just as Shakespeare often proceeded automatically from one image to another in the same 'cluster', simply because some words were connected in the poets' minds with others, synonyms, graphically related words and the like. Thus Keats interchanged silver—silken in *To Hope*, l. 48, and *To My Brother George* (sonnet), l. 10; or sleep—dream in *I Stood Tip-toe*, l. 223, and *Eve of St. Agnes*, l. 281; and Burns such variants as helpless—hapless in the two copies of *On Seeing a Fellow Wound a Hare*, and in *To Robert Graham of Fintry Requesting a Favour* (texts in Burns' Second Commonplace Book).

'Twin' variants, then, trace back to the author in some instances. Are there any in Shakespeare? The curious variation lad(s)—lord(s) (*Troilus*, III.1.101; *Othello*, II.1.20) could be an example. That Shakespeare paused on the word in *Othello* may be confirmed by a later echo:

3 *Gent.* Newes *Lords*, your warres are done:
The desperate Tempest hath so bang'd the Turke,
That their designement halts: (Q)

3 Newes *Laddes*: our warres are done:
The desperate Tempest hath so bang'd the Turkes,
That their designement halts.   (F)

For Othello, when he enters, repeats: 'Newes *friends*, our warres are done, the Turks are drownd' (II.1.200, Q; so F); and Shakespeare could have written Lords—Laddes—friends as well as Lords—friends or Laddes—friends (cf. p. 72, n. 3). In *Troilus* both 'lord' and 'lad' fit the context as well.

If there are any 'twins' in Shakespeare they will be found chiefly among his indifferent variants: the—that, these—those, singular—plural and the like are very common in his printed texts. Doubtless they sometimes look almost identical in Secretary Hand: yet we cannot therefore take it as a matter of course that misreading explains their every occurrence. Burns in writing out his poems very frequently oscillated between the same dialect forms and standard English (to—tae, from—frae, whom—wham, if—gif etc.), as also between that—which, but—yet, singular—plural, etc., and Keats repeatedly changed his mind about trivialities such as thy—thine, the—a, singulars and plurals. Shakespeare too, therefore, could have switched similar words.

(g) Sometimes when an author's second thoughts are discussed it is assumed that they ought to be superior to his first. Because some of Shakespeare's second thoughts would be 'less happy than his first' in such a text as the Q of *Troilus* Miss Walker would not allow that Q could represent Shakespeare's fair copy and include his afterthoughts. 'Neither text is consistently better than the other' she held, therefore neither text, apparently, could be regarded as later than the other, or as a revision.[1]

The word 'revision' may, unfortunately, suggest a more thorough overhauling of the text than would be likely when a fluent poet wrote out his fair copy and in so doing introduced alternative words and phrases (cf. p. 64). In the duplicate holographs of Middleton, Burns, Keats, etc., we do in fact find that very often 'neither text is consistently better than the other'. Alexander's attitude to the variants in *Troilus* therefore seems to me more realistic than Miss Walker's:

> One or two longer passages seem to have been rewritten very hastily, Shakespeare being content to make the passage clear without improving on his first draft.[2]

If we may take the substitutions of Middleton and the others as typical I would add that not only in longer passages but even in the case of single-word variation Shakespeare could have made a change 'very hastily . . . without improving on his first draft', and may even have changed some readings for the worse.

A poet dissatisfied with a line in his first draft might, by the way, substitute for it in his fair copy a makeshift line, neither better nor worse than the original, and in a third or fourth copy continue to tinker. This happened in the holographs of Keats and Burns,[3] and suggests that the fair copies of a fast writer give us not consistently 'better texts' but only 'alternative texts' with some better readings.

---

[1] Walker, *Troilus and Cressida*, pp. 126–7.

[2] Alexander, '*Troilus and Cressida*, 1609' (*The Library*, 1928–9, ix), p. 275.

[3] Keats in Letter 27 began the second stanza of 'O Sorrow' (*Endymion*, IV, 146 ff.) 'O Sorrow / Why dost borrow / The lustrous passion from a Lover's eye'. A second fair copy (Letter 28) gives the last words as 'an orbed eye' and a third as 'a falcon-eye' (Garrod, p. 163). Burns hesitated like this quite often, reaching a record number of variants in *Verses Written in Friars Carse Hermitage* (*I*), l. 12: *idle restless, restles idle, idle airy, airy idle*, and *restless airy* (*Centenary Burns*, II, 348. I have not checked all these readings).

We must remember, too, that patches of 'first draft' may appear within a fair copy—even where the foul papers offer a perfectly acceptable text. The poet could have made an unsuccessful attempt to improve upon his first thoughts: the later text would then incorporate readings that look earlier.[1] Sometimes, also, an author reverts consciously or otherwise to an abandoned first thought in a second or later copy,[2] and this again should warn us not to expect a consistently better text in a fair copy.

(*h*) 'That Shakespeare should not have known which was the better reading is incredible.' This, Miss Walker's view,[3] underlies the assumption (*g*) that a fair copy ought to be consistently superior. Yet even in this narrower formulation Miss Walker's faith in the poet's judgment provokes doubt. For example, Keats in his draft hit on one of his most admired epithets in *The Eve of St. Agnes* and nevertheless struck it out, restoring it, presumably, while the poem went through the press. As printed in 1820 the relevant lines run:

> And diamonded with panes of quaint device,
> Innumerable of stains and splendid dyes,
> As are *the tiger-moth's deep-damask'd wings*;   (st. 24)

In the Harvard holograph we find that Keats arrived at the familiar words I have italicised, not without false starts, yet substituted for the wonderful *deep-damasked* the less satisfactory *deep sunset*, and thus left his manuscript.

> And diamonded with panes ⟨of quaint⟩ device
> Innumerable of stains and splendid dies
> ⌜As is the tiger moths [rich] deep [dama⟨skd⟩)] ⌜sunset⌝ wings⌝
> [As is the wing of evening tiger moths]

Burns dropped, consciously or unconsciously, the improved reading 'Wild tumbling' in *Winter* (cf. p. 56) and restored 'While tumbling'

---

[1] Greg was led by the occasional 'foul' patches in *Antony and Cleopatra*, e.g. a false start, to define the source of F as foul papers, though he agreed that the copy for F was 'very carefully written' (*F.F.*, pp. 398, 402–3). For a 'foul' passage in printer's copy cf. Burns, *The Twa Dogs*, p. 59, above.

[2] In two copies of *Lament of Mary Queen of Scots* (Kilmarnock; National Library, Edinburgh) Burns wrote and deleted *spreading* for *blooming* in l. 2 ('On every [spreading] ⌜blooming⌝ tree'), which looks less like anticipation of *spreads* in l. 3 than an unconscious recollection of an earlier state of the line.

[3] *Problems*, p. 81.

in his first printed text. Either he did not know which was the better reading or the inferior version had fixed itself in his mind before he wrote out the printer's copy, and he reverted to it unintentionally. Sometimes, too, a poet may deliberately tone down a word or line, in order to allow a neighbouring passage to gain in effect. For these and similar reasons an 'inferior' reading will sometimes stand in the later manuscript.

Incidentally, does the critic always 'know the better reading'? Miss Walker herself has changed her mind about the 'better reading'—as will every good critic—and, as I argue elsewhere,[1] the difference between many Shakespearian variants is not one between 'inept' and 'inevitable', but gives a choice between two acceptable alternatives. In such a situation the poets themselves frequently dithered: when the first authorised printed text gives readings that stand undeleted some in this fair copy and some in that (cf. No. II, p. 53 ff.), or when there survive three or more holographs of one work with some readings in the third returning to the first and some to the second (cf. No. VI, p. 57 ff.), the incredible has happened: we see that the poet was genuinely perplexed.

(i) Here again I wish to question a 'logical' assumption and to stress the illogicality of the creative processes. Miss Walker may speak first, on behalf of logic.

It is difficult to suppose that Shakespeare first wrote 'liues' for 'stands' in the peroration to Ulysses [sic] speech on Degree and only on second thoughts altered it to 'stands':

> And 'tis this feauer that keepes Troy on foote,
> Not her owne sinnews. To end a tale of length,
> Troy in our weaknesse stands not in her strength.   (Q)

In the context 'stands' is inevitable. It is one thing to suppose that there were some afterthoughts when a word was the first or an early link in a rhetorical chain, but it is quite different to have to postulate an afterthought in the above lines.[2]

More than a single 'rhetorical chain' holds together the passage in question, however, and F's 'liues' concludes one just as Q's 'stands' does

[1] Cf. pp. 88, 94. The three readings which Miss Walker thought 'incredible' were unanimously preferred by the last editors (Kittredge, Alexander, Sisson), who rejected the substantive alternatives backed by Miss Walker.

[2] Walker, Problems, p. 91, quoting Troilus, I.3.135-7.

the other[1]: I do not therefore find it 'difficult to suppose that Shake-speare first wrote "liues" for "stands" '. Yet even where one reading is truly 'inevitable' and the other ineffective we must not assume, if two arch-texts lie behind the variants, that the author would not have chosen the poorer alternative in the first place. A poet may see in his mind's eye the need for a particular type of word or line to conclude a particular argument, attitude, or 'chain', a *mot juste* that is implied by the context—and nevertheless may fail to hit on the 'inevitable'. Not every writer can afford to drag words out of himself as slowly as a perfectionist like Flaubert, and many were content with makeshift words, with approximations, even in important lines. Shelley represents an extreme case, no doubt,[2] yet poets temperamentally closer to Shakespeare be-haved similarly. To us, judging after the event, 'drowsed' seems in-evitable in *To Autumn*, yet Keats temporised with 'dozed' and 'dazed'.

Quite apart from the common habit of authors of putting up with words that they feel to be less than perfect we must, in addition, take into account the many poems given their finishing touch long after their first composition.[3] A word or line implied by the context or the 'rhetorical chain' seems, when at last committed to paper, inevitable, in spite of which the poem circulated, won praise, and presumably satisfied many others if not the poet.

To label a reading at the end of a 'rhetorical chain' *inevitable*, and thus to insist, as does Miss Walker, that it stood in the author's text from the beginning, is to run a variety of risks. The 'inevitable' will not always come immediately to the poet. It could also be argued that poetry does not admit of 'rhetorical chains' as rigidly deter-ministic as logic would prescribe: on the other hand, if the idea of a 'chain' has any relevance whatever, great poetry will often resolve

---

[1] F's *liues* concludes a chain dealing with sickness-health, living-dying: 'O, when degree is shak'd . . . The enterprise is sick'; 'This chaos, when degree is suffocate, / Follows the choking'; 'And 'tis this fever that keeps Troy on foot' etc. Both Nestor and Agamemnon in their replies summarise Ulysses' speech in terms of sickness-health, not standing-falling ('Most wisely hath Ulysses here discover'd / The fever whereof all our power is sick.')

[2] Cf. the quotation from Neville Rogers, p. 48.

[3] More than twenty years after the first writing of *The Prelude* Wordsworth added the marvellous two lines that conclude a paragraph in the 1850 version: 'The antechapel where the statue stood / Of Newton with his prism and silent face, / *The marble index of a mind for ever / Voyaging through strange seas of Thought, alone.*' (III, 60–3) Coleridge omitted many of the most famous lines of *The Ancient Mariner* in the first edition, presumably because they only came to him later (e.g. 'The sun's rim dips, the stars rush out . . .').

itself into more than a single chain, as in the example from *Troilus*.[1]

(*j*) I turn, finally, to an assumption about variants in neighbouring lines involving repetition. It is sometimes said that such variation (for instance, *x* and *y* in one line, and *z* and *x* in another nearby) lends itself to only one interpretation, being typical of memorially contaminated texts.[2] Yet authors no less than copyists indulged in this form of substitution. Only one of my extracts exhibits something like it (VII, (*a*), lines 4 and 16: *cantraip*), but here are two more examples, from Burns.

(i)   Awake thy last, sad voice, my harp,
    The voice of woe & wild despair;
Awake, resound my latest lay,
    Then sleep in silence evermair!
And thou, my last, best, only friend,
    That fillest an untimely tomb,
Accept this tribute from the Bard,
    Thou brought'st frae fortune's mirkest gloom.

(*Lament for James, Earl of Glencairn*, st. vii;
    Glenriddell Manuscripts I, 152; fair copy)

In the Bixby[3] fair copy the last two lines were changed to read:

Accept this lay from him thou brought'st
Frae hapless fortune's mirkest gloom.

Burns then noticed that 'lay' appears twice in the stanza, so he crossed out the word in line 3:

Awake, resound my latest [lay,] song,

(ii)   Pitying the propless Climber of mankind,
She cast about a standard-tree to find;
And to support his helpless woodbine state,

(*To Robert Graham of Fintry, Requesting a Favour*,
    lines 43–5; National Library of Scotland; fair copy)

Viewing the propless Climber of Mankind,
She cast about a standard-tree to find;
In pity for his helpless woodbine-state,

(*Glenriddell Manuscripts* I, 120; fair copy)

---

[1] I resume the subject of rhetorical continuity on p. 159 ('Verbal Balance').

[2] Miss Walker, *Othello*, p. 126; cf. below, p. 108.

[3] Available in facsimile in *Poems and Letters in the Handwriting of Robert Burns*, ed. W. B. Stevens (privately printed, Saint Louis, for the Burns Club, 1908), between pp. 70, 71.

An intermediate copy demonstrates that these two texts, linked by the word 'pity', do not suffer from a 'copyist's' memorial confusion. For the Second Commonplace Book transmits the lines as in the first version, then scores out 'Pitying' and 'And to support his', interpolating 'Viewing' and 'In pity for his'. If we possessed only the two fair copies of this passage, nevertheless, it might be argued that the Glenriddell text is the earlier and that in copying this Burns or another 'anticipated' *pity* in the first line, substituting 'Pitying' for 'Viewing' unconsciously, and then changing 'In pity for his' to 'And to support his'. If the two texts survived only in print a scribe or compositor would be blamed.

Like Burns, Shakespeare tended to repeat words unintentionally: in the one scrap of dramatic composition available to us in his hand he observed one such repetition (*warrs* in *Sir Thomas More*, D, l. 113) and deleted it, which suggests that in his printed texts, where a repeated word is replaced in the second printed version by a synonym, both variants may sometimes be authorial. It could also happen that, like Burns, in making a change in the fair copy Shakespeare unconsciously caught up a word from the adjacent lines, so that the second text carries the inferior reading.[1]

---

[1] As, apparently, in *Troilus* (cf. p. 89, *bounties*). In this play too Shakespeare seems to have repeated *count* at V.3.19–21, but at once changed his construction: 'doe not count it holy, / To hurt by being iust; it is as lawfull: / For we would *count* giue much *to as* violent thefts' (F only; *to as* is usually emended to *to use*, and *count* is dropped). In Timon's epitaph Shakespeare changed *wretches* to *Caitifs* to avoid repetition (cf. p. 43).

VI

Troilus and Cressida

★

THE old Cambridge editors thought F a revised text, and were followed by several competent authorities.[1] In 1928 an article by Alexander submitted that, on the contrary, Q (1609) printed the revised text, a fair copy by Shakespeare, and that F was a composite version, a reprint of Q corrected with the aid of the foul papers.[2] Chambers, in 1930, no less intransigent than in his British Academy lecture of 1924, brushed aside 'revision' in either copy and put the blame for the many variants on the two printers, the sophisticating editor of F and a Q scribe.[3] Very cautious assent to the 'revised Q' theory came from Greg in 1942:

> It looks therefore as though Q had been cleaned up . . . I think the copy used for Q may have been a transcript made from the foul papers . . . in a few instances the Q and F readings both have a Shakespearian flavour (as in *Othello*): and if some of the variants are really thought to imply revision, we might conjecture that the transcript was made by Shakespeare himself. I am not disposed to rule out the possibility.[4]

Miss Walker, however, in an article of 1950 and more fully in her book of 1953,[5] denied

> that the transcript from which Q was printed can have been by Shakespeare, a point on which her arguments, though not conclusive, deserve consideration. This forces her to account for what she admits to be the general inferiority of the F readings by supposing considerable corruption by compositor *B*.

[1] Cf. the New Variorum *Troilus and Cressida*, 1953, pp. 335 ff., 344.
[2] P. Alexander, '*Troilus and Cressida*, 1609' [in *The Library*, 4th Series (1928–9), vol. IX].
[3] E. K. Chambers, *W. Sh.*, I, 439 ff.
[4] Greg, *Ed. Problem*, pp. 113–14.
[5] 'The Textual Problem of "Troilus and Cressida" ' (*M.L.R.*, 1950, vol. 45), p. 462, n. 3; *Problems*, p. 76.

So Greg commented, in a note in his book of 1955 (p. 350), a book in which he restated at greater length his hypothesis of 1942.

> This copy [underlying Q] Shakespeare wrote from the foul papers himself, observing of course his alterations, but making inevitably many small changes in the text. Whenever he was dissatisfied with an expression he doubtless altered it if on the spur of the moment he could devise a better . . .[1]

Two years later Miss Walker reaffirmed her position in the most detailed study to date.[2] In reopening the case I shall therefore concentrate on Miss Walker's publications on the one hand, since no living expert is more deeply committed against 'revision', and on Alexander's and Greg's on the other.

*   *   *

The possibility that Q includes authorial revision is only touched upon in passing in Miss Walker's article of 1950. Alexander, she mentioned in a footnote, argued 'on the evidence of orthography and punctuation' that Shakespeare himself wrote out the fair copy behind Q—but Miss Walker demurred, agreeing rather with Chambers that spelling and punctuation 'might show through a transcript as well as a print'.[3] Since Miss Walker again stressed Alexander's dependence on this form of evidence in her books of 1953 and 1957[4] it should be pointed out at once that, whether or not we accept Greg's ingenious rescue-operation on behalf of Q's Shakespearian spellings,[5] the possibility of a 'show-through' in transcript may be conceded without prejudice to the main line of defence which is, in Greg's words, the Shakespearian flavour of the variants.

[1] F.F., p. 347.

[2] Her C.U.P. edition of the play, 1957, hereafter referred to as Miss Walker's *Troilus and Cressida*. All Miss Walker's comments, and all my line-references to the play, are taken from this edition in the present chapter, unless I state otherwise.

[3] *Op. cit.*, p. 462; Chambers, *W. Sh.*, I, 441.

[4] *Problems*, p. 76; *Troilus and Cressida*, p. 125.

[5] 'We assume . . . that eccentric spellings were not introduced by a compositor or an inexperienced scribe . . . supposing that there is a one-in-ten chance of a peculiar spelling being reproduced by a scribe or a compositor, the chance of its surviving in a print set up from a transcript is only one in a hundred.' (F.F., p. 148, referred to in *ibid.*, p. 342, n. 9.) Greg therefore concluded that if we find a considerable number of eccentric spellings in a print 'the likelihood is great that it was set up from the author's own manuscript and not from a scribal copy.' Unfortunately Greg throws out the notion of a one-in-ten chance without any serious justification of the figure.

More telling, at first glance, are Miss Walker's observations upon the 45 lines or part-lines found in F but not in Q:

> The impression they convey is that they were not 'cuts' (the longest of them amounts to no more than half a dozen lines) but the omissions of a copyist and / or compositor and that their restoration may be due to someone primarily interested in cues.[1]

This impression derives from the fact that the 45 lines consist of 19 items of which all but six come at the end of speeches.

Here, again, one may well begin with a concession. Some of the 19 Q omissions do appear to be the result of carelessness (e.g. II.3.55–9, IV.5.206, V.2.69). But about half can be defended as probably deliberate: and if enough Q omissions turn out to be defensible, the hypothesis of a copyist other than Shakespeare loses force, as no one will dispute that the Q compositors, like others of the profession, may have lost *some* lines through negligence.

On a later occasion Miss Walker also made a concession, and a most damaging one, as I think, to her general argument. Annotating III.3.161–3 in 1953 and 1957 she came to the conclusion that Q's omission gave the true text, and that F's recovery 'was intended for cancellation'—since both the metre and the main line of thought are disrupted in F. One asks immediately: if F prints an 'intended cancellation' here, why not elsewhere? And a second instance will leap to the notice of every reader of Miss Walker's *Textual Problems*, for she could not fail to agree with earlier commentators that Troilus' farewell to Pandar must have been moved by Shakespeare from the end of V.3 (where only F gives it) to V.10.32 (where both texts have it).[2] The 'impression' that Q omissions should be ascribed to 'a copyist and / or compositor' begins to grow hazy if, on Miss Walker's own showing, there are important exceptions. Indeed, as I contend in Note A (p. 96), several more exceptions can be claimed and, if this is so, Q omissions speak not for but against Miss Walker.

*   *   *

Returning to the 'revision' of *Troilus and Cressida* in 1953 Miss Walker developed another line of attack, Q's 'unreliable speakers' names'.

We know that Shakespeare was careless about speech prefixes in the course of composition . . . Some negligence would not be out of

---

[1] *Op. cit.*, p. 459.   [2] *Problems*, p. 74; *Troilus and Cressida*, p. 221.

character, but persistent negligence of the kind exemplified in Eld's quarto is not evident elsewhere in the quartos or Folio.[1]

Three years earlier Miss Walker wrote of the same prefixes:

> They cannot be author's ★ [★ Not at any rate in the process of composition. An author making a fair copy might, of course, have done as other copyists did.] or actors' muddles, nor are they likely to have originated in such numbers in the printing house.[2]

As Alexander and Greg looked upon Q not as a first draft but as the work of an 'author making a fair copy', Miss Walker answers herself. The charge that the 'persistent negligence' in Q 'is not evident elsewhere in the quartos or Folio' nevertheless deserves some attention.

Unreliable speakers' names may be put into two significant groups. (i) 'Interpolated' prefixes. Those for Helen at III.1.85 and Diomedes at V.2.82 'are hardly likely to have been the compositor's and are best explained', Miss Walker thought, as the insertions of a copyist who wrote the dialogue first and then added speech prefixes too hastily—so that some were 'omitted, interpolated, or out of alinement'.[3] It is, however, possible to hold that these 'interpolated' prefixes represent the genuine text. At III.1.85 most editors follow Heath and Capell and continue Pandar's preceding speech, instead of assigning the line to Helen, as in QF ('Hel. You must not know where he sups'). Apparently they think that Pandar speaks privately to Paris, excluding Helen from their talk. But as Helen persistently butts in and cannot be shaken off there is absolutely no reason to emend. Among recent editors Alexander and Sisson return to QF.

At V.2.77-84 I would also retain the QF prefixes, rather than drop two (Dio: and Cres: in lines 82, 83) and thus give lines 78-83 to Cressida.

> Cres: O all you gods; O pretty pretty pledge!
> Thy maister now lyes thinking on his bed
> Of thee and mee, and sighes, and takes my gloue,   [80]
> And giues memoriall dainty kisses to it, as I kisse thee.
> Dio: Nay do not snatch it from me.
> Cres: He that takes that doth take my heart withall.
> Dio: I had your heart before, this followes it.   (Q)

In modern, emended texts Cressida gives the pledge (l. 67), takes it back (l. 71), then Diomedes snatches at it (l. 82), and succeeds in retrieving it after the coquettish invitation, 'He that takes that doth take my heart

---

[1] *Problems*, p. 78.   [2] *Op. cit.*, p. 461.   [3] *Problems*, p. 77.

withal.' In QF Diomedes pulls away the pledge as Cressida kisses it, and mockingly anticipates her next words (l. 82)—so that her following speech (l. 83), coming after the fact, displays a coquetry less aggressive than resigned to the inevitable. (She says in effect: 'Now I am yours and you must take me.') The triumphant jeer in Diomedes' 'Nay do not snatch it from me' is in character, being on a par with l. 84 ('I had your heart before, this follows it'), and with the ugly derision of his replies in IV.4.116–35.

(ii) Omitted prefixes. These seem to me comparatively unimportant if we accept the Alexander-Greg hypothesis that Shakespeare transcribed the Q copy. Indeed, a run of omissions surely designates the author who, we happen to know, sinned thus elsewhere, rather than a professional scribe whose incompetence might lead to loss of employment.

It is instructive, incidentally, to trace the distribution of the omitted prefixes. What will arouse wonder is the frequent absence of prefixes before short speeches that begin in the middle of a verse line, or after a short speech that would leave room for the next speech on the same line, as at I.3.304, II.1.36–41, II.3.218–20, V.2.86—as also confusion in the same circumstances, as at V.2.14. This suggests that each new speech was not begun on a new line, an inference borne out by other Q errors where speech prefixes following half-lines are treated as dialogue.[1] If the 'negligence' in Q is 'not evident elsewhere in the quartos or Folio' this may mean no more than that Shakespeare attempted a different lay-out for the text, and that, accustomed to running his eye down the margin to fill in prefixes after writing out the speeches, he missed some prefixes that should have gone into the main column of his dialogue.

*   *   *

Another attack against the theory of holograph copy for Q was pressed far too hard by Miss Walker in 1953—as she herself seems to have recognised four years later. Selecting three Q readings decisively

---

[1] At II.1.36–7 'Aiax' is a mistake in Q ('*Ther.* Thou shouldst strike him. *Aiax Coblofe*,'), as F shows. The Q compositor thought the name part of the speech because in his copy it stood in the same line as the previous speech. At III.1.52 ff. Q reads '. . . you shall peece it out with a peece of / your performance. *Nel.* he is full of harmony': / (F: '. . . performance. *Nel*, he . . .'). Alexander follows an anonymous conjecture in the Cambridge ed. and takes '*Nel.*' as a speech prefix ('*Helen.* He is full of harmony').

inferior, as she maintained, to their F counterparts, Miss Walker submitted that they

> seem to exonerate the quarto compositor. In all three it looks very much as if the transcriber of the quarto manuscript had been faced with first and second thoughts in the foul papers and had chosen badly.

The last of the three is typical of the rest:

> At IV.v.187, the Folio's 'And seene thee scorning forfeits and subduments' is again rhetorically better as holding the thread of the *anaphora* running through IV.v.183–96 and leading up to its culmination in
>
> > ... This haue I seene,
> > But this thy countenance (still lockt in steele)
> > I neuer saw till now.
>
> The quarto's 'Despising many forfeits and subduments' not only loses the key-words but loses force through the qualification implied in 'many'.[1]

'I cannot see Shakespeare as either the transcriber or reviser in the three rhetorically poorer quarto readings', Miss Walker continued; yet in her edition she commented on IV.5.187: 'as compositor *B* set this F. page, the F. reading may be a typical perversion'. The huge difference between Q and F, beyond which Miss Walker could not see in 1953, dwindled in 1957 to nothing, and the incomparably better reading may be the worse, 'a typical perversion'!—All three of the examples upon which Miss Walker pinned her faith in 1953 belong to the class discussed in chapter IX under 'Verbal Balance' (p. 159 ff.); that is, Miss Walker insists on a rhetorical chain whereby an earlier word or phrase is repeated, and she rejects the paraphrase or variation (believe-think, deserves-merits, etc.). The answer to such a rigid procedure must follow the general course indicated below (pp. 156–62), and will also bring out that, supposing Q in these three readings has 'chosen badly' (a view not backed by the latest editors[2]), we have seen that authors writing out a fair copy do sometimes resurrect first thoughts or insert weaker alternatives (cf. p. 73).

*   *   *

[1] *Problems*, pp. 79, 80.

[2] Kittredge, Alexander and Sisson prefer Q in each of the three readings, and the Cambridge editors in the last two (IV.1.42, 55; IV.5.187).

Her third survey of Q in 1957 led Miss Walker to stress some further points. (i) 'Q. certainly reveals some bodging'—though she added that this 'need not have been extensive, and there is certainly no evidence that it was'.[1] (ii) A comparison of compositor-analysis and presswork-analysis suggested

> that the Q. manuscript presented no obstacles to rapid composition and, therefore, that the troubles that led to bodging . . . were encountered when the manuscript was copied from the foul papers. [A footnote continues:] This seems to me to point away from Shakespeare as the transcriber . . .[2]

Behind these arguments, and indeed behind all Miss Walker's work on the play, there lies the assumption that Alexander and Greg take Q to represent an 'authoritatively revised version' which would be all of a piece—so that 'F.'s authority would be inferior to Q.'s throughout'.[3] What they in fact said was not so sweeping in implication: 'The Quarto gives a later draft of the play' (Alexander), and 'Shakespeare wrote [the Q copy] from the foul papers himself . . . making inevitably many small changes in the text. Whenever he was dissatisfied with an expression he doubtless altered it . . .' (Greg).[4] In short, though they class Q as a 'fair' copy they allow for the possibility that in transcribing Shakespeare might change his mind and might thus introduce 'foul' and inferior patches—precisely what we find in some fair copies of a later period.[5] If the passages requiring bodging were not numerous, as Miss Walker admits, we may suppose the more readily that some very few 'foul' patches in Shakespeare's fair copy were illegible or confusing to the compositor and that, nonetheless, the manuscript *as a whole* 'presented no obstacles to rapid composition'.

*   *   *

I turn now to the dialogue variants which hold, as everyone concurs, 'the key to the mystery'. Even those opposed to the notion of second thoughts grant that some 'first shots' have infiltrated into F. Miss Walker, for example, besides ceding that F prints some passages 'intended for cancellation' (cf. p. 80), added, in the notes in her edition, several other possible instances: II.2.51-2 (Q: 'Brother, shee is not

---

[1] *Troilus and Cressida*, p. 127.
[2] *Ibid.*, p. 130.   [3] *Ibid.*, pp. 127, 125.
[4] Alexander, p. 274; Greg, *F.F.*, p. 347.   [5] Cf. p. 73.

worth, what shee doth cost the *keeping*'; F: *holding*); II.2.58 (Q: attributiue; F: inclineable); II.3.129 (Q: 'course, and time'; F: 'pettish lines'); IV.5.96 ('the obvious explanation is that they [the words in F omitted in Q] are a first thought, which Shakespeare at once discarded.'). At II.1.14 (Q: 'vnsalted'; F: 'whinid'st') she envisaged a possible 'first shot' in Q. In *Textual Problems* Miss Walker also indicated other places where 'it looks very much as if the transcriber of the quarto manuscript had been faced with first and second thoughts in the foul papers and had chosen badly'.[1]

Obviously if Miss Walker will go so far it becomes an urgent question to find out upon what principles she proceeds, and why she stops where she does. I feel that if one can stretch one's credulity to accept 'keeping' as Shakespeare's substitute for 'holding' one cannot logically deny the same *possibility* with dozens of other minor variants.

Of course, in the uncertainty about QF variants Miss Walker held on to an anchor. As Greg pointed out, she placed the responsibility for a great many variants on F's careless Compositor B.[2] Where Q and F diverge repeatedly, as in the 'merchant'-simile, this to Miss Walker 'looks very much like a typical piece of muddling on the part of Compositor B'[3]—a verdict which must be scrutinised very carefully together with her acknowledgment that when Compositor B's copy can be checked (as in the first three pages of *Troilus*, and in *Richard III*) no such muddling occurs.[4] The anchor is not as firm as one would like.

Even if we could share Miss Walker's confidence regarding the methods of Compositor B this would only solve half the problem. For, however negligent we prove the compositor, supposing the 'substitutions' in his text resemble those in authorial copies, as is often the case in *Troilus*, we cannot decide whether author or compositor made 'good' changes if it is allowed that authorial variants are also transmitted in the texts. We cannot decide—unless the allegations of 'muddling' are justified.

Miss Walker's strategy seems to be to discredit one of the alternatives wherever both Q and F offer attractive or possible readings, thus enforcing that only one arch-text existed. Here are a few typical annotations.

[1] *Problems*, p. 79. [2] Cf. p. 78, above. [3] *Troilus and Cressida*, p. 162.
[4] *Problems*, p. 91. Hinman, however, assigned the first three pages of *Troilus* to Compositor E.

(a)   And therefore is the glorious planet Sol,
    In noble eminence enthron'd and spherd,
    Amidst the other; whose medcinable eye,
    Corrects the influence of euill Planets,
          (I.3.89–92, Q)
    (*Corrects the ill Aspects of Planets euill,* (F))

'I see no point in F.'s inversion of the last two words . . . "ill" suggests interpolation in anticipation of "evil", leading to the perhaps unconscious substitution of "aspects" for "influence" ' (Miss Walker). If, on the other hand, one keeps an open mind on the subject of two Shakespearian drafts it could be that behind F's inversion there lies a very simple motive—the desire to avoid too many adjective-plus-noun constructions (glorious planet, noble eminence, medcinable eye, ill Aspects—Planets euill), a desire possibly still at work when *influence* replaced *ill Aspects* in the Q version.

Greg thought this line 'perhaps the crucial case' in the argument—a slight overstatement—and observed that while F 'is much the more colourful reading and has naturally appealed to editors' it remains 'open to criticism in respect of style and sense alike'.[1] In short, F looks like a first shot and Q like an 'improved' second.

(b)   Achilles meete not Hector let vs like Marchants
    First shew foule wares, and thinke perchance theile sell;
    If not; the luster of the better shall exceed,
    By shewing the worse first: do not consent,
          (I.3.358–61, Q)

    Let vs (like Merchants) shew our fowlest Wares,
    And thinke perchance they'l sell: If not,
    The luster of the better yet to shew,
    Shall shew the better. Do not consent,   (F)

'The F. version of the lines . . . looks very much like a typical piece of muddling on the part of Compositor B, due to his having fouled the metre at the beginning of the speech after dividing the first line' (Miss Walker). Who, then, fouled Q's metre, which is just as bad? Long and irregular lines, especially when the speaker changes in the middle, are so common in Shakespeare, that it is unsafe to blame the compositor rather than the author. Perhaps the second *shew* in F is a compositor's unconscious substitution. But to suggest that this man muddled the

---

[1] F.F., p. 346, n.

rest of the speech because he fouled the metre of the first line is to assume that he was willing to fake the words for the sake of the metre—which is not likely, since two of his four lines are not regular pentameters.

(c)   Nor feeles not what he owes but by reflection:
       As when his vertues *ayming* vpon others,
       Heate them and they retort that heate againe
       To the first giuers.
               (III.3.99–102, Q; F: *shining*)

'F. seems better to accord with the idea of reflected heat' (Miss Walker). Greg, however, preferred Q, as 'more pointed'.[1]

(d)   *Patro.* Thy Lord Thersites. Then tell mee I pray thee, what's
      Thersites?   (II.3.46–7, Q)

Miss Walker drops the second *Thersites* and reads *thyself* (with F) on the ground that *Thersites* was 'caught from earlier in the speech'. It must be remembered, however, that Q's 'what's *Thersites?*' follows immediately two speeches ending 'what's *Agamemnon?*' and 'whats *Achilles?*' As repetition is the essence of the verbal game played by the characters I find it difficult to rule out Q, or to explain the variation with certitude.

It will have become patent that my object is not so much to establish the superiority of those readings swept aside by Miss Walker as simply to defend them as possible first or second shots. Consequently the opinions of the most competent recent editors are very relevant here. To avoid any impression of prejudice I accept a short-list drawn up by Miss Walker herself: the old Cambridge editors, W. J. Craig (the Oxford editor), Kittredge, Alexander and Sisson.[2] How do Miss Walker's expert witnesses react to the variants stigmatised by her as pointless and bungled?

(a) Q: Miss Walker.
      F: Cambridge, Craig, Kittredge, Alexander, Sisson (and Greg).
(b) Q: Miss Walker.
      F: Cambridge, Craig, Kittredge.
      F with some modification from Q: Alexander, Sisson.

---

[1] *F.F.*, p. 345.
[2] Cf. Miss Walker's *Othello*, p. 126 ff., *Troilus and Cressida*, p. 129. Craig does not appear in the second. I have added in brackets Greg's verdict on those few variants which he picked out for discussion (*F.F.*, p. 338 ff.).

(c) Q: Kittredge, Sisson (and Greg).
     F: Cambridge, Craig, Alexander, Miss Walker.
(d) Q: Alexander.
     F: Cambridge, Craig, Kittredge, Sisson, Miss Walker.

There is no unanimity, except in so far as all the experts part company with Miss Walker in (a) and (b), where she dismisses their text with least hesitation. In brief, these four cruxes split the authorities, as do many, many more: the differences between variants are not as clear-cut and indisputable as Miss Walker would like to compel us to believe. It should be added that quite often Miss Walker herself vacillates between the two texts and chooses one 'doubtfully', or says of the rejected one that 'it may be right'[1]: indeed, she has reversed her judgment in some cases,[2] an even surer sign of doubt. On such occasions she usually finds fault with both F and Q, which are 'foolish' or 'bungling' or 'vulgarised'—since it would embarrass her thesis to admit that *both* could pass as Shakespeare's. In reading such uncompromising judgments we must remember that the best editors frequently preferred the variant branded by Miss Walker, as also that the language of the play is often deliberately difficult.

Let us see now what more can be said on the other side, on behalf of the 'Shakespearian flavour' of both texts in some of their variants.

(e)   I haue a roisting challenge sent amongst
              The dull and factious nobles of the Greekes,
              Will *shrike* amazement to their drowsie spirits,
                         (II.2.208–10; F: *strike*)

(f)   They clap the lubber Aiax on the shoulder
              As if his foote were one braue Hectors brest,
              And great Troy *shriking*.
                        (III.3.139–41; F: *shrinking*)

The 'short-list' of editors prefers F in the first (e), and divides between F and Q in the second (f); Miss Walker votes for F both times. The special interest of these two passages is that they were set by different Q compositors (Eld B and A), and that *shrike* (= shriek), which also survives in Q at II.2.97 (F: *shreeke*) is a Shakespearian spelling[3] not very

---

[1] Cf. the notes on I.2.259, I.3.293, 294, 352, etc.
[2] Cf. p. 83, above. In 1950 Miss Walker thought Q's *pale* inferior to F's *stale* at II.2.79 (*op. cit.*, p. 460), but in 1957 she preferred *pale*: and there are other changes of the same sort.
[3] As in *Romeo* IV.3.47, V.3.189 (Q2 and F), *MND.* I.2.68.

common in 1609. Moreover, as Malone recognised, 'Troy shrieking' in
(*f*) ties up with 'Hark how Troy roars! how Hecuba cries out!'—and,
indeed, with Shakespeare's source.[1] Those who throw out the Q variants therefore ask us to believe that a copyist or different compositors
changed the text and produced an unusual spelling, a Shakespearian
spelling, which both times makes excellent sense. I submit that, whichever reading we select as better, we must allow a strong presumption
that *shrike* in both (*e*) and (*f*) came from Shakespeare.

(*g*)   As Hectors leisure, and your bounties shall
         Concurre together, seuerally entreate him
         To taste your bounties, let the trumpets blowe,
         That this great souldier may his welcome know.
              (IV.5.273–6; F: *Beate lowd the Taborins*)

Most editors, including Miss Walker, follow F, which avoids the
awkward repetition of 'bounties'. Yet, as Miss Walker noted, 'the Q.
phrase might certainly have been written by Shakespeare since its like
occurs twice in *Timon of Athens*'.[2] If we assume revision in Q, she continued, 'the verdict of the editors suggests that . . . Shakespeare's second
thoughts were less happy than his first', therefore 'an equally strong
case could be made for revision in F.' But is the position then, as she
concludes, 'one of stalemate'? Miss Walker overlooked that authors in
copying or revising do sometimes catch a word from a neighbouring
line, and may insert some inferior variants influenced by adjacent words
(cf. pp. 76–7). When editors prefer one text, as here, and the other
reproduces an unusual phrase employed elsewhere by the author, this
argues for two arch-texts much more strongly than an inferior second
thought argues against.[3]

(*h*)   . . . venerable Nestor (hatcht in siluer)
         Should with a bond of ayre strong as the Axel-tree,
         (*On which heauen rides*) knit all the Greekish eares
         To his experienc't tongue
              (I.3.65–8, Q; F: *In which the Heauens ride,*
                              knit all Greekes eares)

[1] Cf. *Troilus* V.3.83, and V.10.16. Also Chaucer's *Troilus and Criseyde*, Bk. 5,
stanzas 223, 224.

[2] *Troilus and Cressida*, p. 126, quoting *Timon*: 'And taste Lord Timon's bounty'
(I.1.276), 'Having often of your open bounty tasted' (V.1.56).

[3] Similarly, when Miss Walker rejects an unusual word like acerbe (*Othello*,
I.3.348), which occurs in the play's source, this may indicate two arch-texts: cf.
p. 106.

Choosing Q Miss Walker calls F 'a typical compositor *B* perversion'. Yet in the same scene the plural 'heavens' and not the singular reappears:

> The heauens them-selues, the plannets and this center
> Obserue degree, prioritie and place,
>   (I.3.85–6, Q; so F)

And plural 'heavens' in l. 67 would naturally take 'the' with it, upsetting the metre—so that there are two syllables less for the end of the line. Leaving aside *In* for *On*, the 'typical compositor *B* perversion' rests on a usage vouched for by repetition (a form of 'evidence' much respected by Miss Walker: cf. p. 159), from which springs the subsequent variation.[1]

Here as elsewhere Miss Walker paints a black picture of Compositor B's tinkering: 'weak substitutions are a prevalent feature of B's work'.[2] Barring the initial *In*, is F really weaker?

If B was sometimes careless, which I am willing to believe, one would expect a fairly even spread of variants in his work. Yet now and then there occur longish stretches without error and suddenly a few lines crammed with new readings. For example

(i)   If then one is, or hath *a* meanes to be,
        That one meetes Hector: if none else *I am he*.   [290]
            Nest. Tell him of Nestor, one that was a man
        When Hectors grand-sire suckt. He is old now,
        But if there be not in our Grecian *hoste*,
        A noble man that hath *no* sparke of fire
        To answer for his loue, tell him from me,   [295]
        Ile hide my siluer beard in a gould beauer,
        And in my *vambrance* put *my* withered *braunes*
        And meeting him *tell* him that my Lady,
        Was fairer then his grandam, and as chast,
        As may bee in the world, (his youth in flood)   [300]
        Ile *proue this troth* with my three drops of bloud,
            Æne. Now heauens *for-fend* such scarcity of *men*.
                    (I.3.289–302, Q; F: *or* (l. 289), *Ile be he* (l. 290),
mould (l. 293), *One . . . one* (l. 294), *Vantbrace . . . this . . . brawne*
(l. 297), *wil tell* (l. 298), *pawne this truth* (l. 301), *forbid . . . youth* (l. 302))

---

[1] Cf. also Tofte's *Laura*, 1597: 'The heavens their restless sphere do always move . . .' (Pt. 2, no. 40).
[2] *Problems*, p. 92.

Has Compositor B gone suddenly mad? And, incidentally, have Q's two compositors gone suddenly mad at the same point?[1] In fourteen lines the three men yield a crop of ten variants, most of them possible readings in both texts, whereas in the preceding fourteen they have only one (*couple*—*compasse*, l. 276. I count as one connected variants like *this* ... *brawne*). The fact that editors committed to the theory of a single arch-text here put the blame for 'corruption' equally on Q and F is, I need hardly emphasise, of considerable importance (it exonerates Compositor B), as is the choice of variants from both texts by the other side. (Miss Walker prints *or* (F), *I am he* (Q), *host* (Q), *One* ... *one* (F), *this* ... *brawn* (F), *will tell* (F), *prove* (Q), *truth* (F), *forfend* (Q), *youth* (F). So, too, the Cambridge editors (except for one reading: *forbid*), and Alexander (except for one reading: *mould*).)

From this multiple 'corruption' in both Q and F anyone who believes in a single arch-text will draw the obvious inference that Shakespeare's papers gave difficulty—so that the Q 'scribe' and F corrector both resorted to some guessing. This is possible, but one could then press that the trouble will have started with deletions and substitutions by the author—in which case a few of the variants could represent second thoughts, or simply authorial alternatives. I think, however, that Middleton's two holographs of *A Game at Chesse* shed more light on the problem. Repeatedly Middleton copied stretches of dialogue absolutely correctly, and then, all at once, as in *Troilus*, embarked on a series of variants. (To save space I quote only variant passages: cf. p. 59 ff.) One substitution brought on another, often for no discernible reason: I feel that, like Middleton, Shakespeare could have switched to many of Q's alternatives, *I am he, hoste, A* ... *no, my* ... *braunes, troth, for-fend*, perhaps even *proue* (*pawne* seems just possible) and *men* (over-looking the jingle with the next word, *Amen*). Q has only two very probable errors (*a*, l. 289: misreading; *him tell*, l. 298) and no F reading is impossible (except, perhaps, *pawne*).[2]

*   *   *

Alexander and Greg are in substantial agreement about the motives for Shakespeare's changes in Q.

Sometimes a flat and commonplace reading in F appears to have been

---

[1] Eld's Compositor A takes over from Eld B at l. 296 (Miss Walker, *Troilus and Cressida*, p. 129).

[2] O.E.D. shows that *vantbrace-vambrace* and *truth-troth* were interchangeable.

replaced by one with more flavour in it; sometimes a forced and obscure expression gives place to simpler and directer manner of speech; sometimes we can detect other good reasons for the change.[1]

If the study of authorial substitutions in manuscripts has taught me anything it is that very often we *cannot* 'detect . . . good reasons for the change'. How many of Middleton's variants in *A Game at Chesse* could one explain on rational grounds? Consequently, and because I disagree with Greg's opinion that 'most of the changes were probably unconscious' (cf. p. 66), it seems to me imperative not to stop short after the self-evident examples of second thoughts—some of them conceded by Miss Walker—but to enquire what minor variants could have the same provenance. For, as we have seen (p. 63 ff.), whenever authorial fair copies introduce new readings minor or 'indifferent' variants may vastly outnumber those that are obvious.

(i) Synonyms could be substituted by Shakespeare (cf. p. 64): 'is not birth, beauty, good shape . . . liberallity *and such like*' (I.2.255, Q; F: *and so forth*); 'Breakes scurrell iests, / And with ridiculous and *sillie* action, / . . . He pageants vs' (I.3.149, Q; F: *aukward*); 'Achilles . . . / Cries excellent; 'tis Ag memnon [*sic*] *right*, / Now play me Nestor' (I.3.164, Q; F: *iust*); 'I begin to relish thy aduise, / And I will giue a taste *thereof* forthwith' (I.3.388, Q; F: *of it*).

(ii) Cognate words, and singulars and plurals, could be substituted by Shakespeare (cf. p. 69): 'the spice & salt that *season* a man' (I.2.256, Q; F: *seasons*); 'Trumpet blowe *alowd*' (I.3.256, Q; F: *loud*); 'who may you elce oppose, / That can from Hector bring *those honours* off, / If not Achilles' (I.3.334, Q; F: *his Honor*); 'Way you the worth and honour of a King: / So great as our dread *fathers* in a scale / Of common ounces?' (II.2.27, Q; F: *Father*); 'Adde to my *clamours*: let vs pay be-times / A moytie of that masse of mone to come:' (II.2.106, Q; F: *clamour*).

Sometimes we may guess at a reason for the change. At IV.1.58 Q's *soyle* for F's *soylure* avoids rhythmical awkwardness:

> Hee merits well to haue her that doth seeke her,
> Not making any scruple of her *soyle*,

Merits—haue her—seek her—making—scruple—soilure, all stressed on the first syllable, have an unfortunate tripping effect.

(iii) Shakespeare could transpose words and phrases (cf. p. 65): 'I shall *say so* to him' (II.3.82, Q; F: *so say*); 'A hoarson dog that shall palter *with vs thus*, would he were a Troyan?' (II.3.230, Q; F: *thus with vs*); 'I loue you now, but *till now not* so much / But I might maister it' (III.2.119, Q; F: *not till now*). There are also more extensive rearrangements:

> I would be gone:
> Where is my wit? I know not what I speake,
> > (III.2.149–50, Q)
> Where is my wit?
> I would be gone: I speake I know not what. (F)

(iv) Shakespeare could substitute literally related words (cf. p. 67):

> Take but degree away, vntune that string,
> And harke what discord followes, each thing *melts*
> In meere oppugnancie:
> > (I.3.110, Q; F: *meetes*)[1]

> He hath a Lady, wiser, fairer, truer,
> Then euer Greeke did *couple* in his armes,
> > (I.3.276, Q; F: *compasse*)

> *Æn.* Good, good, my lord, the secrets *of neighbor Pandar*
> *Haue* not more guift in taciturnitie.
> > (IV.2.72–3, Q; F: *of nature | Haue*)

Of the last Miss Walker says 'F.'s "nature" and Q.'s "neighbor" were clearly readings of the same word (possibly MS. "nabor")'. Yet the editors have been anxious to hold on to the wittiness of 'the secrets of nature', with some emendation, or at least to 'nature' (cf. the New Variorum Edition, 1953, p. 209).

These are only a few examples from each class of minor variants. I do not, I repeat, claim them as definite authorial variants: my purpose is only to insist that *they and many more could be authorial*. Precisely the same types of variation were also introduced, we may take it, by the compositors: yet, even when a compositor is proved to have had a strong tendency towards one class of substitution we must not rule out the possibility, in a text or group of texts presumed to include second thoughts, that authorial afterthoughts apparently of the same class may survive in that compositor's work. Time and again we simply cannot

---

[1] 'F. is more forceful' (Miss Walker). But is the idea of 'meeting' not contained in 'oppugnancy'? That 'each thing melts' when degree is taken away seems to me not only a more pregnant image but also links with the later one (l. 124) **of appetite eating up himself.**

tell upon whom to fasten the responsibility for a trivial alternative word or phrase: not to acknowledge our helplessness is to risk grave miscalculations in editorial policy.[1]

*   *   *

In the final analysis the various differences outlined above are governed by general assumptions, about authorial texts and textual criticism, in which I diverge sharply from Miss Walker. It will be useful to set out these assumptions, for more is at stake than the one play.

(i) Miss Walker holds that supposing Shakespeare made out a fair copy of a play this would be 'an authoritatively revised version' and 'consistently better' than the foul papers.[2] I believe that an authorial transcript hurriedly written would frequently substitute variants not markedly superior to the original version (especially when the dramatist, Middleton, Heywood, or Shakespeare, composed swiftly), would sometimes interpolate inferior substitutions—and also some 'foul' patches which might fall below the standard of the original.

(ii) It seems significant to Miss Walker that 'there is nowhere so much as a line which differs wholly from its counterpart' in Q and F: strange, she implies, if Shakespeare was the Q copyist. Yet single-word substitution without more detailed revision is not at all uncommon in final authorial drafts.[3]

(iii) Repeatedly Miss Walker gives the impression that the choice between Q and F is clear-cut, that one is 'inept' and the other 'inevitable'. In doing so she ignores a very strong editorial tradition, which sometimes favours the discarded variant and sometimes divides between the two: indeed, she fails to draw the obvious conclusion from her own expressed doubts about some cruxes. I believe that Miss Walker editorialises against perfectly acceptable variants and that her 'corrective' methods are, in turn, based upon largely unsound assumptions (cf. 'Corrective Editing': p. 153 ff.).

(iv) Like other editors Miss Walker agrees that some F readings are first shots and some Q readings authorial substitutions. If it could be established that Q was printed from a holograph Miss Walker's position would become untenable, and therefore she tries very hard to head off this danger. Her search for more and more counter-arguments (cf. pp.

---

[1] Cf. Chapter XII.
[2] *Troilus and Cressida*, p. 127.
[3] *Ibid.*, p. 126; and cf. p. 64, above.

79–84) suggests that she does not regard her own case as proved: and some of her arguments are certainly shaky. On the other hand, the survival of Shakespearian spellings such as 'shrike' (cf. p. 88), especially when 'harder readings', together with Greg's calculations about the diminishing returns of unusual spellings in copies of copies (cf. p. 79), gives some support to the theory that there were two holographs.

(v) Miss Walker insists that all Shakespeare's first and second thoughts stood in a single arch-text from which both the Q and F texts derive. We are therefore asked to believe that the F editor, with Q in front of him, several times over saw fit to delete Shakespeare's second thoughts and insert first shots of poorer quality *though the Q 'copyist' reading the same manuscript chose correctly at the very same points*. If the Q 'copyist' was not misled, why was the F editor? It would be sheer perversity to change these readings. But if Shakespeare wrote out the play twice and the F editor had access to a different manuscript (the foul papers) he would naturally restore first shots if told to follow copy.

(vi) Nowhere does Miss Walker show any awareness of the similarities of compositors' errors and authorial substitutions. Even if only a single holograph lies behind Q and F (that is, if 'second shots' stood in the foul papers) we are often unable, I maintain, to identify attractive variants as the product of the one rather than the other—though we would have to assume, in the case of Shakespeare, that most of the variants were non-authorial. But if there exists at least a possibility (Greg thought it a probability) that Shakespeare supplied a second arch-text, the editor, I believe, should deal respectfully not only with such 'good' alternatives as *attributive* and *inclineable*, and other glaring examples, but also must keep an open mind about the provenance of 'good' but comparatively 'indifferent' variants. That Shakespeare, like Middleton in *A Game at Chesse* and many other writers, might introduce hundreds of alternative readings in the course of transcribing a play does not, however, enter into Miss Walker's deliberations.

Note A (page 80)

TROILUS AND CRESSIDA:
QUARTO OMISSIONS AND ADDITIONS

Though Miss Walker thought that the 45 lines or part-lines found in F but not in Q 'were not "cuts" ... but the omissions of a copyist and/or compositor', she admitted that some of F's recoveries were 'intended for cancellation'.[1] (In all quotations below I italicise the words omitted from Q.)

(a)   Like to an entred Tyde, they all rush by,
                       And leaue you hindmost:
                       Or like a gallant Horse falne in first ranke,
                       Lye there jor pauement to the abiect, neere
                       Ore-run and trampled on: then what they doe in present,
                                  (III.3.159–63)

'I think it very likely that this recovery was intended for cancellation. It not only disturbs the metre but is also somewhat irrelevant to the main thought . . .' (Miss Walker).

(b)   *Pand. Why, but heare you?*
                       Troy. Hence brother lackie; ignomie and shame
                       Pursue thy life, and liue aye with thy name.
                                (V.3.112+)

These lines were transferred to V.10.32–4 where they 'occupy the position in which Shakespeare finally intended them to stand' (Miss Walker).

(c)   *Aga. Speak Prince of Ithaca, and be't of lesse expect:*
                       That matter needlesse of importlesse burthen
                       Diuide thy lips; then we are confident
                       When ranke Thersites opes his Masticke iawes,
                       We shall heare Musicke, Wit, and Oracle.
                                (I.3.70–4)

'It would seem natural for Ulysses to wait for permission to proceed, but the compliment paid to him is so cumbersome that this may explain Q.'s omission' (Miss Walker).

(d)   *Vlis.* The yongest sonne of Priam, a true knight,
                       Not yet mature, yet matchlesse firme of word,
                                (IV.5.96–7, Q)
               Vlis. The yongest Sonne of Priam;
               A true Knight; *they call him Troylus;*
               Not yet mature, yet matchlesse, firme of word, (F)

[1] That MS. cancellations were sometimes printed has long been known. It is assumed that the printer was told to ignore cancellations, possibly because his text contained some by the book-keeper, and that he then accidentally restored the author's deletions as well. Cf. Greg, *Documents*, p. 363 ('The passages marked for omission in the manuscript are retained in the print'), Sisson, *New Readings*, I, 23 ff. For the discussion of Q omissions cf. also the New Variorum edition, 1953, p. 339 ff.

'Since the words are here extra-metrical and occur again in Q. and F. at l. 108, the obvious explanation is that they are a first thought, which Shakespeare at once discarded' (Miss Walker).

★   ★   ★

(e)   The Grecian youths are full of qualitie,
         Their louing well compos'd, with guift of nature,
         Flawing and swelling ore with Arts and exercise:
                       (IV.4.76–8)

If (a)–(d) resurrect passages in the foul papers intended for deletion we may account for F's 'Their louing . . . Flawing' on the same hypothesis. The words disturb F's metre, and were dropped, I imagine, because they bring up his fear of a 'loving' Greek too indelicately for Troilus. He raises the subject of a rival as indirectly as possible: *louing* in l. 77 is premature coming before the self-accusing 'Alas, a kind of godly jealousy' (l. 80).

(f)   Nor you my brother, with your true sword drawne
         Oppos'd to hinder me, should stop my way:
         But by my ruine.
               Enter Priam and Cassandra.
         Cass. Lay hold vpon him Priam, hold him fast:
                       (V.3.56–9)

'But by my ruin' does not fit into the metrical scheme and ends a speech of defiance on an unfortunate note of anticlimax. Without the four words the speech hangs together perfectly; and Q's comma at the end of l. 57 is of no account, for many other speeches finish with commas in Eld's text (and in other plays). Deletion in the foul papers in the course of writing seems, therefore, as likely as accidental omission from Q.

(g)   *Vlys.* I haue a young conception in my braine,
         Be you my time to bring it to some shape.
          Nest. What is't?
          Vlysses. This 'tis:
         Blunt wedges riue hard knots: the seeded Pride
         That hath to this maturity blowne vp
                      (I.3.312–17)

Q avoids a mincing repetition ('What is't?'—'This 'tis:') out of keeping with the elevated tone; one two-syllable break in blank-verse does no harm, but a second one, and especially an echo, as here, sounds faintly ridiculous. Again F could have printed an intended deletion.

(h)   *Aga.* Worthy of Armes: as welcome as to one
         That would be rid of such an enemie.
         But that's no welcome: vnderstand more cleere
         What's past, and what's to come, is strew'd with huskes,
         And formelesse ruine of obliuion:

> But in this extant moment, faith and troth,
> Strain'd purely from all hollow bias drawing:
> Bids thee with most diuine integritie,
> From heart of very heart, great Hector welcome.
> (IV.5.163–71)

As in (c), an involved speech by Agamemnon is cut in Q, leaving three lines of F's nine. In the result we lose to the extent that Agamemnon says welcome only twice (in Q) instead of thrice (in F). It should be noticed, too, that the omitted lines repeat unnecessarily the laboured wisdom of Ulysses in an earlier scene (III.3.145 ff.). Both passages stress that honour is a thing of the present and that past deeds cannot rise above the present.

(i)   a man distill'd
        Out of our Vertues; who miscarrying,
        What heart from hence receyues the conqu'ring part
        To steele a strong opinion to themselues,
        Which entertain'd, Limbes are in his instruments,
        In no lesse working, then are Swords and Bowes
        Directiue by the Limbes.
           Vlys. Giue pardon to my speech:
        Therefore 'tis meet, Achilles meet not Hector:
                              (I.3.350–8)

Q rephrases l. 352 as 'What heart receiues from hence a conquering part', and, because the first speech ends with a complete pentameter relines the second:

           Vliss. Giue pardon to my speech? therefore tis meete,
        Achilles meete not Hector let vs like Marchants

'F.'s recovered lines are a prolonged metonymy of the part for the whole.' 'The lines are essential to the argument' (Miss Walker). I cannot agree. Miss Walker observes that 'Ulysses takes up Nestor's two points at once' in his reference to 'our honour and our shame' (l. 363): these two points were, however, clearly made before the Q omission ('for the success . . .' (l. 340), 'who miscarrying . . .' (l. 351)), therefore F's three lines are the more dispensable (because they are too involved, and because *Which entertain'd* after *who miscarrying* is a stylistic lapse). If it is felt that Nestor must pursue his thesis to its logical conclusions, Ulysses' apologetic 'Give pardon . . .' could count as an interruption.

The two versions of the merchant-simile, which follows the three omitted lines, complicate the issue. If both versions are Shakespeare's, as many think (cf. p. 86), F's short first line ('Giue pardon to my speech: / ') would be his as well: the lineation of both Q and F is then determined by the omission or inclusion of F's three lines, and confirms Shakespeare's responsibility for both texts. In short, the two passages, I.3.354–6 and I.3.357–61, belong together in Q and in F.

All the F recoveries, incidentally, are linked by several lines of evidence. Sometimes the scansion supports the shorter Q text (*a, d, e, f, g, i*)[1]; sometimes F's extra lines seem obscure or irrelevant (*a, c, h, i*); sometimes they repeat ideas used elsewhere (*b, d, h*); or they occur where neighbouring dialogue also shows signs of instability (*c, g, i*), which has its importance in so far as one authorial change often attracts another (cf. p. 63).

Exploring the reasons for Q's omissions Miss Walker raised two possibilities: 'cuts'—or carelessness on the part of Q's 'copyist' and / or compositor. She preferred the latter rather than 'cuts' on the ground that 'the longest [omission] amounts to no more than half a dozen lines' (cf. p. 80). Manifestly she allowed for only one type of cutting—theatrical cutting designed to clip a long play for a smaller company or a shorter performance-time. But authors also cut in copying if dissatisfied with their first draft, and delete passages in their foul papers immediately after writing them. As Miss Walker grants that F erroneously prints four deletions (*a-d*) I cannot understand why other Q omissions of precisely the same stamp are blamed on the Q copyist / compositor—except, of course, that this suits Miss Walker's general argument that Shakespeare was not the Q copyist. It seems to me that, leaving aside the question of the Q copyist, Shakespeare's responsibility for these nine Q omissions is hard to deny (either he deleted the passages in his foul papers, if there was only a single arch-text—or he dropped them in making his fair copy, if there were two arch-texts). At any rate, it is risky to use Q's omissions to argue as Miss Walker does, against Shakespeare's having been the Q copyist.

*   *   *

One might expect some substantial *additions* in Q if Shakespeare changed his text as he transcribed. Of the few lines found in Q but not in F some, however, look like accidental omissions from F and hardly any like afterthoughts (II.1.28–9 could just possibly be one). We may account for the absence of new lines in Q on the assumption that the F editor decided to keep the whole Q text, adding when his MS. contained more (i.e. 45 lines or part-lines) but not subtracting when his MS. contained less. This would accord with his habit of printing even MS. deletions: he wanted to bring out the fullest possible text.

[1] I base no arguments on metrical irregularity unsupported by other evidence (cf. p. 155).

VII

Othello

★

Up to 1958 the argument about the text of *Othello*—whether or not there are first and second thoughts embedded amongst the corruptions of Q and F—had remained for some years the private property of Greg and Miss Walker, who adopted the same positions as with *Troilus*. Miss Walker, however, working on the two plays in close conjunction (her editions of both appeared in the same year, 1957) took a much stronger line when she turned to *Othello*, dismissing without ceremony the idea of divergent strains which she considered as a possibility in *Troilus*:

> The significant *Othello* variants are not of this kind ... What we have in the *Othello* variants is not evidence of the same mind working at the same level, first tentatively and then with greater assurance of what was apt, but of different minds: the first (in the Folio reading) Shakespeare's, firm in characterization and expression; the second (in the quarto reading) that of an interpreter, losing the appropriateness of Shakespeare's art in approximations.[1]

Initially Greg presented his views not without qualms and reservations.

> My belief is that both Q and F go back fairly directly to foul papers, and rather confused and illegible ones at that ... I do not think that all the differences of reading between Q and F can be due to error or misunderstanding. I suspect that some alternative readings were left undecided or imperfectly deleted in the foul papers ... If not, it will be difficult to avoid bringing in an element of reporting, and the texts are too good for that.[2]

Seizing on Greg's alternative of an 'element of reporting' Miss Walker attempted to show, in her three discussions of the play, 'that

[1] *Problems*, pp. 138–9. Greg, of course, felt differently: 'The variation of the texts [of *Othello*] recalls to some extent that found in *Troilus and Cressida*' (F.F., p. 358). [2] *Ed. Problem*, p. 109.

the well-recognized inferiority of the Quarto text was due not to scribal errors but to memorial contamination', and that 'vulgarisation is persistent throughout the quarto'.[1] With the word 'vulgarisation', it will be observed, we enter the realms of opinion.

There could be no fairer opponent than Sir Walter Greg, who, because of the pioneer quality of so much of his work, not infrequently changed his mind and generously acknowledged his errors. By 1955 Greg had heard Miss Walker state her thesis twice, without any other effect, apparently, than to convince him that she was wrong. Comparing variant passages in the two texts he was driven again and again to the same conclusion.

> It will be noticed, incidentally, that in the case of many of the variants Q's reading might very well be the original one, later superseded by the better reading of F, supposing that the text at some time underwent revision.

> The impression is of deliberate revision in F rather than of corruption in Q.

> A whole essay might be written on these two lines, but what strikes one most is the Shakespearian quality of both versions ... Everything ... points to F's version having been reached by way of Q's, rather than Q's being a corruption of F's.[2]

Is this too no more than 'opinion'? A most carefully reasoned opinion, at the very worst: the latest editor of *Othello*, won over by Greg, praised his discussion of the play in the highest terms.

> In no piece of his work are his scrupulous attention to detail, his fairness, and his refusal to burke one or other of conflicting pieces of evidence, more clearly and more salutarily displayed.[3]

In the last resort the argument boils down to a question of taste, as in *Troilus and Cressida*. Shakespearian flavour in the variants, or vulgarisation? Miss Walker recognised that the subjective element looms large[4]: we must proceed, therefore, to the variants themselves and decide whose taste is the sounder, Greg's or Miss Walker's.

Fortunately some experts have anticipated me. M. R. Ridley ranged

---

[1] See 'The 1622 Quarto and the First Folio Texts of *Othello*' (*Sh. Survey* 5, 1952, pp. 16–24); *Problems*, chap. vii; and Miss Walker's edition, 1957, p. 121 ff. I refer to the last as Miss Walker's *Othello*: line numbers in the present chapter derive from this edition, and all Miss Walker's comments not otherwise identified come from its Notes.   [2] Greg, F.F., pp. 365–71.

[3] M. R. Ridley, *Othello*, p. xxxix.   [4] *Problems*, p. 162.

himself firmly behind Greg in his thoughtful edition of *Othello*—and did so partly on the strength of his knowledge of poetic manuscripts. This I regard as an important qualification for the textual critic, and it may be no accident that Greg too devoted many years of his life to manuscripts while Miss Walker, so far as one can judge from her publications, has concentrated always on printed texts. Ridley and Greg, at any rate, adopt a far less romantic attitude to the dramatist's 'first thoughts' than Miss Walker—who writes as if a first thought that is 'commonplace or inept' is out of the question in Shakespeare.[1] (Are there not a few 'commonplace or inept' readings in Shakespeare's best work? or, to by-pass the counter-argument that these readings must be textually corrupt, in the autograph manuscripts of the greatest poets?) Alexander has also expressed doubt about Q's 'vulgarisation', and about Miss Walker's faith in 'decorum' as a sufficient cover for emendation. There is no point in repeating the arguments of Greg, Ridley and Alexander,[2] who fastened on Miss Walker's most vulnerable allegations, but it may be useful to show that Q is defensible in less obvious cases as well.

(*a*)   I saw Othelloes vissage in his minde,
          And to his Honors, and his valiant parts
          Did I my soule and fortunes consecrate:
          So that deere Lords, if I be left behinde,
          A Mothe of peace, and he goe to the warre,
          The *rites for which* I loue him, are bereft me,
                              (I.3.252–7, Q; F: *Rites for why*)

Most editors retain *rites*, which Miss Walker finds indelicate in the sense 'love's rites', substituting *rights* (i.e. 'what Desdemona is asking for is the privileges ('rights') of sharing the hazards of war').[3] Now *right* was not often spelt *rite* in the seventeenth century, therefore if *rites* replaces Shakespeare's *rights* Q might arguably have vulgarised (F presumably followed Q)—*if 'rites' must mean 'love's rites'*. But why should it? The 'rites of Warre' (*Hamlet*, V.2.391, F; Q: *right*) are clearly implied by the context, the pride, pomp and circumstance which Desdemona sees as an extension of Othello's personality: and these 'rites' do not vulgarise the play.[4]

---

[1] *Ibid.*, p. 138.
[2] Greg, *F.F.*, p. 364 ff.; Ridley, *Othello*, pp. xxxvi ff., 218 ff.; Alexander, *R.E.S.*, 1958, IX, 188 ff.   [3] *Problems*, p. 141.
[4] Ridley, p. 36, defended *rites* as 'love's rites', which is also implied, I think, but not the primary meaning.

(b)   tis not to make me iealous,
To say my wife is faire, *feedes well*, loues company,
Is free of speech, sings, playes, and *dances well*;
Where vertue is, these are more vertuous:

(III.3.185–8, Q; F: *Dances*:)

'An irrelevant interpolation' is Miss Walker's comment on *feedes well*, which she thought a 'common error' in QF, taking the passage as an 'enumeration of Desdemona's attractions'.[1] Attractions? Othello lists the sociable, uninhibited tendencies of a woman's nature, those which could easily make a husband jealous, *free* being a key word: a theme to which Shakespeare reverts when Desdemona's hand 'argues *fruitfulness* and *liberal* heart' (III.4.38), which refers back to 'She's framed as *fruitful* / As the *free* elements' (II.3.334–5), which refers back to 'She is of so *free*, so kind, so apt, so *blessed a disposition*' (II.3.312 ff.), which refers back to 'she's full of most *blest condition* . . . Blest fig's-end . . . Blest pudding . . . Lechery' (II.1.245 ff.). In such a context *feedes well* is not irrelevant, for Shakespeare and his contemporaries associated a hearty appetite with lechery.[2] According to Miss Walker *feedes well* is as 'vulgarly' intrusive as in III.3.342 ('I slept the next night well, *fed well, was* free, and merrie' F; Q: *was*), but she did not notice that the ideas of food and freedom or choice make a miniature 'cluster' elsewhere (I.3.349–50, II.1.229, II.3.338–40). Images of food and eating[3] are, indeed, so important in the play as to provide a second defence for *feedes well*: the words fit into the immediate line of thought—and into a larger pattern. The fact that they occur in an alexandrine carries little weight (cf. p. 155) so long as they do not seem suspicious in themselves.

(c)   If to preserue this vessell for my Lord,
From any *hated* foule vnlawfull touch,
Be not to be a strumpet, I am none.

(IV.2.84–6, Q; F: *other*)

Hated displeases Miss Walker as 'ruinous exaggeration'.[4] It seems to me that *other* is a more inappropriate word, for it implies that Othello's touch is foul and unlawful as well (unlawful, i.e. against the law of

[1] Walker, *Othello*, p. 184; cf. *Sh. Survey 5*, 1952, 16–17.
[2] Cf. J. Leeds Barroll, 'Antony and Pleasure' (*J.E.G.P.*, 1958, LVII), p. 709.
[3] Cf. *unbitted lusts* (I.3.330), *sated with his body* (l. 349), *Her eye must be fed, give satiety a fresh appetite, heave the gorge . . . abhor the Moor, diet my revenge, gnaw my inwards* (II.1.222 ff.) etc. Othello is 'infected' by Iago's food imagery: *tasted her sweet body, Till that a capable and wide revenge / Swallow them up* (III.3.348, 461), etc.   [4] *Problems*, p. 150.

nature), especially if the line is spoken quickly, as it must be. *Hated* could represent a first thought, replaced by a second shot even less happy; on the other hand, Desdemona tends to speak with exaggeration where her chastity is concerned, and *other* could equally well be corrupt.

(d)   Em. 'Twill out, 'twill: I hold my peace sir, no,
     I'le be in speaking, liberall as the ayre, (Q)

     Emil. 'Twill out, 'twill out. I peace?
     No, I will speake as liberall as the North; (F)
                    (V.2.223–4)

'What strikes one most is the Shakespearian quality of both versions,' thought Greg: but Miss Walker found two faults in Q which she could not pardon.

> there is certainly interpolation in Q. when Emilia addresses Iago as 'sir', and to speak as liberally as the air is too feeble for a Shakespearian first shot. For comparison with the gale of Emilia's passion, the wind is wanted. The air may move freely, but it does not 'speak aloud' (cf. 2.1.5) like the storm.[1]

O.E.D. should have settled the second difficulty: *air* could mean 'wind' before Shakespeare, and was used in this sense in *Hamlet*, I.4.41 ('Bring with thee airs from heaven or blasts from Hell'), *Henry V*, I.1.48 ('when he speaks, / The air, a charter'd libertine, is still'), etc. As for the first, Emilia's 'sir', this is one of the attractions of Q rather than the reverse. In each of his three replies to Gertrude in their first scene together Hamlet coldly holds her off with a 'madam' ('Ay, madam, it is common', 'Seems, madam!', 'I shall in all my best obey you, madam'), and Emilia's *sir*, like Lydia Languish's damned monosyllable, is designed to create distance, to express repudiation, in precisely the same way.

(e)   Oth. Villaine, be sure thou proue my Loue a whore,
     Be sure of it, giue me the oculer proofe,
     Or by the worth of *mans* eternall soule,
     Thou hadst bin better haue beene borne a dog,
     Then answer my wak'd wrath.
                    (III.3.361–5, Q; F: *mine*)

'The particularity of F.'s asseveration (the most solemn Othello could make) seems preferable to the Q. generalization' said Miss Walker, choosing F. Here, however, the context suggests that Othello refers to

---

[1] Walker, *Othello*, p. 216; cf. Greg, *F.F.*, p., 368.

Iago's soul (as in Q) rather than to his own (as in F), for he goes on

> *Oth.* If thou doest slander her, and torture me,
> Neuer pray more, abandon all remorce.
> On horrors head, horrors accumilate:
> Do deeds, to make heauen weepe, all earth amaz'd,
> For nothing canst thou to damnation ad greater then that.
>
> (Q: so F)

In short, if Iago slanders Desdemona he would have been better born as a dog, which has no 'eternal soul', than as a man, for being a man his soul will be doomed. This thought, of course, anticipates Othello's later preoccupation with the soul's life in death ('I would not kill thy soul' (V.2.33), 'Sweet soul, take heed, / Take heed of perjury: thou art on thy death-bed' (V.2.53–4)), and would be quite lost in F where the 'dog' idea can only imply physical violence to Iago.

To illustrate that there is 'persistent blurring of the sense by vulgarization' in Q Miss Walker gives a list of typical examples.[1] Some of the examples are highly debatable.

(f)
> That by your vertuous meanes, I may againe
> Exist, and be a member of his loue,
> Whom I, with all the *duty* of my heart,
> Intirely honour
>
> (III.4.115–18, Q; F: *Office*)

(g)
> For if she be not honest, chaste, and true,
> There's no man happy, the purest of *her Sex*
> Is foule as slander.
>
> (IV.2.17–19, Q; F: *their Wiues*)

(h)
> Therefore confesse thee freely of thy sinne,
> For to deny each article with oath
> Cannot remoue, nor choke the strong *conceit*,
> That I doe groane withall: thou art to die.
>
> (V.2.56–9, Q; F: *Conception*)

Are these Q variants really 'vulgarised'? Why is 'conceit' more vulgar than 'conception', when both words could mean exactly the same thing? In (f) 'office' is more attractive than 'duty', but could be a second thought: and in (g), if *her Sex* is indeed more vulgar than *their Wiues* so much the better, since the speech belongs to Emilia. To cite

---

[1] *Othello*, p. 124.

such examples of 'blurring' and 'vulgarisation' in a short list is to admit a dearth of evidence.

Miss Walker is at her most unconvincing in discussing the 'vulgarised' oaths in Q, which are softened or deleted in F. For she admits that an expurgator banished some such oaths from the F text and at the same time urges that others not found in F were added to Q![1]

(i)   Oth. Thinke my Lord? *By heauen he ecchoes* me.
           As if there were some monster in *his* thought:
           Too hideous to be shewne: thou didst meane something;
                    (III.3.109–11, Q; F: *Alas, thou ecchos't*; *thy*)

Miss Walker condemns Q as guilty of a 'bad blunder on two scores: that its indirectness is out of character, and that it loses the dramatic irony of "as if there were some monster . . ." ' (p. 181). These 'blunders' have not offended the great majority of the editors, like whom I find Q perfectly acceptable. F's *Alas*, however, seems a ludicrously weak expletive for a general irritated by his ensign's echoing, and is best explained as one of this text's many expurgations.

(j)   It were not for your quiet, nor your good,
           Nor for my manhood, honesty, or wisedome,
           To let you know my thoughts,
           Oth. *Zouns.*
                    (III.3.155–7, Q; F: *What dost thou meane?*)

We are told by Miss Walker that only memorial error will explain Q's use of 'dramatically objectionable oaths as stop-gaps'. But is it not more likely that Shakespeare wrote *Zouns, what dost thou meane?*, that the F expurgator scored out *Zouns*, like so many other oaths in his manuscript, and Q simply lost four words (which happened sometimes in the best texts)? That *Zouns* is dramatically objectionable is a mere assertion.

The extent of Miss Walker's prejudice against Q emerges most clearly, perhaps, from a reading where, for once, there is no alleged 'vulgarisation'.

(k)   The food that to him now, is as lushious as Locusts, shall be to
           him shortly as *acerbe as the* Colloquintida.
                    (I.3.347–8, Q; F: *bitter as*)

Miss Walker 'thinks the commoner word (almost proverbially associ-

---

[1] Miss Walker, *Othello*, pp. 131–2, 125; cf. Ridley's *Othello*, note on *Zouns* (Q; F: *Away*) at III.4.95 (102).

ated with coloquintida) appropriate to Iago'—although Dover Wilson, her fellow-editor, strongly backed *acerbe*, which occurs in the play's source, is a 'rare word most unlikely to be invented by the transcriber', etc.[1] Subsequently Harold Brooks clinched the matter by observing that uncommon words are not inappropriate to Iago 'in soliloquy or in talk with Roderigo—does not this help to mark that his bluff plainness is assumed, not native to him?'[2]

★   ★   ★

Miss Walker has not dealt kindly with the *Othello* Quarto. It suffers, perhaps, from some memorial corruption—as do other comparatively good texts[3]—but she has grossly exaggerated the case for 'vulgarisation'. Again and again one senses in her exegesis a 'determined parti pris', which troubled Ridley,[4] the hostility of an advocate rather than the impartiality of a judge. She discredits Q variants without giving them a sympathetic hearing, and often suppresses them without any hearing whatsoever.[5] To discredit a text is, unfortunately, not difficult, and therefore I would not be surprised if Miss Walker misleads countless readers. I am surprised, however, that she misled herself, for the stern opposition of her experienced co-editor should surely have pulled her up short, and her own occasional wavering between Q and F should have had the same effect.[6]

As with *Troilus and Cressida* (cf. p. 87), my purpose is not to argue that all the Q variants rejected by Miss Walker are superior to F, only that Q has been maligned and contains much more 'Shakespearian flavour' than Miss Walker allowed. Especially when Q readings spring from a characteristic mode of thought of the speaker—as in (*c*), (*e*)—or tie up with the play's imagery,[7] or reproduce an unusual word from the source, it seems dangerous to abandon them, and even more dangerous not to record them.

The 'vulgarisation' in Q can be interpreted in more than one way. Let us compare Miss Walker's attitude with Greg's.

---

[1] Cf. Miss Walker's *Othello*, p. 160.   [2] Cf. Ridley's *Othello*, p. 42.
[3] Cf. Greg on the *Othello* Quarto (quoted below, p. 108). An element of memorial contamination is present in many good texts since both scribes and compositors would 'memorise' as they worked.
[4] *Othello*, 1958, p. 222.   [5] Cf. p. 152.
[6] For Dover Wilson's opposition cf. notes on I.2.21, I.3.348, II.1.11, III.3.152 in Miss Walker's edition. Significantly, Wilson here champions Q readings.
[7] As in (*b*). Cf. also p. 152 n. 2.

> The memorial errors of the *Othello* quarto go much deeper than can reasonably be postulated as the substitutions of a compositor ... The corruption is evident in the speeches of all characters and persists throughout the play ... In the *Othello* quarto we have, I think, ... the work of a bookkeeper who saved himself time and trouble by using his memory rather than his eyes in making a transcript of the prompt-book. (Miss Walker)

> [Q errors] are, so far as they are unconscious, the very kind of substitutions, often vulgarizations, that compositors and transcribers commonly make when they attempt to carry too many words in their heads at once.

> ... nor indeed is there anything to suggest that the Q transcriber was the book-keeper once we realize that there is no need to credit him with an intimate knowledge of the play. (Greg)[1]

Miss Walker believes that memorial contamination is much more serious than would be likely in a text that has passed through the normal channels of transmission. Greg believed in the 'normal channels'— largely because he also believed in two authorial strains. To which Miss Walker replied:

> One of the fundamental weaknesses of his [Greg's] theory is the assumption that a scribe would arbitrarily substitute 'know' (Q.) for 'warrant' at 3.3.3 and then alter 'I know't' to 'O sir' (Q.) seven lines later. If we explain variants of this kind as memorial errors when we find them in bad quartos or Q. *Richard III*, we must be consistent in our assumptions and explain the numerous variants of this kind in Q. *Othello* in the same way.[2]

Miss Walker seems to have missed the interdependence of Greg's two conclusions. Since Greg argued for *authorial* changes in the text, besides the possibility of scribal ones, there is no 'fundamental weakness' in his theory: authors frequently indulged in 'double substitution' of precisely the same sort as Miss Walker's example.[3]

On the other hand Miss Walker's whole case rests on what seem to me to be two fundamental miscalculations. She takes the Q text to have been set up by a single compositor working from copy written out by a single scribe. The single scribe (i.e. the book-keeper responsible for most of Q's 'perversions') is the corner-stone of her argument, for, as

---

[1] Miss Walker, *Problems*, pp. 142, 151; Greg, *F.F.*, pp. 365, 369.
[2] *Othello*, p. 126.   [3] Cf. p. 76.

she states quite unequivocally, the *Othello* Quarto 'suggests one thought-less mind rather than many imperfect memories, a single contaminator rather than many'.[1] Yet it looks as if we can distinguish at least two compositors and two scribes—which, if correct, disposes of the careless book-keeper, or forces us to invent a second book-keeper or scribe with the same bad habits.[2] If Miss Walker erred regarding both the 'compositor' and the 'book-keeper' it becomes difficult to put faith in her speculations about the working habits of these two individuals; and, indeed, many of her incidental arguments would crumble with her theory of transmission.

*   *   *

Greg's attitude to the *Othello* Quarto seems more satisfactory than Miss Walker's for four principal reasons.

(i) Miss Walker has seriously exaggerated the badness of the text. Her special interest in QF 'common errors' helped her to give Q a poor character: granting that 'the evidence is insufficient to enable us to determine what the [F] collator's margin of error was', Miss Walker assumed that roughly 'one quarto error out of every ten escaped notice' and therefore departed from Q (i.e. from QF) forty-six times.[3] Leaving aside the flimsiness of her preliminary reckonings (the margin of error is a mere guess), Miss Walker's 'corrective' methods arouse misgivings and very many of her emendations are probably unnecessary.[4] On the two counts of 'common errors originating in Q' and the all-important one of 'vulgarisation' Miss Walker has painted a black picture of the text which is, I think, largely unjustified.

(ii) Very little is done by Miss Walker to meet Greg's claim that sometimes QF variants have a 'Shakespearian flavour' in both versions (cf. p. 101).

(iii) Miss Walker misunderstood Greg's theory in finding a 'fundamental weakness'. Miss Walker's own assumptions about authorial substitutions seem less true to the facts than Greg's once authorial manuscripts are examined (cf. p. 108).

(iv) Grounding her editorial work on the belief that 'one thoughtless mind rather than many imperfect memories' corrupted Q, Miss Walker

---

[1] *Problems*, p. 151.
[2] Cf. Note A (p. 112). Greg thought, on other grounds, that 'the transcriber . . . cannot have been the book-keeper' (*F.F.*, p. 366 n.).
[3] *Problems*, pp. 157–8; *Othello*, pp. 133–4.
[4] Cf. 'The New Corrective Editing', pp. 153–65 below.

cannot easily accommodate the new evidence pointing to two or three compositors and two scribes in place of her single compositor and single scribe (cf. p. 112). The 'manifest' errors in Q grow less perplexing when we see how many men were involved in the transmission, while Miss Walker's 'book-keeper who saved himself time and trouble by using his memory rather than his eyes' becomes as otiose as the theory of 'persistent vulgarisation'.

One cannot regard Greg's case as proved beyond all doubt, but the weight of probability seems to incline heavily to his side. That is all I seek to establish: a strong presumption that the variants in *Othello* include authorial afterthoughts. As soon as that is granted, we must admit that there is no knowing how many of the 'trivial' variants came from Shakespeare himself. Accordingly, as in *Troilus and Cressida*, there is no end to the 'good' variants which then require open-minded reconsideration.

(i) Synonyms could be substituted by Shakespeare: 'as *faithfull* as to heauen... / So iustly to your graue eares I'le present, / How I did thriue' (I.3.122, Q; F: *truely*); 'And all indigne and base aduersities, / Make head against my *reputation*' (I.3.274, Q; F: *Estimation*); 'And he shall our Commission bring to you, / *With* such things else of quality *or* respect, / As doth *concerne* you.' (I.3.281–3, Q; F: *And, and, import*).

(ii) Cognate words, and singulars and plurals,[1] could be substituted by Shakespeare: 'bearing with franke appearance / Their purposes *towards* Cypresse' (I.3.39, Q; F: *toward*); 'I ran it through, euen from my boyish dayes, / Toth' very moment that he *bade* me tell it' (I.3.133, Q; F: *bad*); 'That I would all my pilgrimage dilate, / Whereof by *parcell* she had something heard,' (I.3.154, Q; F: *parcels*).

(iii) Shakespeare could substitute literally related words. Some of these 'related' variants in *Othello* are out-of-the-way and would not spring to the mind of every copyist or compositor: *provulgate—promulgate* (I.2.21), *enscerped—ensteep'd* (II.1.70).[2] Some form phrases used elsewhere by Shakespeare:

[1] Miss Walker suggested that Q's 'frequent mistakes in number were due to some peculiarity of the transcriber's hand' (*Problems*, p. 149). How then do we explain F's 'frequent mistakes in number'? Often Q or F is wrong, but equally often both are possible.

[2] Miss Walker classed Q's *enscerped* as 'probably a misreading' since ' "congregated sands" can only be sandbanks, dangerous to navigation because they are hidden rather than because they are (somehow) "scarped" '. Scarped rocks and sandbanks are dangerous because, beneath the surface, they seem deep at one point and turn out to be shallow near-by. Both *enscerped* and *ensteep'd* are first

> *Des.* That I did loue the Moore, to liue with him,
> My downe right violence, and *scorne* of Fortunes,
> May trumpet to the world:
>
> (I.3.248–50, Q; F: *storme*)

Miss Walker here supports Q, which is certainly attractive, but F gives a Shakespearian phrase: 'valour's show and valour's worth divide / In storms of fortune' (*Troilus*, I.3.46–7). That *storm* and *scorn* were, apparently, misread in Shakespeare's hand in *Troilus* ('as when the Sunne doth light a scorne', I.1.37, QF) does not render it impossible for Shakespeare to have interchanged the two words.

(iv) Shakespeare could transpose words and phrases, and rearrange his lines in some details in the process of transcription:

(a)   Beseech you now, to the affaires of the state. (Q)
 I humbly beseech you proceed to th' Affaires of State. (F)
 (I.3.220)

(b)   *Oth.* Your voyces Lords: beseech you let her will,
 Haue a free way, I therefore beg it not (Q)

 Othe. Let her haue your voice.
 Vouch with me Heauen, I therefore beg it not (F)
 (I.3.260–1)

(c)   *Bra.* Looke to her Moore, haue a quicke eye to see,
 She has deceiu'd her father, may doe thee. (Q)

 Bra. Looke to her (Moore) if thou hast eies to see:
 She ha's deceiu'd her Father, and may thee. (F)
 (I.3.292–3)

(d)   I thinke the issue will be, I shall haue so much experience for my paines, as that comes to, and no money at all, and with that wit returne to Venice. (Q)

 And I thinke the issue will bee, I shall haue so much experience for my paines; And so, with no money at all, and a little more Wit, returne againe to Venice. (F)
 (II.3.359–61)

recorded in this play: in view of Shakespeare's partiality for coining new words with the 'en-' prefix (cf. p. 135) we should accept both as his.

POSTSCRIPT. In Nevill Coghill's *Shakespeare's Professional Skills* (October, 1964), which appeared when the present book was already at the printer's, it is also argued, in an important chapter on the text of *Othello*, that Q is not 'vulgarised', and that F represents a second Shakespearian version.

Note A (page 108)

THE *OTHELLO* QUARTO: COMPOSITORS AND COPYISTS

Was the *Othello* Quarto set up by a single compositor, and the copy written by a single scribe, a book-keeper, as we are told in the New Cambridge edition? Spelling tests and typographical evidence bring into doubt both these conclusions.

COPYISTS. The variation between centred and marginal entries coincides with a number of variations in spelling, sometimes roughly page against page and sometimes in stints of a different length. Excluding entries at the commencement of scenes, which would be centred as a matter of course, one series of entries falls in or near the right-hand margin even when several persons are brought on or the direction occupies two lines:

Put into circumscription and confine
For the seas worth,   *Enter* Cassio *with lights, Officers,*
But looke what lights come yonder   *and torches.*

$(B_4{}^a)$

With remarkable consistency the man responsible for these marginal entries (whom I shall call Scribe A) preferred the spellings 'though', 'bin', 'ha' (= has, hath, have), while the man who centred his entries (Scribe B) chose 'tho', 'beene' and dispensed with 'ha'. Also, B tolerated 'Ile' and 'ile' besides 'I'le', whereas A stuck to 'I'le'; and likewise B used the long double 's' when writing 'Cassio' in the dialogue ('*Caſſio*') beside the more normal '*Cafsio*', the latter being A's form throughout. On the other hand, A sometimes wrote ''em', which never occurs in B.[1]

$B_1{}^a$— / $B_1{}^b$ bin; 'em [A] / $B_2{}^a$ tho; tho; Ile; centre [B] / $B_2{}^b$— / $B_3{}^a$ Tho; centre [B] / $B_3{}^b$ Ile; Ile; Tho [B] / $B_4{}^a$ side; bin [A] / $B_4{}^b$ Ile; centre; [Ha misread, l. 57]; ile [B] / $C_1{}^a$ though [A] / $C_1{}^b$ side; side [A]; centre [B] / $C_2{}^a$ tho [B] / $C_2{}^b$— / $C_3{}^a$— / $C_3{}^b$ centre [B] / $C_4{}^a$ ha [A]; tho [B] / $C_4{}^b$ Ile [B] / $D_1{}^a$— / $D_1{}^b$ ha [A] / $D_2{}^a$— / $D_2{}^b$ ha; ha [A] / $D_3{}^a$ centre; *Caſſio*; tho [B] / $D_3{}^b$ side; side [A]; centre [B] / $D_4{}^a$ centre; *Caſſio* [B] / $D_4{}^b$ ha; ha [A] / $E_1{}^a$ tho; *Caſſio*; *Caſſio*; beene [B] / $E_1{}^b$ centre [B] / $E_2{}^a$ [tho misread the]; beene [B] / $E_2{}^b$ tho [B] / $E_3{}^a$— / $E_3{}^b$ centre [B]; ha [A] / $E_4{}^a$ side; 'em [A] / $E_4{}^b$ ha; side [A] / $F_1{}^a$ *Caſſio*; centre; ile; centre [B] / $F_1{}^b$— / $F_2{}^a$ Tho [B]; ha [A]; *Caſſio*; Tho [B] / $F_2{}^b$ side; ha; ha [A] / $F_3{}^a$— / $F_3{}^b$ side [A] / $F_4{}^a$ ha; bin; ha [A]; *Tho* [B]; ha; bin [A] / $F_4{}^b$ ha; side; ha; bin; ha [A]; Ile; centre [B] / $G_1{}^a$— / $G_1{}^b$ centre; beene [B] / $G_2{}^a$— / $G_2{}^b$ beene [B] / $G_3{}^a$ Though [A] / $G_3{}^b$ Though; bin [A] / $G_4{}^a$— / $G_4{}^b$ tho [B] / $H_1{}^a$ Tho; Tho; centre [B] / $H_1{}^b$ ha; side [A] / $H_2{}^a$ bin; side; bin [A] / $H_2{}^b$ [*bin and beene on same*

---

[1] Bowers suggested privately to Greg that the spellings ''em' and 'ha' might be compositorial, which Greg denied because 'the forms '' 'em'' and ''ha'' are certainly not characteristic of any of the habitual Folio compositors' (*F.F.*, p. 357, n. 6). Greg here confused Q and F. For other compositor-studies of play-texts from Okes' printing-house (where the *Othello* Q was printed) cf. articles by Philip Williams, J. R. Brown and Robert K. Turner in *S.B.* vols. I (1948–9), VIII (1956), XIII (1960) and XIV (1961).

line] [?] / $H_3{}^a$ ha [A] / $H_3{}^b$ tho [B] / $H_4{}^a$— / $H_4{}^b$ side [A] / $I_1{}^a$— / $I_1{}^b$ centre [B] / $I_2{}^a$ Tho [B] / $I_2{}^b$ side; bin [A] / $I_3{}^a$— / $I_3{}^b$ side [A] / $I_4{}^a$— / $I_4{}^b$ side; Ha [A] / $K_1{}^a$ side [A] / $K_1{}^b$ centre [B] / $K_2{}^a$ tho [B] / $K_2{}^b$— / $K_3{}^a$ 'em; ha; ha [A]; centre [B] / $K_3{}^b$— / $K_4{}^a$ bin; side; ha [A] / $K_4{}^b$ ha; bin; side; ha [A] / $L_1{}^a$ side [A] / $L_1{}^b$— / $L_2{}^a$ centre [B] / $L_2{}^b$— / $L_3{}^a$— / $L_3{}^b$ side; bin [A]; centre; centre; centre [B] / $L_4{}^a$ centre [B]; bin [A] / $L_4{}^b$ though; side; bin [A] / $M_1{}^a$— / $M_1{}^b$— / $M_2{}^a$ bin; 'em [A] / $M_2{}^b$ ha; side [A] / $M_3{}^a$ bin [A] / $M_3{}^b$ Tho; centre [B] / $M_4{}^a$— / $M_4{}^b$— / $N_1{}^a$ centre [B] / $N_1{}^b$— / $N_2{}^a$— /

Several clues on the same page may confirm a change-over from one scribe to the other (e.g. on $F_4{}^b$). And quite often, where A and B split a page, there are signs of the man who began the page on the preceding one, or signs of the man who finished the page on the one following (compare $C_1{}^a$ to $C_2{}^a$, $C_4{}^a$ to $C_4{}^b$, $D_3{}^b$ to $D_4{}^a$, $L_3{}^b$ to $L_4{}^b$), while even more often there is scribal continuity from page to page. Spellings that look like exceptions to the rule occur only occasionally ($F_2{}^a$, $F_4{}^a$, $H_2{}^b$; italicised above), and suggest that the shorter forms stood in the scribes' copy and were occasionally retained despite the scribes' general policy. This is borne out by two interesting mis-interpretations of 'ha' and 'tho'.

(i)   *Ia.* Hee's married,
    Cas. To who?
    Enters Brabantio, Roderigo, and others with lights and weapons.
    Ia. Marry to. - - - - Come Captaine, will you goe?
    Oth. Ha, with who?   ($B_4{}^b$)

For the last line F reads: '*Othel.* Haue with you.' Here Q's Scribe B overlooked that 'ha' in his copy might represent 'have', and carelessly made Othello enquire with whom to go. We can excuse the blunder when we realise that this is probably the first time B has met with 'ha' in his copy.

(ii) A subtle slippery knaue, a finder out of occasions; that has an eye, can stampe and counterfeit the true aduantages neuer present themselues.
                                                      ($E_2{}^a$)

Instead of 'the true' F reads 'though true'. Here, despite his familiarity with 'tho' (which he had already employed eight times) Scribe B misread 'tho' as 'the' in a passage which gave him other difficulties but which he evidently transcribed as faithfully as he could. All in all, a high degree of consistency can be claimed as compared with recently published 'compositor tests' for, as is well known, scribes and compositors rarely repeated their preferred spellings entirely without exception.[1]

COMPOSITORS. (i) *Dashes.* To the end of Act II ($F_4{}^a$) dashes consist of three or four hyphens, thereafter chiefly of two hyphens (up to $M_1{}^a$, the end of Act V sc. 1). The first series (Compositor X) began with fours (i.e. - - - -) to $C_4{}^b$ (five times), and one three (i.e. - - -); then follow 28 threes and 3 twos

---

[1] 'There will be exceptions' Charlton Hinman warned in 'Principles Governing the Use of Variant Spellings as Evidence of Alternate Setting by Two Compositors' (*The Library*, Fourth Series, 1940, XXI, p. 82).

(i.e. - -) to $F_4{}^a$.[1] Of the three twos, two were dictated by spacing in prose lines, but nevertheless the preference for threes and fours as against twos up to $F_4{}^a$ stands at 34:3.

From III.1 to V.1 inclusive ($F_4{}^a$ to $M_1{}^a$) dashes are made from two hyphens or one, with some threes but no fours. Twos and ones predominate over threes at the rate of 23:7 (Compositor Y).[2]

Sheets M-N (Act V sc.2) have one four, three threes, three twos, one one: this might be the work of X, but the other facts outlined below make it likely that a third man is responsible (Compositor Z).

(ii) *Abbreviated names.* Both Y and Z frequently abbreviate names, in entries as in exits. Only once does this happen with X, in an exit immediately following the full name in the preceding line:

> *Iag.* How now Roderigo   *Enter* Roderigo.
> I pray you after the Leiutenant, goe.   *Exit Rod.*
> ($E_4{}^b$)

(iii) *Spaces with centred entrances.* Excluding entrances at the top of the page and entrances at the opening of an act, X put spaces above and below centred entrances ten times, and no spaces twice. In Y's work the figures are reversed: eleven entrances have no spaces, two have them above and below.[3] The four centred entrances in Z's sheets are all without spaces.

(iv) *Speeches per line.* Y followed short speeches with a second speech in the same line four times, as on $G_2{}^b$:

> *Iag.* Honest my Lord? *Oth.* Honest? I honest.

This happens only once in X's pages, for a special reason—the next line begins a song.

> *Mon.* Good faith a little one, not past a pint,
> As I am a souldier.   *Iag.* Some wine ho:
> *And let me the Cannikin clinke, clinke,* ($E_4{}^a$)

Z never printed two speeches in one line.

(v) *'Descriptive' entrances.* Excluding directions for lights and noises, X and Z give us several descriptive touches in entrances which are entirely lacking in Y: $B_2{}^a$ 'Brabantio *at a window.*'; $B_3{}^a$ '*Enter* Barbantio [*sic*] *in his night gowne . . .*'; $B_4{}^b$ '*Enters* Brabantio, Roderigo, *and others with lights and weapons.*'; $C_1{}^a$ '*Enter* Duke and Senators, *set at a Table . . .*'; $D_2{}^b$ '*Enter* Montanio, *Gouernor of* Cypres . . .'; $E_3{}^a$ '*Enter a Gentleman reading a Proclamation.*'; $F_1{}^a$ '*Enter* Cassio, *driuing in* Roderigo'[4]; $F_1{}^a$ '*Enter* Othello, *and Gentlemen with weapons.*'

---

[1] It is possible that Y only took over with Iago's entrance on $F_4{}^b$, since there is a three-hyphen dash just before and a two-hyphen one just after: but the form of the Act-opening (cf. p. 115), and the convenience of dividing work by acts, makes it more likely that Y began on $F_4{}^a$.

[2] Possibly $L_2{}^a$ was set by X: it has three threes, and spaces above and below a centred entry.

[3] Both X and Y have some entrances with spaces *either* above *or* below the direction, but these do not affect the general picture.

[4] Cf. *Tp.,* V.I.256, s.d.: '*Enter* Ariell, *driuing in* Caliban . . .'

Evidently Y thought such information superfluous. Z later added: $M_4{}^b$ '*The Moore runnes at Iago. Iago kils his wife.*' (centred, but not an entrance); $N_1{}^a$ '*Enter . . . Cassio in a Chaire.*'

(vi) *Directions after speeches.* Directions after a speech referring to the speaker or other characters on stage (as distinct from directions for noises etc.) run as follows: $E_1{}^b$ 'they kisse', $F_1{}^a$ 'they fight' [X] / $H_3{}^b$ 'he kneeles', 'Iago kneeles', $I_3{}^b$ 'He fals downe' [Y] / $M_1{}^a$ 'He kisses her', $M_2{}^a$ 'he stifles her', $M_3{}^a$ 'she dies', $M_3{}^b$ 'Oth. fals on the bed', $M_4{}^b$ 'The Moore runnes at Iago. Iago kils his wife', $M_4{}^b$ 'she dies', $N_2{}^a$ 'He stabs himselfe', 'He dies' [Z] / . Considering that Y's third direction was added by the press-corrector,[1] and that X and Y set five sheets each and Z only one sheet and three pages (B—$F_4{}^a$; $F_4{}^a$—$M_1{}^a$; $M_1{}^a$—$N_2{}^a$), Z clearly displayed more concern for these directions than his colleagues. The Folio, incidentally, offers only *one* direction equivalent to all those in Z's pages ('Smothers her' = 'he stifles her'). The difference between $E_1{}^b$ 'they kisse' and $M_1{}^a$ 'he kisses her' may also point to the compositors: probably only imperatives stood in the copy (*kisse, fight,* etc.), X inserting 'they' twice and Y and Z choosing 'he' etc.

(vii) *Act division.* The five acts open as follows:

1. Enter *Iago* and *Roderigo.*
    Roderigo.
    TVsh, neuer tell me, I take it much vnkindly

2. *Actus 2.*
    Scœna I.
    Enter Montanio, *Gouernor of* Cypres, *with two other Gentlemen.*
    Montanio.
    WHat from the Cape can you discerne at Sea?

3. *Enter Cassio, with Musitians and the Clowne.*
    Cas. MAsters, play here, I will content your paines.

4. *Actus.* 4.
    Enter Iago and Othello.
    Iag. Will you thinke so?

5. *Actus.* 5.
    Enter Iago *and* Roderigo,
    Iag. Here stand behind this Bulke, straite will he come,

X centred his first speech prefix (Acts I and II), and put no full stop after *Actus*: Y differed in both particulars (Acts III to V). It seems, too, that X intended to give both 'Actus' and 'Scœna' for act-openings, a procedure not adopted by Y. Though no third act is formally noted the large capital suggests that it was indicated in the copy: and if the large capital was selected by Y simply to commence his stint—which is not very likely—the decision to change compositors at the very place where F begins Act III again suggests that act-division was marked in the copy.

---

[1] Cf. Miss Walker, *Othello*, p. 128.

(viii) *Signatures and pagination.* Act III sc.1 begins near the bottom of $F_4{}^a$: this is the only fourth leaf in the sheet in Q without a signature, an anomaly probably occasioned by the change of compositors (X to Y). Curiously, the change from Y to Z led to a similar oversight in the pagination. Sheets L and M are the only ones with errors. L starts correctly on p. 73 ($L_1{}^a$) but goes on: 78 or 84 (for p. 74), 77 or 85 (for p. 75), 76, 77, 80 (for p. 78), 81 (for p. 79), 80. Pagination for 81–88 is missing (except that 81, 84, 85 were used earlier), sheet M commencing on p. 89 and continuing thence quite regularly. The gap of exactly eight pages between the last on sheet L (p. 80) and the first on sheet M (p. 89) makes one suspect 'casting off', i.e. the pagination on sheet M accidentally allows for two sheets where only one preceded. This inference is supported by another irregularity. The 'M' in 'Moore' in the running-titles of the four rectos of each sheet appears as a swash capital once in every full sheet in Q—except in sheet L. It seems that Compositor Z was called in to speed up the printing and worked on sheet M while Compositor Y set up sheet L, borrowing Y's running titles and leaving Y to put together new ones.[1]

All the evidence so far cited centres on lay-out or typography. Spelling-tests divide Q in the same way.

(ix) Compositor X tolerates some spellings normalised by Y and Z: (a) 'hee'le' and 'shee'le' ($D_4{}^b$, $E_2{}^b$, $E_4{}^b$. Cf. 'youle' ($B_2{}^b$, thrice), and the misspelling 'Weele' ($B_4{}^a$))[2]; (b) italic '*Caſſio*' (the double s ligature) ($D_3{}^a$, $D_4{}^a$, $E_1{}^a$ (twice), $F_1{}^a$, $F_2{}^a$); (c) 'Ile' and 'ile' ($B_2{}^a$, $B_3{}^b$ (twice), $B_4{}^b$ (twice), $C_4{}^b$, $F_1{}^a$, $F_4{}^b$).[3] Here (b) and (c) probably go back to Scribe B spellings (cf. p. 112), and (a) and (c) look like Shakespearian spellings (cf. p. 117).[4]

X never prints 'Oh' or 'oh', which are found in Y and Z: $G_3{}^b$, $H_3{}^a$, $I_2{}^b$, $K_3{}^b$ (twice), $M_3{}^b$ (thrice).

Z has several peculiarities. (a) The spelling 'damned' or 'damn'd' with an 'n': $M_3{}^a$, $M_3{}^b$, $M_4{}^b$, $N_1{}^a$, $N_1{}^b$. Previously there was a decided preference for alternative spellings—'dambd' ($B_1{}^a$, $B_4{}^b$, $K_3{}^b$, $L_4{}^a$), 'damb'd' ($K_1{}^b$), 'dam' ($H_4{}^a$ (twice), $K_3{}^b$), and 'damme' ($D_2{}^a$). Only once before do we find 'damned' ($G_3{}^b$). (b) After his first mention ($C_1{}^b$ 'Montano') the leading Cypriot becomes consistently 'Montanio' ($D_2{}^b$, $E_4{}^a$, $F_1{}^a$, $F_1{}^b$, $F_2{}^a$) but in the pages set up by Z reverts to the correct form, 'Montano' ($M_3{}^b$, $N_1{}^a$). (c) Special care is taken throughout Q to print the apostrophe before 's' when this stands for 'is'. In the 80 pages set by X and Y there are hardly any errors, but Z in his 11 pages was careless, slipping up four times ($M_1{}^a$ 'this sorrowes heauenly', $M_2{}^b$ 'whats the matter', 'murders out of tune', $N_1{}^b$ 'heres another').

Like the change-over of the scribes (p. 113), the change of compositors produced

---

[1] If 'casting off' took place, Z's stint probably began not at V.2.1 but nine lines earlier, at the top of $M_1{}^a$ (i.e. at V.1.122).

[2] With 'Weele' (= Will) cf. *Ham.* III.1.33, Q2 (Wee'le).

[3] 'Ile' on $F_4{}^b$ contradicts my compositor-division. But scribes and compositors sometimes reproduced copy on first running into a strange spelling and normalised thereafter: cf. my notes on 'Ha, with who?' (p. 113), 'madnes' (p. 117), 'Emilla' (p. 117).

[4] X also gives the more usual spellings 'I'le', '*Caſsio*' etc., but his retention of distinctive forms seems significant: Y and Z print '*Caſsio*' more than eighty times but never '*Caſſio*'.

some misreading—in addition to errors with signatures and pagination (p. 116): for example, the spelling 'Emilla' (F_4^b) gives Y's first shot at this slightly out-of-the-way name.

*   *   *

The question now arises whether any other 'copy' intervened between Shakespeare's papers and the MS. written out by Scribes A and B. Do we have to reckon with three versions (autograph MS.; scribal MS.; print)—or with four? Miss Walker is right, I think, in seeing the book-keeper's hand in the text, but not necessarily right in making him the Q copyist. Cuts in the dialogue and early stage directions could be noted by the book-keeper in foul papers or in an 'intermediate fair copy'—for this seems to have happened in other early dramatic manuscripts preceding the official prompt-book.[1]

Standardised spellings, which cut across the scribal and compositorial divisions, do not point to a fourth version either. Someone went through the play and regularised '-ness' suffixes as '-nesse'. No doubt Shakespeare used '-nes', '-ness' and '-nesse', but he had a partiality for '-nes',[2] of which only one instance survives in Q ('madnes' on B_2^b, perhaps the first '-nes' in the text). The mechanical method of the 'corrector' emerges from the following:

O my soules ioy,

If after euery tempest, come such *calmenesse*,
May the winds blow, till they haue wakened death,   (E_1^b)

F reads 'Calmes'. One Q stratum clearly read 'calmnes', and the 'corrector' expanded '-nes', as usual, to '-nesse', the middle 'e' being inserted either at the same time or by the compositor. Such 'normalisation' took place, I imagine, for the benefit of the printed text—the 'corrector' being, quite possibly, Thomas Walkley himself, checking through his scribal copy. Other examples include 'preethee' (so throughout: but 'prethee' escaped twice on L_2^b, and probably stood in the copy—for it is one of Shakespeare's usual spellings); and the apostrophe with italicised names in the possessive (a normalisation not always remembered), and with 's' when ''s' stands for 'is'.

Since both the scribes, the 'corrector', the compositors and (probably in very few instances) the proof-reader levelled spellings it is extraordinary that so many 'Shakespearian' spellings survive in Q: and this inclines me to think that Scribes A and B worked from autograph. On another occasion Miss Walker argued that unusual spellings may be retained in copies, but Greg urged that their chances of perpetuation dwindle with each new copy,[3] a conclusion vindicated by our text: some 'Shakespearian' spellings were tolerated by both scribes but by only one compositor (e.g. 'hee'le', 'shee'le'), some by only one scribe and one compositor (e.g. 'ile '). Other peculiarities were no doubt ironed away, yet Shakespearian spellings—and errors—still stand in Q[4]:

---

[1] Cf. Greg, *F.F.*, pp. 109, 141, 358.
[2] Cf. the 'good' quartos and *More*, l. 52, *stilnes*.
[3] Cf. p. 79.
[4] In this list the first 'good' text is always cited. Thus *Ham.* = *Hamlet*, Q2; *H5* = *Henry V*, F. Line references are to Alexander's edition, except for those good texts available in the Oxford Shakespeare Quarto Facsimiles (*LLL.*, *Rom.*, *Mer. V.*, *Troil.*, *Ham.*).

I.1.39 *tearme* (cf. *LLL.* I.1.16, 131; *Ham.* I.1.103, I.2.91); I.2.64 *ile* (cf. *Rom.* I.2.82, *LLL.* V.2.60, 240); I.2.70 *gardage* (cf. *gard* etc., *Ham.* III.4.104, *Mer. V.* II.2.164, *Troil.* (Q) IV.5.253); I.2.83 *Qu.* (= cue) (cf. *Wiv.* III.2.37, III.3.31, *Ado* II.1.316); I.3.61 *mountebancks* (cf. *Ham.* IV.7.142, *Mountibanck*; *More*, l.39, *banck*); I.3.291 *Adue* (cf. *Rom.* II.2.136, *LLL.* I.2.186, V.2.629); I.3.332 *syen* (cf. *H5* III.5.7, *Syens*; *Wint.* IV.4.93, *Sien*); II.1.48 *Pilate* (cf. *Rom.* II.2.82, *Pylat*); II.1.105 *Ladiship* (cf. *LLL.* IV.2.139, *Mer. V.* III.4.42; *Ham.* II.2.444, *Ladishippe*); II.1.146 *merrits* (cf. *LLL.* IV.1.21, *Ham.* II.2.556, III.1.74); II.1.202 *Honny* (cf. *Ham.* III.1.164); III.3.148 *ghesse* (cf. *Ado* I.1.93, *Meas.* IV.4.6, *Wint.* I.2.403); III.3.221 *groser* (cf. *Ham.* I.2.136, *Sonn.* 151.6, *grose*; *Ham.* III.3.80, *grosly*); III.3.277 *desteny* (cf. *Mer. V.* II.1.15, II.2.64, *Troil.* (Q) V.1.69); III.3.372 *accumilate* (cf. *Sonn.* 117.10); III.4.73 *Sybell* (cf. *Tit.* IV.1.106, *Sibels*; *Shr.* I.2.68, *Sibell*); IV.2.29 *Coffe* (cf. *MND.* II.1.54, *Troil.* (Q) I.3.173); *LLL.* V.2.932, *coffing*); V.2.46 *neather* (cf. *1H4* II.4.397; 111 *neatherstocks*; *Lr.* (F) IV.2.79); V.2.132 *lyer* (cf. *MND.* V.1.424, *Ham.* II.2.118); V.2.320 *catieffe* (cf. *Rom.* V.1.52, *Catiffe*); V.2.368 *ceaze* (cf. *Ven.* 158, *Tit.* I.1.405, IV.2.96).

The unorthodox use of the apostrophe in Q is also very often 'Shakespearian': *t'were* (II.1.187), *t'will* (III.3.287), *T'would* (III.4.62), etc. Compare *Hamlet*[1] II.2.406, 456, 467 (*t'was*); III.1.30, V.2.103 (*t'were*); IV.7.100 (*t'would*). Even more uncommon outside Shakespeare are *i'st* (= is't) (III.3.45, III.4.71, 78, 82) and *bit'h* (= by th') (I.3.399: cf. *bi'th*, V.2.357), with which compare *Hamlet*[1] I.5.117, III.4.116, IV.5.141, V.1.25, V.2.25, 67 (*i'st*), I.5.162 *it'h* = i'th'); *Sonnets* 133.3 (*I'st*), *AYL.* III.2.382 (*i'st*), *Much Ado* I.1.61 (*I'st*).[2] These forms should not be regarded as compositors' errors: the words were clearly written in this way by some people when the increased use of the apostrophe caught on.[3]

As *O.E.D.* will show, most of the above spellings were employed by other writers. Nevertheless they were, generally speaking, out of the common run and therefore one would expect more and more of them to be eliminated with each new copy. Precisely how much levelling took place with every additional copy of a text can be seen in the *Othello* Folio, which was printed wholly or largely from Q.[4] For there every one of the 'Shakespearian' spellings listed above—I have, of course, given only a selection—disappears.[5]

---

[1] These irregular apostrophes in *Hamlet* Q2 are found in the stints of both compositors of the text, according to J. R. Brown's divisions ('The Compositors of *Hamlet* Q2 and *The Merchant of Venice*', *S.B.*, 1955, VII, 19).

[2] F, perhaps from a copy of Q with the same form.

[3] Probably Shakespeare employed irregular apostrophes (like distinctive spellings such as 'scilens') only fitfully: and some of his printers no doubt corrected or dropped them. They occur in his poems as in his plays (*Sonnets* 4.8,12 *can'st*; 24.3 *ti's*; 62.13 *T'is*; *Ven.* 259 *copp's*; 587 *tell's*; 594 *fall's*; etc.). Some of those in *Hamlet* Q2 may derive from Q1, where *i'st*, *t'is* are found. Q1 of *Lear* also shows several of the irregular forms, *it'h* (C₁ᵃ), *it'h*, *at'h*, *it'h* (D₁ᵃ), *i'st* (D₂ᵇ), but by and large they were not common, and the spread of at least *i'st* and *t'were* etc. in so many of his texts makes it likely that these were sometimes Shakespeare's spellings. Misplaced and intrusive apostrophes are found in MSS. too, e.g. in Middleton's.

[4] Greg accepted Miss Walker's thesis (*F.F.*, p. 363).

[5] F reads *terme, Ile, Guardage, Cue, Mountebanks, Adieu, Seyen* (for *Scyen*?), *Pylot,*

This suggests that a further copy at the other end of the chain of transmission, i.e. preceding the transcript by Scribes A and B, would have left far fewer 'Shakespearian' spellings in Q than in fact remain.

Greg thought that 'the frequent spellings " 'em" and "ha" (for "haue" in place of the earlier "a") point to a late Jacobean original'.[1] Both 'em and ha are Scribe A spellings, and the AB transcript was, I believe, 'late Jacobean', yet the credit for *some* of these spellings may go to Shakespeare, who resorted to *ha* several times in *Hamlet*[2] and could have moved further towards Jacobean usage in *Othello*. Therefore the probability that Scribe B misread *ha* on first encountering it (cf. p. 113) does not force us to postulate an earlier scribal copy.

In what circumstances, and with what end in view, was the AB transcript prepared? The rapid alternation of hands would not make for an attractive 'private transcript' nor, indeed, for a serviceable prompt-book. Walkley, the Q publisher, had recently snapped up some other King's Men plays and uttered them against the wishes of the grand possessors[3]: it seems difficult to avoid concluding that the AB transcript was copied out for publication—and very likely for piratical publication. With printer's copy the alternation of hands would not greatly matter. The rapidity of this alternation could mean that the two men wrote out the text simultaneously, and that its leaves were sewn together.

Though they levelled some spellings the Q compositors treated their copy with respect in so far as they retained Shakespearian forms and also the (scribal) lay-out of centred and marginal entries: and turned letters and manifest errors are not in excess of the usual quota in play-texts. The scribes, on the other hand, seem to have worked in haste, and this probably accounts for some of the obvious misreading in Q: their transcript will not have been very legible. Yet, since so very often Q seems almost but not quite correct, even printing nonsense in the effort to reproduce copy,[4] we have every reason to

---

Ladyship, merit, Hony, guesse, grosser, destiny, accumulate, Sybill, Cough, nether, Liar, Caitiffe, seize, as well as *'Twere, 'twill, 'Twould, is't, by'th'*. There are, naturally, some 'Shakespearian' spellings in Q which are kept in F: *prophane, hee'le, shee'le* (common in Sh.); *sterrill* (I.3.324: cf. *Ham.* II.2.310, *sterill*), etc. Many of the words in my list appear several times in the play: I have cited only their first occurrence, but the levelling continued in F with almost every repetition.

[1] *F.F.*, p. 357. Yet 'ha' is common in Dekker's *Satiromastix*, 1602.

[2] II.2.565, IV.7.157, V.1.26, V.2.354 (Q2).

[3] Walkley published *A King and no King* in 1619 from a private transcript, apparently, and *Philaster*, 1620, in a 'bad' text. Greg thought it 'possible that the King's men sought to prevent the publication' of the former, for the S.R. entrance on 7 August, 1618 'is in the name not of Walkley but of Edward Blount, who made the abortive entries of *Pericles* and *Antony and Cleopatra* ten years earlier' (*F.F.*, p. 154, n.). Another King's Men play 'escaped' in 1619 and was entered in the S.R. on *April 28th—The Maid's Tragedy*. This was not Walkley's venture, but it is possible that the letter from the Lord Chamberlain before the Court of the Stationers on *May 3rd*, 1619 was called forth by these first prints rather than, as is usually assumed, by the 'Pavier Shakespeare' reprints. Cf. also Greg, *F.F.*, pp. 362, 151–4, 15; Kirschbaum, *Stationers*, pp. 242–8.

[4] 'The Ottamites . . . doe *resterine* / Their backward course . . .' (I.3.33–8; F: *re-stem*). The MS. no doubt read *restemme* (cf. *stemme* in *MND.* III.2.211, *3H6* II.6.36), and the compositor printed what he thought he saw. So IV.1.76: 'Whilst you were here *ere while*, *mad* with your griefe' (F: *o're-whelmed*).

assume that some 'good' variants transmitted in Q could be authorial. As Greg said, Q variants do not 'imply any general acquaintance with the play',[1] and therefore we need not fear contamination and deliberate falsification on the scale envisaged by Miss Walker. Q looks mangled only if we allow its manifest errors, its superficial wounds, to impress us unduly. If, however, we recognise that most of the obvious misreading resulted from the difficulties of *compositors* trying their honest best to decipher scrawled copy, this superficial corruption should not prejudice us against the reliability of the *scribes* and therefore against the general character of the text.[2]

Finally, what do we know about the manuscript behind the scribes' copy? Greg thought this parent-text foul papers, Miss Walker thought it prompt-copy.[3] Greg's case depends on Q directions such as '*Exit two or three*' (I.3.120), '*and the rest*' (I.3.171), '*Montanio, Gouernor of Cypres*' (II.1.1), while Miss Walker argued that directions such as '*and the rest*' are 'fairly common in bad quartos' and, of course, that the 'scribe' was the book-keeper. Unfortunately the scribes and compositors interfered with Q's directions (the scribes most patently in their centred and marginal entries, the compositors in tests (v) and (vi) (cf. p. 114)), so that we have very little to go on. Nevertheless I attach some importance to '*Montanio, Gouernor of* Cypres' (cf. Note A, p. 44), and I think that Miss Walker is mistaken about the book-keeper (cf. p. 109). These considerations, together with the quality of the 'good' Q variants, tempt me to accept Greg's view that the parent-text consisted of foul papers.

Postscript. Professor Charlton Hinman, in his unpublished doctoral dissertation, *The Printing of the First Quarto of 'Othello'* (University of Virginia, 1941), found 33 variants in 13 copies of this text. It is interesting that all but two were introduced in formes set by the man I call Compositor Y, 30 of them in two formes (Outer H and Inner I). One of the few inconsistencies in my division of the MS. between two scribes, the use of *bin* and *beene* in one line on $H_2{}^b$ (cf. p. 112), occurs on a page with eight press-corrections: we may deduce that here the compositor, working carelessly, normalised either *bin* or *beene*.

I am most grateful to Professor Hinman for giving me permission to see his list of variants as I go to press, and to the Librarian of the University of Virginia, Mr John Cook Wyllie, for sending xeroxes of the relevant chapters at very short notice.

---

[1] *F.F.*, p. 365.

[2] On the evidence of Q's proof-correction Miss Walker argued 'that, by and large, the inferiority of Q. was due to inaccuracies in the copy' (*Othello*, p. 128). Three years earlier she wrote: 'the evidence suggests unusual carelessness on the part of . . . Okes's compositor' and 'the manuscript from which the quarto was printed was legibly and possibly professionally written' (*Problems*, pp. 149-50). Some of the proof-reader's recoveries suggest that the copy was, on the contrary, hard to read ('Conuinced' in place of 'Coniured', IV.1.28; 'vnsuting' in place of 'vnfitting', IV.1.77): cf. my second-last note.

[3] *F.F.*, p. 360 ff.; Miss Walker, *Othello*, p. 125 ff.

VIII

King Lear

*

To extend the argument about Shakespeare's 'second thoughts' to *King Lear* will seem foolhardy to anyone acquainted with the extraordinary complications of the two texts—or, what is more daunting still, with the range of 'solutions' published in the last forty years. I do not offer a full-scale attack, only a footnote to two of the most thorough recent studies, those by Miss Walker and G. I. Duthie.[1]

From 1930 to the 1950's a strong majority classed the *Lear* Quarto as a 'bad' text, a memorially corrupted report of the play as acted.[2] Since the manuscript used in the preparation of the F text was commonly supposed to have been the prompt-book the question of authorial variants hardly arose. Miss Walker, and Duthie in his second edition of the play, reopened a possibility raised before but never fully exploited[3] —that Q, though contaminated by knowledge of the play as performed, goes back not to the prompt-book but to a copy taken by dictation from Shakespeare's foul papers. If this is right some QF variants could, once again, represent first and second thoughts.

Its occasional superiority in metre is the one characteristic of Q to which I wish to draw attention. (I take lines of ten or eleven syllables to be metrically 'regular' or complete, others as short or long.) The passages below are quoted from F: lines not found, or differently transmitted, in Q are italicised.

(*a*)   And here I take Cordelia by the hand,
    Dutchesse of Burgundie.
    Lear Nothing, I haue sworne, *I am firme*.

---

[1] Cf. Miss Walker's article in *M.L.R.*, 1952, XLVII, 376–8, and *Problems*, chap. III; Duthie's C.U.P. *King Lear*, 1960; and also K. Smidt, 'The Quarto and the Folio *Lear*' (*English Studies*, 1964, XLV, 149 ff.).

[2] Cf. Chambers, *W. Sh.*, I, 464, ff.; J. Q. Adams in *Modern Philology*, 1933, XXXI, 135 ff.; Leo Kirschbaum, *The True Text of 'King Lear'* (Baltimore 1945), etc.

[3] Cf. Madeleine Doran, *The Text of 'King Lear'* (Stanford Univ. Pub., *Lang. and Lit.*, Vol. IV, No. 2), 1931; and in *R.E.S.*, 1941, XVII, 474.

> *Bur.* I am sorry then you haue so lost a Father,
> (I.1.243–6)

(*b*)   Ingratitude! thou Marble-hearted Fiend,
More hideous when thou shew'st thee in a Child,
Then the Sea-monster.
Alb. Pray Sir be patient.
Lear. Detested Kite, thou lyest.
My Traine are men of choice, and rarest parts,
(I.4.259–63)

Here *lyest* could be a monosyllable (as Q's *list* perhaps indicates), which leaves Q with eleven syllables in l. 261 ('Then . . . lyest').

(*c*)   *Alb.* I cannot be so partiall Gonerill,
To the great loue I beare you.
Gon. Pray you content. What Oswald, hoa?
You Sir, more Knaue then Foole, after your Master.
(I.4.312–15; Q: *Come sir no more*)[1]

This passage is connected with (*d*), for in F Goneril calls thrice for Oswald (lines 314, 328, 334) and in Q only once (l. 334). This repetition not being strictly necessary it is usually assumed that Q represents the cut, acting version: nevertheless, Shakespeare could have expanded the incident, to underline Goneril's impatience. Her reference to 'that [Q: this] Letter to my Sister' need not imply an earlier mention of a letter any more than 'What, has this thing appear'd again to-night?' implies that we have lost part of the opening of *Hamlet*. What is significant is that in two related passages Q scans each time and F fails to scan each time.

(*d*)   What he hath vtter'd I haue writ my Sister:
If she sustaine him, and his hundred Knights
When I haue shew'd th'vnfitnesse.
                Enter Steward.
How now Oswald?
What haue you writ that Letter to my Sister?
Stew. I Madam.
Gon. Take you some company, and away to horse,
(I.4.332–7, F)

---

[1] The *sir* in Q should stand in the next line, where Q omits it ('Come sir no more, you, more knaue then foole, after your master?'). Duthie (*Shakespeare's 'King Lear'* (Oxford 1949), p. 35) thinks 'Come sir no more' too 'rude' to be addressed to Albany at this stage of the play, but cf. the impatient last words of the scene.

Q has nothing corresponding to I.4.323–34, and begins at l. 335. I have
given it verse lineation, since Q prints as prose.

> *Gon. What Oswald, ho.*
> *Oswald. Here Madam.*
> *Gon.* What, haue you writ
> This letter to my sister?
> *Osw.* Yes Madam.
> *Gon.* Take you some company, and away to horse,

F's 'I Madam' hangs loose from the metrical pattern, Q's 'Yes Madam'
is part of it.

(*e*)　　　I am a very foolish fond old man,
　　　　　Fourescore and vpward,
　　　　　Not an houre more, nor lesse:
　　　　　And to deale plainely,
　　　　　I feare I am not in my perfect mind.
　　　　　　　　　　　(IV.7.60–3)

F's half-line could be an authorial interpolation in the fair copy.

(*f*)　　　　　　　　　If you miscarry,
　　　　　Your businesse of the world hath so an end,
　　　　　And machination ceases. Fortune loues you.
　　　　　　Alb. Stay till I haue read the Letter.
　　　　　　Edg. I was forbid it:
　　　　　When time shall serue, let but the Herald cry,
　　　　　And Ile appeare againe.
　　　　　　Alb. Why farethee well, I will o're-looke thy paper.
　　　　　　　　　　　(V.1.44–50, F)

Q prints partly as prose, and therefore I have re-lined:

　　　　　　　　　　if you miscary,
　　　　　Your busines of the world hath so an end,
　　　　　Fortune loue you,
　　　　　　Alb. Stay till I haue read the letter.
　　　　　　Edg. I was forbid it, when time shall serue let but
　　　　　The Herald cry, and ile appeare againe.
　　　　　　Alb. Why fare thee well, I will ore-looke the paper.

Taking 'I have' as one syllable in both texts (l. 47) we find that F gives
a long line ('Stay...forbid it') and a short one ('And Ile appeare
againe')—whereas Q never exceeds the permitted eleven syllables. In
Q 'Fortune loue you' comes a little abruptly, yet the context justifies

this: Edgar has to rush his words as he holds back a general on the point of battle.

(g)   *Kent.* If Fortune brag of two, she lou'd and hated,
        One of them we behold.
            Lear. This is a dull sight, are you not Kent?
            Kent. The same: your Seruant Kent,
        Where is your Seruant Caius?
            Lear. He's a good fellow, I can tell you that,
                                        (V.3.280–4, F)

        Kent. If Fortune bragd of two she loued or hated,
        One of them we behold. *Lear. Are not you Kent?*
            Kent. The same your seruant Kent, where is your
                                        seruant Caius,
            Lear. Hees a good fellow, I can tell that,
                                        (Q)

F leaves a half-line ('One of them we behold') metrically unassimilated; Q scans regularly (taking 'where is' as one syllable, and making the obvious emendation in l. 284).

My last example is a little more difficult. I have again re-lined Q's prose as verse.

(h)   To make thee seeke it.   *Tucket within.*
            Glo. O strange and fastned Villaine,
        Would he deny his Letter, *said he?*
        Harke, the Dukes Trumpets, I know not wher he comes;
                                        (II.1.77–9, F)

        To make thee seeke it.
                Glost. Strong and fastned villaine,
        Would he denie his letter, *I neuer got him,*
        Harke the Dukes trumpets, I know not why he comes,
                                        (Q)

Duthie (ed. 1949, p. 173) may well be right that 'said he' was marked in the F copy in such a way as to suggest (mistakenly) that 'I neuer got him' was scored out. If so, F gives two consecutive long lines; if not, F has a long and then a short line. On the other hand, Q is perfectly regular (taking 'neuer' as a monosyllable).

One explanation of Q's metrical superiority in such passages as I have quoted may be ruled out at once. Could a pedantic desire to normalise

Shakespeare's irregular metre have interfered in the transmission? As one of the most striking features of Q is its persistent mislineation we cannot postulate a 'corrector'—more especially since four of my eight passages are actually printed in Q as prose. The fact that the verse of *King Lear* suffers, or benefits, from metrical 'loosening', from the employment of occasional long and short lines (in both texts), accordingly fails to solve the problem as well, for, supposing Q to be corrupt in all eight instances, it seems highly unlikely that the men behind Q would repeatedly conform *by accident* to a pattern to which they proved themselves utterly insensitive. In so far as they were accident-prone they erred instinctively in the direction of metrical ineptitude.

Apart from two scenes (I.1 and V.3) which are seriously contaminated, Miss Walker found Q 'very good text', and its oddities 'superficial'. A study of Q's spellings will reinforce this view, and also its corollary, which is important for my argument, that 'the quarto text is much closer to the foul papers than is widely supposed'.[1] Many of its peculiar spellings were scribal or compositorial or Shakespearian, and, surviving in other texts of the period in sufficient numbers, should not be regarded as misprints or 'difficulties in the manuscript'. The apostrophe in such words as *it'h, ot'h, at'h, byt'h, i'st, id'e, tha're*, which are common in Q, can be parallelled, as can the apostrophe in *say's, apeer's* (C_4^a), *repeat's* (D_2^a).[2] On the other hand, the copy's scribe or scribes apparently used some archaic spellings baffling compositor and press-corrector alike, such as *the* for *thee* (B_3^a, C_3^b, D_2^b, F_1^a, H_3^a), which might throw out whole sentences. And other odd spellings could be Shakespeare's own—*far you well* (IV.2.24; cf. *Hamlet*, Q2, I.3.1,81; *Romeo*, Q2, II.2.89, etc.), *bould* (IV.6.233; cf. *Troilus*, Q, I.3.23, 192, *Sonnets* 128.8), *Preheminence* (I.1.130; cf. *Errors*, II.1.23).

The argument that Shakespeare himself introduced metrical irregularities in F gains some support from other second arch-texts. The same seems to have happened in the Folio *Othello*.

(1)   And let me finde a charter in your voyce,
         And if my simplenesse. - - - -
         Du. What would you - - - - *speake.*
                        (I.3.245-7, Q)

         . . .
         T'assist my simplenesse.
         Duke. What would you Desdemona? (F)

---

[1] Miss Walker, *Problems*, p. 67.   Cf. p. 118.

(2)   By his deare absence, let me goe with him.
　　　　Oth. Your voyces Lords: beseech you let her will,
　　　　Haue a free way, I therefore beg it not
　　　　　　　　　　(I.3.259–61, Q)

　　. . .

　　　　Othe. Let her haue your voice.
　　　　Vouch with me Heauen, I therefore beg it not (F)

(3)   And speede must answer, *you must hence to night,*
　　　　Desd. To night my Lord?
　　　　Du. This night.
　　　　Oth. With all my heart.
　　　　Du. At ten i' the morning here weel meete againe.
　　　　　　　　　　(I.3.277–9, Q)

And speed must answer it.
Sen. You must away to night.
Othe. With all my heart.
　　. . .　　　　　　　　　　　　　　　　　(F)

Compare also Emilia's ''Twill out, 'twill out. I peace?' (p. 104, above), and similar disregard of the metre in the second (F) text of *Hamlet*.[1]

If we are willing to accept Q as 'very good text', and some metrically irregular lines in F as afterthoughts, we must ask whether other discrepancies between the two texts point to Shakespeare. I have suggested that Goneril's repeated call to Oswald looks like authorial expansion in F rather than a cut in Q (cf. p. 122): and there follow similar connected variants later in the play.

(i)   I'ld speake with the Duke of Cornewall, and his wife.
　　　　Glo. Well my good Lord, I haue inform'd them so.
　　　　Lear. Inform'd them? Do'st thou vnderstand me man.
　　　　Glo. I my good Lord.
　　　　Lear. The King would speake with Cornwall,
　　　　The deere Father
　　　　Would with his Daughter speake, commands, tends, seruice,
　　　　Are they inform'd of this? My breath and blood:
　　　　　　　　　　(II.4.95–101)

[1] Cf. p. 136. In *Troilus* we cannot expect Shakespeare's additions to be self-evident, since the earlier text (F) was printed last, and could incorporate Q's additions (cf. p. 99); yet when Shakespeare re-wrote several lines he also disrupted the metre, as in the 'merchant-simile' (cf. p. 86).

(*j*)   If you will marry, make your loues to me,
          My Lady is bespoke.
           Gon. An enterlude.
           Alb. Thou art armed Gloster,
          Let the Trmpet sound:
          If none appeare to proue vpon thy person,
                            (V.3.89–92)

In both cases the added lines give edge to the dialogue—and, if we are to regard them as deliberately 'cut' in Q would save very little time. They cannot be accidental omissions in Q, for (*i*) occurs at a point where Q loses no complete lines, let alone two sets of complete lines, and (*j*) yields perfect blank verse without F's two half-lines.[1] Extant dramatic manuscripts with cuts marked in them do not often betray anxiety to preserve the metre.

I think, too, that where F has two metrically irregular lines close together and Q only one at the same point, this may sometimes suggest authorial afterthoughts.

(*k*)   *Reg.* Was he not companion with the riotous Knights
      That *tended* vpon my Father?
        Glo. I know not Madam, 'tis too bad, too bad.
        Bast. Yes Madam, he *was of that consort.*
        Reg. No maruaile then, though he were ill affected,
                (II.1.94–8; Q: *tends*; *was*)

If, rationalising Q, we take ''tis too bad, too bad. / Yes Madam, he was' as one complete line, Regan's half-line with Gloucester's 'I know not Madam' give more than ten syllables, but this was not uncommon at the end of a speech (cf. p. 155). F's *two* irregular lines are less easy to explain.

As well as making insertions and, perhaps, some cuts, a dramatist preparing a fair copy might also decide to re-write short passages. After III.1.21 Q and F print twelve and eight lines respectively which are placed one after the other in modern editions, on the assumption that the F compositor thought F's eight lines, inserted in the margin beside

---

[1] J. S. G. Bolton thinks that 'wear and tear' caused the omission of certain Q passages that fell at the bottom of the page in the MS. (cf. *Shakespeare Quarterly*, 1960, vol. XI). Only (*g*), (*i*) and (*j*), of the passages I quote, are thus explained by Bolton, but he does not take into account that in both (*i*) and (*j*) there are two apparently connected variants, which seems to me to tell against his hypothesis here.

Q's twelve, a substitution for Q's. As the twelve and eight lines cover much the same ground we should ask whether, if the theory of a marginal insertion is viable, the F compositor was not correct in deciding that his eight lines were substituted for Q's.

Since Greg and other competent critics found no room for doubt that the Folio *Lear*, based on prompt-copy, was cut for representation, the theory that Q also follows a cut version, but a different one, is, as all are agreed, 'hard to believe'. Greg thought that 'much of the omission in Q is certainly accidental, and it may all be'[1]—but could accident have produced metrically correct omissions in a text metrically so odd? It is to avoid the embarrassment of 'alternative cutting and two acting versions' that we must assume interference from Shakespeare himself.

[1] Cf. *F.F.*, p. 375, and Miss Walker, *Problems*, p. 51.

IX

Some other Shakespearian Texts

*

MY comments on the 'textual instability' of *Troilus and Cressida*, *Othello* and *King Lear* rest, of course, upon conjecture. Fortunately conjecture need not bombinate in a void, for the authorial habits noticed in the manuscripts of Middleton, Burns, Keats and others serve as a sort of control. Even more fortunately, we can actually compare Shakespearian first and second drafts in some of the 'foul paper' texts, wherever the printer inadvertently reproduced so-called 'false starts': these fully vindicate the assumption that fluent Shakespeare might touch up, in the fair copy as in the foul papers, words and lines that struck him as unsatisfactory, and might introduce quite trivial variants.

(a)   Ah deare Iuliet
      Why art thou yet so faire? *I will beleeue,*
      Shall I beleeue that vnsubstantiall death is amorous,
      And that the leane abhorred monster keepes
      Thee here in darke to be his parramour?
      For feare of that I still will staie with thee,
      And neuer from this pallat of dym night.
      Depart againe, come lye thou in my arme,
      Heer's to thy health, where ere thou tumblest in.
      O true Appothecarie!
      Thy drugs are quicke. Thus with a kisse I die.
      Depart againe, here, here, will I remaine,
      With wormes that are thy Chamber-maides: O here . . .

      .   .   .   .   .

      Heeres to my Loue. O true Appothecary:
      Thy drugs are quicke. Thus with a kisse I die.
                     (*Romeo and Juliet*, V.3.101–20, Q2)

(b)   *From womens eyes this doctrine I deriue,*
      They are the Ground, the Bookes, the Achadems,
      From whence doth spring the true Promethean fire.
      Why vniuersall plodding poysons vp . . .

      .   .   .   .   .

> *From womens eyes this doctrine I deriue.*
> *They sparcle still the right promethean fier,*
> *They are the Bookes, the Artes, the Achademes,*
> That shew, containe, and nourish all the worlde.
>
> *(Love's Labour's Lost,* IV.3.298–301, 346–9, Q)

In (*a*) Shakespeare's changes cause no real difficulty. The editors assume that he deleted *I will beleeue* and substituted *Shall I beleeue* (Q1 *O I beleeue* nevertheless seems to support *I will beleeue*), and that he expanded four lines, slightly altering some phrases but retaining the last line and a half intact. In (*b*) the first and second drafts appear in longer alternative passages (IV.3.292–313, 314–61) which here come very close verbally, and include some unimportant substitution (true-right, Ground-Artes), and inversions. But sometimes it is not so easy to decide what happened.

(*c*)   But Romeo may not. More validitie,
      More honourable state, more courtship liues
      In carrion flies, then Romeo: they may seaze   [35]
      On the white wonder of deare Iuliets hand,
      And steale immortall blessing from her lips,
      Who euen in pure and vestall modestie
      Still blush, as thinking their owne kisses sin.
      This may flyes do, when I from this must flie,   [40]
      And sayest thou yet, that exile is not death?
      But Romeo may not, he is banished.
      Flies may do this, but I from this must flie:
      They are freemen, but I am banished.

                 (Romeo and Juliet, III.3.33 ff., Q2)

(*d*)   *The grey eyde morne smiles on the frowning night,*
      Checkring the Easterne Clouds with streaks of light,
      And darknesse fleckted like a drunkard reeles,
      From forth daies pathway, made by Tytans wheeles,

              .   .   .   .   .

      The grey-eyed morne smiles on the frowning night,
      Checking the Easterne clowdes with streaks of light:
      And fleckeld darknesse like a drunkard reeles,
      From forth daies path, and Titans burning wheeles:
      Now ere the sun aduance his burning eie,

                 (Romeo and Juliet, II.2.188 + (A), II.3.1–5(B), Q2)

Since *Romeo and Juliet* Q2 is riddled with 'false starts' it looks as if the repetition in (c) belongs to the same category. But what came first and what second? Dover Wilson and Duthie suggested

> that ll. 42–4 were Sh.'s first shot, for which he later substituted ll. 33–9 ('But Romeo . . . kisses sin'); writing these seven new lines in the margin or on a slip, and forgetting to delete the three old ones.[1]

This is not likely, for ll. 42–3 were known to the Q1 pirate, whose text prints them without error. Unless the lines were accidentally transferred from Q1, for which there is no supporting evidence (the Q2 compositor consulted Q1 when his manuscript was defective or illegible,[2] but did not introduce duplications—except, possibly, in (d), where such a diagnosis remains doubtful)—we must assume that l. 40 (together, perhaps, with ll. 38, 39, 41, which are missing from Q1) transmits the 'first shot'. The repetition of *But Romeo may not* in such a passage makes one suspicious but need have no significance.

As for (d), Dover Wilson and Duthie dismiss B as 'the collator's'— who, they say, transcribed Shakespeare's four lines in Q1, which served as copy for Q2, but omitted either to indicate where they should be inserted or to delete the Q1 version.[3] They agree with Steevens that 'From forth daies path, and Titans burning wheeles' makes nonsense ('a man may stagger *out* of a path, but not *out* of a wheel'), and regard B in Q2 as a 'careless reprint' of Q1 (which reads 'Checkring', 'flecked darkenes', 'From forth daies path, and Titans fierie wheeles'). One might reply that if an insertion was made in Q1 copy the compositor would have noticed all the more readily that something had gone wrong—for one compositor apparently set both A and B.[4] More important, the articles just cited make it almost certain that Q2 was set from foul papers and not from Q1 copy—except for a few recognisable patches of text—and therefore the attempt to deny that A and B represent alternative authorial versions loses most of its force. Indeed, the repetition in the two passages, close together on the page and nearly identical verbally, is of such mid-day and noon-tide obviousness that its only plausible explanation seems to be that the compositor found them in his copy in the author's hand, a form of guarantee that would override all doubt. Re-examining B with this in mind one can defend

---

[1] *Romeo and Juliet* (C.U.P., 1955), pp. 187–8.
[2] Cf. Richard Hosley's article in *Sh.* Q., 1953, IV, 11–33, and that by P. L. Cantrell and G. W. Williams in *S.B.*, 1957, IX, 107–28.
[3] *Op. cit.*, pp. 160–1.
[4] Cf. Cantrell and Williams (above, n. 2.).

'From forth daies path, and Titans burning wheeles' quite simply: either 'From forth' is used loosely as 'away from', the sense of the parallel in Sonnet 7,[1] or we mentally carry over *path* to the end of the line: 'From forth . . . Titans burning wheeles' [path]'. The *Oxford English Dictionary*, incidentally, records *checking* and *fleckled* with the same meaning as *chequering* and *flecked*, so that we need not reject these words as corrupt in B. In fact, *fleckted* in A is best explained as a misreading of *fleckled*: where, otherwise, did its *t* come from? We may conclude, then, by crediting three changes between A and B to Shakespeare: 'Checkring' to 'Checking' (doubtful: could be a misprint); 'darknesse fleckled' to 'fleckeld darknesse' (more probable); and 'From forth daies pathway, made by Tytans wheeles' to 'From forth daies path, and Titans fierie wheeles'.[2]

To trace other 'false starts' the reader may refer to the index of Greg's *The Shakespeare First Folio*, and to Dover Wilson's indispensable New Cambridge edition. Two straightforward examples and two more controversial ones are sufficient for my purposes. They reinforce the warning that the trivial variants which form so large a part of the 'editorial problem' in many Shakespearian plays, synonym substitution, the substitution of 'indifferent' alternatives, inversion and so on, may often have originated with the author himself—as they did quite incontrovertibly in the texts of Middleton, Burns and Keats.

*   *   *

So far I have restricted the argument to authorial alternatives in 'good' or 'fairly good' texts. Nevertheless we learn from *King Lear* that we ought to go further afield, even though sceptics will tend to explain away attractive variants in 'bad' texts as accidental omissions from the better version, or as the reporter's patch-work.

(*a*)   But feare the maine intendment of the Scot,
        Who hath been still a giddy neighbour to vs: [145]
        For you shall reade, *that* my great Grandfather
        Neuer went with his forces into France,
        But that the Scot, on his vnfurnisht Kingdome,
        Came pouring like the Tyde into a breach,   ˎ   [149]

        .   .   .   .   .

[1] 'Like feeble age he reeleth from the day' (of the setting sun).
[2] Q2 reads *burning wheeles*, but *burning* looks like anticipation of the next line, and therefore editors emend from Q1.

That England being emptie of *defence*,   [153]
Hath shooke and trembled at *th' ill neighbourhood*.
(Henry V, I.2.144–54, F)

But feare the mayne entendement of the Scot,
For you shall read, *neuer* my great grandfather   [146]
Vnmaskt his power for France,
But that the Scot on his vnfurnisht Kingdome,
Came pouring like the Tide into a breach,
That England being empty of *defences*,   [153]
Hath shooke and trembled at *the brute hereof.*
(Q)

Apparently lines 150–2 were cut for the text underlying Q, and Q seems to have lost l. 145 accidentally: otherwise the texts are almost the same. Q, however, contains a magnificent line (l. 147) which looks like Shakespeare (except that the reporter may have dropped a word or two), and, if Shakespeare did indeed change the mediocre line found in F (a text based on foul papers), it could be urged that the substitution of *the brute hereof* for *th' ill neighbourhood* (l. 154), avoiding the repetition of *neighbour* (l. 145), also points to the author.

(*b*)   *Fal. I will* not lend thee a penny.
          Pist. Why then the world's mine Oyster, which I, with sword will open.
          Fal. Not a penny: I haue beene content (*Sir,*) you should lay my countenance to pawne . . .
(Merry Wives, II.2.1 ff., F)
          Fal. Ile not lend thee a peny.
          Pis. I will retort the sum in equipage.
          Fal. Not a pennie: I haue beene content you shuld lay my countenance to pawne . . .   (Q)

(*c*)   See where she comes.
          So light of foote nere hurts the troden flower:
          Of loue and ioy, see see the soueraigne power.
          Iul: Romeo.
          Rom: My Iuliet welcome. As doo waking eyes
          (Cloasd in Nights mysts) attend the frolicke Day,
          So Romeo hath expected Iuliet,
          And thou art come.
          Iul: I am (if I be Day)
          Come to my Sunne: shine foorth, and make me faire.

Rom: All beauteous fairnes dwelleth in thine eyes.
Iul: Romeo from thine all brightnes doth arise. . . .

(*Romeo and Juliet*, II.6.16 ff., Q1)

This last passage differs surprisingly from its equivalent in *Romeo and Juliet* Q2, yet many critics think it as good as, or better than, the definitely Shakespearian text. Nonetheless there are those who insist that Q1 simply throws together images and phrases recollected from other parts of the play.[1] It seems possible, however, that while one or two phrases stem from the reporter the passage as a whole, and its splendid lyricism, represents substantially what Shakespeare himself wrote. The fact that the imagery of *eyes, day, night* and *sun* recurs elsewhere in the play surely counts for less than the poetic quality of the lines—for, after all, these are the 'iterative' images of the play: why should Shakespeare not mention the sun once more, having already done so fifteen times?

The three passages which I have quoted from 'bad quartos' (there are, of course, many more with 'Shakespearian flavour') will scarcely have been omitted from the good texts accidentally: all of them take the place of equivalent lines. If we believe in the 'flavour' we are driven inevitably to one conclusion. Greg commented on (*b*):

> This phrase ['I will retort the sum in equipage'] can only be worked into F on the assumption of partly overlapping omissions in both texts. Such coincidence may be thought unlikely, but the alternative is to suppose that the text underwent some no less improbable literary revision before the printing of F.[2]

Provided that we clear from our minds the associations of the impressive word 'revision' and think, instead, of minor authorial afterthoughts inserted *currente calamo* in the course of transcription, the alternatives are not so perplexing.

*   *   *

This chapter must not close without a word on the 'textual stability' of the play that more than any other has troubled the editors. Though Greg and Dover Wilson lost much of their enthusiasm for the theory of

---

[1] Cf. Harry R. Hoppe, *The Bad Quarto of 'Romeo and Juliet'* (New York 1948), p. 184 ff., G. I. Duthie, 'The Text of Shakespeare's *Romeo and Juliet*' (*S.B.*, 1951, IV, 3–29).

[2] *F.F.*, p. 335. Greg conceded an element of revision in F, indicated by the change of the name Brooke to Broome (*ibid.*, p. 337).

second thoughts in *Hamlet*, Greg's very plausible diagnosis of a double false start in Q2 at III.2.177–8[1] suggests that this text may harbour less obvious first thoughts as well: indeed, there are various additional reasons for thinking that Shakespeare retouched the text underlying F which support my discussion of the play's variants.[2] In view of the complexity of the problem I restrict myself, however, to some purely exploratory notes.

F. W. Bateson[3] has recently championed authorial second thoughts at I.4.49:

> Let me not burst in ignorance, but tell
> Why thy canoniz'd bones hearsed in death
> Haue burst their cerements? why the Sepulcher,
> Wherein we saw thee quietly *interr'd*
> Hath op't his ponderous and marble iawes,
>   (Q2; Q1: *interr'd*; F: *enurn'd*)

Bateson urged that the weaker variant of Q2, *interr'd*, fits in with the facts of Old Hamlet's death as described in this very speech and elsewhere, that he was *buried* and his bones *hearsed* and wrapped in *cerements*. F's *enurn'd* contradicts this picture of a body laid to rest, implying, instead, the urn-burial of ashes; yet this, the stronger reading, must also be Shakespeare's, for the word is first recorded in *Hamlet* and Shakespeare had a weakness for coining new words with the 'en-' prefix (enclog, endart, enrank, enridge etc.). There is only one slight weakness in the argument, the possibility that *enurn'd* was used metaphorically (and Q2 *interr'd* contaminated by unauthorised Q1, like some other Q2 readings in Act I): but, according to Bateson, to impute to Shakespeare 'unconsciousness of the cremation-image latent in the word is indeed a desperate conjecture'.

At III.4.50 both the variants are again very attractive.

> Heauens face doth glow,
> Yea this solidity and compound masse,
> With *tristfull* visage as against the doome,
> Is thought-sicke at the act.
>   (F; Q2: *heated*)

---

[1] *F.F.*, p. 314.

[2] Cf. J. R. Brown, 'The Compositors of *Hamlet* Q2 . . .' (*S.B.*, 1955, VII, 31); E. A. J. Honigmann, 'The Date of *Hamlet*' (*Sh. Survey* 9, 1956, 26–9); Bowers, *Editing*, pp. 96–7, and his articles in *S.B.* VII and VIII (1955, 1956).

[3] 'Shakespeare's Laundry Bills: The Rationale of External Evidence' (*Shakespeare Jahrbuch*, 1962, vol. 98, 51–63).

Many will agree with Dover Wilson that 'while I find it hard to believe that "heated" can have come from any other pen than Shakespeare's, "tristfull" may well have done so likewise'.[1]

Despite the multitude of patently corrupt variants in *Hamlet* it may be, then, that some of the indifferent or trivial alternatives are authorial. And some of the extra-metrical half-lines in the second (F) text, without which the earlier (Q2) version gives perfect sense, could be so too, as in the case of *Othello* and *Lear* (cf. pp. 124, 125 ff.), though Q2 admittedly loses words elsewhere through sheer carelessness. I italicise the words missing in Q2.

(*a*)   Remorselesse, Treacherous, Letcherous, kindles villaine!
         O Vengeance!   (II.2.576–7, F)

(*b*)   That he, as 'twere by accident, may there
         Affront Ophelia. Her Father and my selfe (*lawful espials*)
         Will so bestow our selues, that seeing vnseene
                                          (III.1.30–3, F)

(*c*)   His madnesse is poore Hamlets Enemy.
         Sir, in this Audience,
         Let my disclaiming from a purpos'd euill,
                                          (V.2.231–3, F)

---

[1] *The Manuscript of Sh.'s Hamlet*, I, 167.

X

Shakespeare's Alternative Numbers

*

THERE is nothing magical about numbers to put them in a class of variants of their own, indeed, so far as I know, variant numbers in the canon have never been examined as a group. But they deserve to be. It has been assumed that the trifling difference between four and five, or nine and ten, could hardly trace back to indecision on the part of easy-flowing Shakespeare, and therefore the one or the other number was thrown out as a corruption. Yet, if indifferent variants such as 'the: this' or 'you: thou' were interchanged by Burns and Keats and, as I think, by Shakespeare, why not numbers as well? Other great poets worried about the numbers in their texts, and there are so many variants of this sort in Shakespeare that I believe some of them must point back to the author. It cannot be proved absolutely and beyond cavil, but if shown to be likely will strengthen the general case for 'second thoughts' in Shakespeare.

I begin with a play that gives, at first glance, only the flimsiest support to my argument. The bad reputation of the *King Lear* Quarto may prejudice one against any unnecessary *secundum quid* to explain the divergences in I.1.173 ff.:

> Fiue (Q: Foure) dayes we do allot thee for prouision,
> To shield thee from disasters (Q: diseases) of the world,
> And on the sixt (Q: fift) to turne thy hated backe
> Vpon our kingdome . . .

It is no doubt conceivable [wrote Greg, *Ed. Problem*, p. 92] that a compositor might print 'diseases' for 'disasters' or *vice versa*, or even that an author might substitute one for the other in revision. But the numbers, indifferent in themselves, are consistently varied, and here neither explanation seems satisfactory.

Let us leave *King Lear* for the moment and pass on to some other examples.

137

(1) At nine (Q: ten) i' th' morning, here wee'l meete againe.
     (*Othello*, F, I.3.279)

(2) Marry this Sir is proclaim'd through al our host,
     That Hector by the fift (Q: first) houre of the Sunne,
     Will with a Trumpet, 'twixt our Tents and Troy
     To morrow morning call some Knight to Armes, . . .
     (*Troilus*, F, II.1.117 ff.)

Nothing much can be said of the *Othello* variants: nine or ten will do equally well in the context. The pair from *Troilus* has divided the editors: the majority follows F because 'it is broad day when the exchange of Cressida for Antenor takes place (4.3.1, 'great morning') and Thersites gives 11 o'clock as the time for the fight at 3.3.294'.[1] But there is some inexactness here, for Thersites refers to 11 o'clock as the probable time of the end of the fight, not of its commencement,[2] and before Aeneas's question at IV.5.67 ff. a clash 'to the edge of all extremity,' that is, a long, drawn-out encounter, remains a distinct possibility—since any other Greek but Ajax, his cousin-german, would have tempted Hector to a more gory emulation (IV.5.119 ff.). I think, consequently, that Q's 'first' can be defended, as can F's 'fift'. Both readings cohere with other elements of the play, just as the two time-schemes of *Othello* run side by side as independent systems. If in *Othello* the 'double time' goes back to Shakespeare, as is almost universally agreed, the same may be true of the variants in *Troilus and Cressida*.

To proceed to some single-text plays. In consecutive scenes in *The Winter's Tale* we learn from Time, the chorus, 'I slide / Ore sixteene yeeres' (IV.1.6) and from Camillo, 'It is fifteene yeeres since I saw my Countrey' (IV.2.4). A flat contradiction, since Camillo's absence from Sicilia is the longer span of the two.[3] Similarly in *Measure for Measure* a different number occurs in adjacent scenes. Angelo, the deputy, enforces laws

> Which haue (like vn-scowr'd Armor) hung by th' wall
> So long, that ninteene Zodiacks haue gone round,
> And none of them beene worne;
>
> (I.2.160–2)

---

[1] *Troilus and Cressida*, ed. Alice Walker, p. 167.

[2] 'If to-morrow be a fair day, by eleven of the clock it will go one way or other.'

[3] Probably the same number should have been given both times: the gap between Camillo's departure (Act I) and the end of Act III (to which the chorus refers) could only be a matter of weeks.

yet the Duke confesses that the state's 'strict statutes and most biting laws' have been 'let slip' for 'this foureteene yeares' (I.3.21). Such divergent numbers could be the result of revision, or of composition on loose sheets of paper,[1] or of the dramatist's indecision at the time of writing.

Again, in *Titus Andronicus* four sons enter with Titus at I.1.70, he having buried twenty-one (l. 195) of the twenty-five (l. 79) he had fathered. But later Titus exclaims

> For two and twentie sonnes I neuer wept,
> Because they died in honours loftie bed
> (Q, III.1.10–11)

Horst Oppel observed that twenty-two sons also died in battle in the Titus Andronicus ballad and chap-book, which were printed later than Shakespeare's tragedy and yet (this is perhaps more true of the chap-book) follow his source or sources. It looks therefore as if Shakespeare switched from twenty-two to twenty-one dead sons in the course of writing.[2]

That Shakespeare changed his mind about the talents in *Timon* no one can doubt after a perusal of Spencer's and Maxwell's comments.[3] In parts of the play Timon's *insouciance* finds illustration through gifts and loans of a small number of talents, five (I.1.98), three (I.1.144), five (II.2.226, 229); in other parts the number is huge, fifty (II.2.193, III.1.18, III.4.93), and a thousand (II.2.199). Elsewhere an indefinite number is mentioned, 'so many talents' (III.2.12, 23, 35), and an extraordinary number, 'fifty fiue hundred Talents' (III.2.37). Of this last Spencer wrote that it is 'unsuitable and arithmetically abnormal. This phrase also may be explained as revealing Shakespeare's uncertainty; it represents his manuscript indication for "*either* fifty *or* five hundred . . ."'. According to Spencer, Shakespeare became aware after he had begun on *Timon* that he did not know the value of a talent, checked up, and then in several places put his figures right: Maxwell added the interesting further point that of Shakespeare's chief sources

---

[1] Cf. p. 144.

[2] Cf. Horst Oppel, *Titus Andronicus* (Heidelberg, 1961: *Schriftenreihe der deutschen Shakespeare-Gesellschaft*, Neue Folge, IX), pp. 22–3. Possibly, however, Titus is meant to refer in III.1.10 to the twenty-one plus Mutius.

[3] Terence Spencer, 'Shakespeare Learns the Value of Money: the Dramatist at Work on *Timon of Athens*' (*Sh. Survey* 6, 1953); J. C. Maxwell, *Timon of Athens* (C.U.P.), 1957, pp. 93–7.

one (Lucian) refers to small numbers of talents, the other (Plutarch) to vast sums. Spencer held that Shakespeare corrected some earlier numbers, Maxwell that the use of the two sources adequately explained the facts and that correction was 'not proved'.[1]

Whichever explanation we prefer, we are left with unmistakable signs of the author's hesitation in 'so many talents' and 'fifty fiue hundred Talents'. Writers of every kind stumbled against the same sort of obstacle. For years Tennyson

> was vexed that he had written 'two and thirty years ago' in his 'All along the Valley' instead of 'one and thirty years ago,' and as late as 1892 wished to alter it since he hated inaccuracy.[2]

Wordsworth in *The Prelude* changed the length of a journey (from two days to three), his own age (from nine to ten), the number of his brothers at his father's funeral (from two to three), etc.[3] To get nearer to Shakespeare in poetic temperament, Keats's Hyperion 'breath'd fierce breath' for 'full three dewy hours'—which was changed to six in the holograph; his Enceladus saw 'a hundred eyes / Wide glaring for revenge'—which was changed to a thousand in the holograph; and the disappearance from one authorised version of the 'Kisses four' with which the Knight-at-arms shut the eyes of La Belle Dame Sans Merci is familiar to all. (Keats was worried about the 'four' from the start. He wrote in a letter, 'Why four Kisses— you will say—why four because I wish to restrain the headlong impetuosity of my Muse . . .')[4]. Again, in *The Eve of St. Mark*, Keats could not make up his mind whether 'Twice' (or 'Thrice') 'holy was the Sabbath-bell'. Closer to Shakespeare in time we meet with Ben Jonson changing various sums of money for the Folio version of *Every Man Out of his Humour*: three or four score pounds became three or four hundred, twenty, thirty and twenty-five pounds become fifty, a hundred and two hundred, and three thousand marks become pounds. Though these are examples of 'revision' rather than of a swift writer's casual alterations in the act of copying, they help to illustrate that authors worry

---

[1] Cf. also p. 145.

[2] *Alfred Lord Tennyson A Memoir* By His Son, 2 vols., 1897, I, 475 (footnote), referring to 'In the Valley of Cauteretz'.

[3] *The Prelude*, ed. E. de Selincourt and Helen Darbishire, 1959, I, 114; I, 311; XI, 367; (A-text lineation).

[4] Keats's journal-letter of February-May, 1819.

about numbers and may change them for the most trivial reasons.[1] In the past editors felt disinclined to consider alternative numbers as Shakespeare's in two-text plays, chiefly because, as Greg said, such variants are 'indifferent'—and indifferent variants merited no serious attention. We have seen, however, that poets with some temperamental kinship to Shakespeare, as Shakespeare himself in his 'false starts', freely altered 'indifferent' readings in transcription, and that several proved themselves remarkably sensitive and irresolute about numbers; and we shall see (p. 144 ff.) that some of the variant numbers in one-text plays discussed in this chapter almost certainly connect with other discrepancies and point straight to Shakespeare. Consequently the possibility of authorial afterthoughts must be kept in mind—even in a play like *King Lear*, where the latest trend is towards the reinstatement of Q. Alternative numbers in two-text plays, such as four and five, nine and ten, are a matter of supreme unimportance to most editors, but they can be taken to represent all Shakespeare's much-neglected indifferent variants: if we wish to think precisely on the event we must therefore be prepared to find quarrel in such straws.[2]

---

[1] Cf. *Jonson*, III, 492, 533, 596. In 1611 the value of the coinage was changed by one tenth, but the sums in *E.M.O.H.* were not changed by one tenth and there was no real need to tamper with them. (Cf. H. de Vocht, *Comments on the Text of Ben Jonson's 'E.M.O.H.'* (Materials for the Study of the Old English Drama) (Louvain 1937), p. 75.)

[2] I have given only a selection of variant numbers in Shakespeare: there are other examples even in the plays I have quoted. In *Lr.* II.4.70 ('*Foole . . .* ther's not a nose among *a 100.* but can smell him thats stincking, let goe thy hold . . .' Q; F: *twenty*): Q's hundred may be contaminated by the hundred knights, yet a sly reference to the disappearance of the knights would be very much in character. For the confusion in *Meas.* IV.2 between four and eight o'clock cf. the New Cambridge edition, p. 100.

XI

Order of Writing

★

Iт is usually assumed that scarcely-blotting Shakespeare wrote his plays from the first line to the last following the order of scenes with which we are now familiar. Clearly implied in Greg's casual remark that it 'is unlike Shakespeare to repeat at II.1.1 the details already given in a previous scene',[1] this assumption, of course, tags after the larger one concerning the 'unblotted papers'. Yet Heminge and Condell's words in no wise rule out the possibility of a less orderly proceeding—a possibility that is worth exploring since it could affect our textual criticism in several important ways.

If 'irregular' composition were rarely encountered it might appear that I propose to tackle a difficulty of my own invention. But, whereas it sounds injudicious to build houses by beginning at the roof and working downwards to the foundations (a technique laughed at by Swift, yet employed of late in a revolutionary building programme), it is a fact that writers, composers and the like, especially those engaged on longish projects, in very many cases prefer to work on whatever chapter, scene or movement happens to excite them rather than to advance step by step. The advantages of such 'irregularity' are manifest: the artist can suit his mood in his work, he need not compose what is uncongenial while his 'spirit is fevered in a contrary direction' (as Keats put it), he can pursue a particular person, sub-plot or theme into a later section without losing his impetus, and so on. Examples will spring to the mind of every reader: *Gulliver's Travels*, *The Prelude*, *In Memoriam*, *The Waste Land*, Goethe's *Faust*, to name some of the most famous. Fast writers as well as laborious ones: Goethe seems to have composed, when thus inclined, with fluency, and even more facile authors, such as Sheridan and Burns, fathered bits and pieces which they fitted together 'irregularly'.[2]

---

[1] *F.F.*, p. 277. Cf. also G. I. Duthie on 'scene-sequence' in *The 'Bad' Quarto of Hamlet'* (Cambridge 1941), pp. 206–19, and A. L. Rowse, *William Shakespeare*, 1963, pp. 302, 403.

[2] Sheridan's *School for Scandal* is an amalgam of two separately worked out

There is no need to heap up further examples, for there can be little doubt that the conditions in which Elizabethan-Jacobean plays were produced would encourage piecemeal writing. As Henslowe's diary shows, a great many plays resulted from collaboration, which could take various forms: the play is divided in the middle or by acts (*Gorboduc*), the sub-plot is divided from the main plot (supposedly a common practice), or a play-patcher helps out with just a scene or two (Hand D in *Sir Thomas More*). Such a division of labour would be difficult without a firmly executed author-plot: and there is no reason to believe that a playwright dispensing with collaborators would be any less careful in preparing his plot, for some companies seem to have checked through this before permitting their dramatists to start on the dialogue—and, in any case, those accustomed to plots would think out their plays in advance with or without a co-author.

Here it is of interest that Shakespeare's 'collaborations' are mostly split up by the critics into Shakespearian scenes and episodes interspersed amongst scenes by another, a *modus operandi* which would suggest willingness to abandon sequential writing. Thus Shakespeare is credited with I.2.90 ff., II, IV.4 of *Edward III*, with I.1,2, II.3,4, III.2.1–203, V.1 of *Henry VIII*.[1] Whether or not we accept all such divisions, no one disputes that they are theoretically possible. I find even more interesting, then, Chambers's concurrence in the 'disintegration' of *Henry VIII* and his comment that 'Shakespeare starts most of the themes'.[2] For in discussing *Timon* Chambers submitted that 'Shakespeare seems to have worked chiefly on the beginning and end of the play, and to have left the middle acts in a very imperfect state', adding: 'I do not suggest that *Timon* throws much light upon Shakespeare's normal methods of working'.[3] If Shakespeare worked 'irregularly' in *Henry VIII* and *Edward III* and *Timon* this would throw several beams of light in the same direction.

Like Chambers, Greg tried to brush aside *Timon* as not necessarily typical of Shakespeare's 'normal methods'—understandably, since the

---

playlets, *The Slanderers* and *The Teazles*. Burns composed the middle portion of his second epistle *To Robert Graham, Esq., of Fintry* before the rest (*Letters*, I, 241: 'I intend inserting them, or something like them, in an epistle I am going to write . . .'), and copied out 'embryotic parts of what may, perhaps, one day be a Poem' (*ibid.*, I, 267).

[1] Cf. the various divisions indicated in Kenneth Muir's *Shakespeare as Collaborator*, 1960, and Chambers's *W. Sh.*

[2] E. K. Chambers, *W. Sh.*, I, 496–7.   [3] *Ibid.*, pp. 482–3.

play presents an embarrassing obstacle to the view that 'Shakespeare doubtless composed fluently and seldom went back over what he had written', and therefore to his general account of Shakespeare's foul papers and fair copies.[1] Yet of late the representativeness of the text of *Timon* has been taken more and more seriously,[2] and with good reason. Even if *Timon* is exceptional in having been left unfinished—a doubtful proposition, for Heminge and Condell may simply have failed to lay hands on Shakespeare's latest text, just as they failed for a time to track down copies of *The Winter's Tale* and *Troilus*[3]—it by no means follows that Shakespeare's writing methods were exceptional before he 'abandoned' the play. On the contrary, one would expect the author of thirty dramas to have become more or less set in his ways.

Since Elizabethan-Jacobean plays were written on loose sheets of paper[4] a fluent dramatist wishing to start a scene before its turn has come could easily take up a new sheet, make a 'foul' draft—and later insert this material in its proper place. Anyone as careless as Shakespeare about 'loose ends' and 'inconsistencies' could well leave traces of such a crab-like progress, for if he sketched out Act V before commencing Act I he might use 'first shot' names etc. in Act V and finalised ones later in Acts I–IV—especially if he intended to make a fair copy of the whole text himself and then to rectify such anomalies.

Unfortunately the matter is not quite so straightforward. Shakespeare, as has been seen (chap. IV), not infrequently left a trail of inconsistencies in his plays. What we must look for, therefore, is a series of two or more inconsistencies at odds with another textual unit—if possible a contiguous one.

One does not have to search far. The numerical contradictions in *The Winter's Tale* IV.1.6 (sixteen years) and IV.2.4 (fifteen years), as those in *Measure for Measure* I.2.161 (nineteen years) and I.3.21 (fourteen years),[5] are in both cases accompanied by other signs of dislocation. In *The Winter's Tale* IV.1 'Time, the Chorus' continues:

---

[1] Cf. p. 15, chap. III (from which I now continue the subject of the 'unblotted papers'), and Greg, *Ed. Problem*, p. 149, F.F., pp. 408–9.

[2] Cf. Terence Spencer in *Sh. Survey* 6, 1953, p. 75; Bowers, *Editing*, p. 26; H. J. Oliver, *Timon of Athens* (New Arden ed.), 1959, p. xxviii.

[3] Cf. Honigmann, '*Timon of Athens*' (in *Sh. Q.*, 1961, vol. XII, p. 3 ff.).

[4] 'The usual practice seems to have been to write the plays on separately folded sheets, in units that is of four pages, and several manuscripts are so numbered' (Greg, *Documents*, p. 205).

[5] Cf. p. 138.

> remember well,
> I mentioned a sonne o' th' Kings, which Florizell
> I now name to you
>
> (IV.1.21-3)

Yet Time has mentioned no such person, for this is his first appearance in the play—in the play as we have it. Accordingly J. M. Robertson deduced that Time's words imply 'a previous prologue, which has been dropped'.[1] I would not be surprised if such a prologue existed, perhaps as an alternative to the play's first scene—which, unlike all Shakespeare's expository openings written at the same time or thereafter, fails to melt into a larger perspective but stands in the Folio ruled off and separate.[2] Thus IV.1.6 and 22 indicate that the whole scene is textually distinct from its neighbours.

In *Measure for Measure* the signs are even more decisive. The reference to nineteen years in I.2, conflicting with the fourteen years of I.3, occurs in a scene exhibiting multiple confusion about Claudio's crime: (i) the bawd informs the men (including Lucio) that Claudio has been sentenced 'for getting Madam Iulietta with childe' (lines 58-77); (ii) the bawd asks the clown why Claudio has been sentenced, and he tells her what she has just told the others (Lucio is not present at this duologue) (lines 78-109); (iii) Lucio asks Claudio the reason for his restraint, and is left to guess that it is fornication (line 110 ff.). Quite patently (ii) and (iii) belong together, and were composed separately from (i)—this explains the muddle that both the bawd and Lucio know and then do not know the facts. As (ii) and (iii) fail to connect with (i), which precedes, and also with the immediately following scene (in the matter of the fourteen and nineteen years), the case for textual dislocation is complete.[3] Accordingly the muddle later on in the play about 4 a.m. and 8 a.m. (cf. p. 141) may very well stem from the same 'irregularity' in the writing.

A third explanation will now suggest itself for the huge and small sums of talents in *Timon* (cf. p. 139). The middle portions of the play, less finished than the earlier scenes, were perhaps roughed out before

---

[1] Quoted in the C.U.P. edition, p. 159.

[2] Cf. especially *Lr.* I.1.1-32, *Ant.* I.1.1-10; also *Tim.* I.1.1-97, *Cor.* I.1.1-48, *H8* I.1.1-114. In *Cym.* the Folio also divides off the 'exposition scene', but this is clearly linked by its last words (I.1.68-9) to F's 'Scena Secunda': not so in *Winter's Tale*.

[3] Some of the ideas in this paragraph are borrowed from Dover Wilson's C.U.P. *Measure for Measure*, pp. 99, 120.

Shakespeare realised his mistake: 'so many talents' and 'fifty fiue hundred Talents' in III.2 would then indicate the point where doubt arose in his mind, and I.1 and part of II.2 would belong to a later phase of composition.

Inconsistencies of another sort distinguish the last scene of *Merry Wives* from its predecessors. To quote Greg:

> One curious feature of V.v in F is that Evans drops his dialect, and yet Falstaff is able to recognize him by his speech: 'Heauens defend me from that Welsh Fairy' (l. 85). Perhaps, writing hastily, Shakespeare did not trouble to supply the dialect, leaving it to the actor to make good his negligence. If so the actor failed him, for the indications of Welsh pronunciation in Q are of the slightest . . . But the trouble goes deeper than this: Evans's speeches are quite out of character.[1]

A play that closes with a series of discoveries will sometimes invite writing 'from the roof downwards'. The dramatist must keep one eye on his 'unravelling' and therefore it may help him to write towards a foregone conclusion rather than to worry about his crucial scene till the very last. No one will believe for a moment that the ingenious contrivances in Act V of *Cymbeline* are simply a series of lucky strokes by a fatigued Shakespeare anxious to tie up his 'loose ends': a great deal of careful planning goes into any chain reaction. It is possible, therefore, that the last scene of *Merry Wives* was composed out of order, though, character not always being sustained in the final frivolities of comedy, I do not regard this as anything like certain.

Love's Labour's Lost provides another baffling example. In IV.2 survive allusions to the princess's alternative status as a queen (IV.2.124, 132) inside speeches confusing the names of the schoolmaster and the curate. These, together with similar inconsistencies (e.g. Ferdinand's being a king or a duke), are textual disturbances too embrangled to be discussed in a few sentences, yet it may be that they signify not 'an earlier play', as Dover Wilson and Greg suggested, but merely two 'states' of the play dating from one continuous act of composition.

The variation between 'Titus Lartius' and 'Titus Latius' in *Coriolanus*, a variation which goes back to Plutarch (cf. p. 42), provides the first clue for one of the best examples of 'irregular composition' in Shakespeare. At II.1.153 the stage direction reads

---

[1] *F.F.*, p. 334, n. 2.

A Sennet.   *Trumpets sound.*
Enter Cominius the Generall, and Titus Latius: be-
tweene them Coriolanus, crown'd with an Oaken
Garland, with Captaines and Soul-
diers, and a Herauld.

As P. A. Daniel observed, Titus Lartius should not be in this scene, for he was left in command in Corioli (I.9.75 ff.), is still there when we reach II.2.35 ff., and only reappears in Rome at III.1.1: moreover, though his name figures in the direction he never speaks in II.1. Nevertheless, H. C. Beeching added, 'betweene them' in the direction, and Menenius' words at II.1.177–8 ('You are three / That Rome should dote on'), show that Shakespeare himself assumed Titus Lartius' presence in Rome in II.1: the direction is not a compositor's error.[1] What happened? As soon as we bring the 'Lartius'—'Latius' discrepancy into the picture we begin to understand. Shakespeare, I suggest, adopted the form 'Titus Latius' and had written several scenes before spotting the misprint in his Plutarch, namely II.1.153 ff. and III.1 (and possibly parts of I.1).[2] Thus II.1.153 ff. fails to fall in with the assumptions made in I.9 and II.2.35 ff. concerning the whereabouts of Titus Lartius because these other scenes were written together but II.1 came into existence separately. On their own these two independent 'inconsistencies' more or less clinch the case, yet there is a third clue. Very commonly Shakespeare identified a character at his first entrance with a label stating his rank, profession, or relationship to another character. These labels are repeated so rarely that, as I have said, Greg specially drew attention to an instance in *Much Ado* ('It is unlike Shakespeare to repeat at II.i.1 the details already given in a previous scene.')[3] In *Coriolanus* such a label is repeated—and, what is even more extraordinary, not in its original form. The direction at II.1.153 includes 'Cominius the Generall', that at II.2.35 calls him 'Cominius the Consul':

---

[1] For Daniel and Beeching cf. the New Variorum Edition, 1928, p. 195.

[2] Greg (*F.F.*, p. 407, n. 2) thought that the misprint 'Titus Lucius' (for Titus Lartius) at I.1.237 points to 'Latius' in the copy.

[3] Cf. p. 142. The directions at I.1.1 and II.1.1 read: '*Enter Leonato gouernour of Messina, Innogen his wife, Hero his daughter, and Beatrice his neece, with a messenger.*' and '*Enter Leonato, his brother, his wife, Hero his daughter, and Beatrice his neece, and a kinsman.*' It seems possible that II.1, or the first page or two of II.1, was composed before I.1, and perhaps that it was intended as the play's opening: II.1 has more than its fair share of 'expository' chat, but might be moved to its present position to make way for a more brilliant attack upon the audience by Beatrice in the all-important first scene.

this confirms that the two adjacent scenes were not originally written one after the other.

A number of Shakespearian texts printed from foul papers transmit directions that read like authors' notes. Greg hazarded that they found their way into the text from the author's plot,[1] but surely some are too unimportant to have stood there. In the almost total absence of information about these plots it is not safe to dogmatise, yet how many plotters would mark the fact that at a particular point 'She [the heroine] addresses her to a Lord' (*All's Well*, II.3.60)? Greg made no attempt to collect all examples: had he done so he might well have concluded that some of these notes are memoranda supplementary to the plot (or, possibly, memoranda made in lieu of a plot) left by the author when he broke off writing. A dramatist who composes 'irregularly' would find such notes all the more useful, since he might abandon half a dozen scenes as fragments, or might have to piece together scenes written out of order: an idea for the next episode jotted in the margin could impress the compositor as a stage direction, and thus reach print. It will hardly be an accident, I think, that the play showing the clearest signs of piecemeal composition, *Timon of Athens*, is also richest in 'author's notes'.[2]

One reason for the assumption that Shakespeare wrote his plays sequentially is probably to be found in the 'ghost' characters and 'character labels' frequently supplied with the stage direction when the character first enters—as in *Much Ado*. They suggest an author still feeling his way: and they are most numerous in the opening scenes of Act I. Even for 'irregular' playwrights there would be advantages, however, in fixing the tone of their first scenes and accordingly of their whole drama early on in the time-table of their writing—the early composition of the opening scenes thus scarcely guarantees that the story advanced thereafter from beginning to middle to end. Both 'ghosts' and 'labels' turn up, in fact, in later sections of Shakespeare's plays,[3] but cannot be pressed as evidence for 'irregular composition'

---

[1] *F.F.*, p. 164.

[2] 'Enter Lord Timon, addressing himselfe curteously to euery Sutor', 'Enter ... Ventigius which Timon redeem'd from prison', 'Flaminius waiting to speake with a Lord from his Master . . .' etc.

[3] 'Beaumont' is a 'ghost' in *Henry V* (IV.2.1), 'Kent' in *2H4* IV.4.1(Q); 'labels' are repeated in *Timon* IV.3.457 ('Enter the Steward to Timon'), *Ant.* II.5.3 ('Enter Mardian the Eunuch'), etc. I wonder, too, whether *Hamlet* IV.7.36 ff. was written earlier than its present position suggests. A messenger tells Claudius (who figures simply as 'King' throughout the scene in Q2 and F) that 'Claudio' brought

unsupported by other clues, since abridgment might produce ghosts, and an author could repeat the label needlessly.

Only a startling change in the plot can on its own indicate 'irregular' writing in an author as inconsistent as Shakespeare. At *1 Henry VI* V.1.28 ff. Exeter deplores Winchester's recent elevation to a cardinalate, though Winchester was addressed in I.3 as a cardinal. Greg commented that 'the author of V.i . . . can hardly have read, still less have written, I.iii, in which he already appears in full canonicals'.[1] Had there been only a passing reference to Winchester's canonicals earlier one might have taken the passage in V.1 as an instance of forgetfulness: but the subject is dwelt upon several times and with the maximum of effect (I.3.36, 49, 84: 'I'll canvass thee in thy broad cardinal's hat', 'Under my feet I stamp thy cardinal's hat', 'This Cardinal's more haughty than the devil'). Forgetfulness seems out of the question. Greg and others therefore embrace a theory of multiple authorship—which readers of Hereward T. Price's admirable lecture[2] will wish to avoid, and can avoid by assuming 'irregular' composition.

*　　*　　*

Disintegrators like J. M. Robertson, when they met with inconsistencies of the sort outlined in this chapter and in chapter IV, knew exactly what had to be done: they applied stylistic tests and 'demonstrated' in a twinkling that half a dozen dramatists collaborated in a *Julius Caesar* or a *Macbeth*. Dover Wilson recognised some of the dangers and often argued, instead, for authorial revision—in doing which he put forward an astonishing number of fascinating and rewarding ideas. A further step was taken by Greg, who countered in case after case that inconsistencies might infiltrate into a text during the original composition.[3] Greg clearly believed in 'regular' writing which, to be sure, may often have been Shakespeare's method, but this would not give rise to all the inconsistencies accepted by Greg as part of the original composition. The hypothesis of 'irregular' writing provides, I think, a useful compromise between Greg and Dover Wilson.

It will also incline us to take a cautious view of the subject of 'heterogeneous copy'. The foul papers of a play could, after all, contain scenes

---

the letters from Hamlet. If Shakespeare had already determined on 'Claudius' as the king's name, would he have called the messenger 'Claudio'?

[1] Greg, *F.F.*, p. 186.

[2] As in n. 1, p. 39. Cf. also A. S. Cairncross's New Arden *1 Henry VI*, 1962, pp. xiv, xxviii–xxix.　　　　[3] Cf. p. 4, n. 2.

or sheets of fair copy and, contrariwise, the fair copy could well take over some of the cleaner sheets of the foul papers—especially if these last were not always surrendered to the players as a matter of course (cf. p. 20). Hence we may find certain parts of a text like *Romeo and Juliet* Q2 or *Love's Labour's Lost* Q1 crammed with 'false starts' and similar indications of foul papers—and yet may decide that a few sections of the same text read like fair copy. This last appears a likely outcome with a fast writer, whose first drafts would sometimes satisfy but who, nevertheless, would also discard inferior material on occasion: the dismembering of the foul papers to piece out a fair copy seems, on the other hand, unlikely as a common practice, for if the later printing of a play was contemplated the author or company would value a second complete text.

If texts were not always all of a kind and if, in addition, scenes were sometimes written out of order, a sharp distinction should be made between heterogeneous copy pointing to two or more scribes and heterogeneous copy pointing merely to shifting authorial processes. Greg thought that distinctive textual features found only in the fly-scene (III.2) of *Titus Andronicus*, a scene first printed in the Folio, namely the speech prefix 'An.' (for 'Titus') and the spelling 'Tamira' (for Tamora), argue 'at least a different scribal origin from Q1'.[1] Philip Williams, in a brilliant paper[2] that gives a foretaste of the results to be expected from future studies, showed that variations in spelling, such as Burgundy—Burgonie and Puzel—Pucell in *1 Henry VI*, cut across the compositor-divisions and therefore 'the copy for *1 Henry VI* was almost certainly heterogeneous'. In view of Shakespeare's notoriously 'unstable' spelling one or two variations in a textual unit, even if consistently maintained, seem to me insufficient as proof of an hetero-geneous manuscript. The last editor[3] of *1 Henry VI* has, indeed, sug-gested that the *Burgundy* and *Pucelle* variations may simply trace back to the play's sources, and, if so, we need not postulate scribal interfer-ence or revision. The late publication of the *Titus Andronicus* 'fly-scene' lends more weight to this example: nevertheless with a writer such as Shakespeare we should beware of assigning a text to different scribes, or to different periods of composition, unless the evidence very positively demands it.

[1] *F.F.*, p. 204.
[2] 'New Approaches to Textual Problems in Shakespeare' (*S.B.*, 1956, VIII, 3–14).   [3] A. S. Cairncross, *op. cit.*, pp. xiii–xv.

XII

Editorial Policy

*

ALL the experts of the last few decades, from Greg to Miss Walker, have agreed that there are 'second thoughts' in Shakespeare: they have disagreed only about particular texts and readings. Yet the serious editorial implications of 'second thoughts', whatever their distribution, remain to be thrashed out. Because the extraordinary similarities between authorial substitutions and post-authorial corruptions were not recognised, and because so much exciting work on corrupting agents has been produced, attention strayed away from an issue as richly embarrassing in some Shakespearian texts as the private fads of their compositors.

Whenever we admit the existence of a single authorial substitution in a text we must concede the probable presence of others which will always escape detection. A poet like Shakespeare might change 'Goe softly on' to 'Go safely on' (*Hamlet*, IV.4.8), 'promulgate' to 'provulgate' (*Othello*, I.2.21), or the other way round, and also, more or less consciously, 'the' to 'this', 'my' to 'mine', etc. Both substantive and indifferent variants must become suspect, though our chances of proving Shakespeare's hand behind indifferent variants approach vanishing point. In short, an editor alive to his responsibilities must take into account an unknowable and go softly on—and should warn his readers that he cannot go safely.

The pessimistic position I take up with regard to the unknowable in Shakespeare's text has something in common with another argument now in progress. Were the Folio texts analysed by Miss Walker in *Textual Problems* printed directly from earlier Quartos—or were the Quartos only 'occasionally consulted'? The latter view made Miss Walker impatient.

> There is about this escapist solution that an earlier print was 'occasionally consulted' a lack of logic and realism because, since we have no means of knowing how often or when it was referred to, no reading common to the two texts escapes suspicion.[1]

---

[1] P. 4.

Like advocates of the 'occasionally consulted' theory I suggest that a large number of readings in some texts must come under suspicion (for a different reason, of course), and I can supply no easy answers. I do not, however, regard myself as an 'escapist'—on the contrary, my purpose is to oppose an insidious form of escapism. It seems to me more realistic to grant the presence of an unknowable than to deny its existence because it happens to be inconvenient.

How, then, can editors come to terms with the unknowable? A critical edition offering notes and collation ought, I think, to cite all variants in substantive texts that are not manifest misprints or nonsense. (I refer to editions like the New Cambridge and the New Arden, which invite the reader to think things out for himself where the text is in doubt, rather than to more selective ones like the New Temple.) Of late there has grown a tendency to trim the collation, encouraged, perhaps, by compositor-studies, since these gave the editors confidence in their power to identify error. The value of the New Cambridge Shakespeare, for example, is greatly impaired by the silent suppression of innumerable attractive variants from the substantive texts. In *Othello* Act II scene 1 we are kept in the dark about alternatives such as *hauen*: *Heauen* (l. 3), *does speake*: *hath spoke* (l. 5), *when the huge mountaine meslt*: *when Mountaines melt on them* (l. 8), *chiding*: *chidden* (l. 12), *euerfired*: *euer-fixed* (l. 15), and so on, though some of the rejected readings make excellent sense.[1] To suppress such variants, some of them the choice of perceptive editors, is to take a grave risk under any circumstances—and if there is a possibility that authorial afterthoughts lie hidden among the play's corruptions, an inexcusable one. It has been urged that too much dead wood in the *varia lectio* burdens an edition unduly: but, as Tannhäuser's pope discovered, seemingly dead wood may spring to life unexpectedly. If *some* of the variants in a play derive from Shakespeare, *all* the variants in that play spring to life—in the sense that all of them deserve pondering as possible first or second shots.[2]

Another policy that should recommend itself to the editor of a play

---

[1] Especially 'And quench the guards of th' *euer fired* pole' (Q), a reading unnoted in the C.U.P. *Othello* despite its 'parallel' in 'you ever-burning lights above' (III.3.467) and in *Lear* III.7.58–60 ('The sea . . . would have buoy'd up And quench'd the stelled fires.').

[2] A student of Shakespeare's imagery may find that a rejected variant belongs to a 'cluster' (cf. my last note): he will therefore wish to see all the variants of a play, and has the right to expect them in an edition as far-ranging and as expensive as the New Cambridge *Shakespeare*.

probably harbouring 'second thoughts' will be to give the collation on the same page as the text. If the rejected lections recorded in the apparatus are not putative corruptions but possibly authorial alternatives, so much the more need for the reader to keep them in sight.

It may appear that I am campaigning on behalf of one of the two major British editions of Shakespeare now nearing completion, the New Arden, which scores on these two counts against the New Cambridge. (The New Cambridge collations are defective and arbitrary, and are tucked away at the end of the book.) Not so; neither edition can replace the other: I admire them both, though both have their faults. Therefore, to keep the balance even, I shall discuss the more disturbing problems of 'policy' with reference to each in turn.

The New Corrective Editing

Together with the great advances in bibliographical technique in recent years there has arrived a new enthusiasm for corrective editing comparable in many ways to the excesses of Pope and Warburton. At first glance the new correctors appear to have built upon rock—that is, upon bibliographical facts—but on inspection the rock melts away all too easily.

The new school, the leadership of which has been claimed by Miss Walker, takes as its starting-point the calculation of probable errors in F texts.[1] Greg has conveniently summarised Miss Walker's thesis—as applied to *Richard III*.

> The bulk of F was printed from Q6, and we know the number of errors that had accumulated in Q6 in the course of successive reprintings after Q1, and also the percentage of these errors that were corrected in F. (Where F failed to correct an error of this sort we can of course confidently substitute the reading of Q1.) But Q1 must also have contained errors, and we know the number of cases in which F altered a reading of Q1 (disregarding evident misprints in F). Presumably the percentage of Q1 errors that F corrected was the same as that of the accumulated errors in Q6 that it eliminated. We are therefore in a position to calculate the probable number of Q1 errors that F overlooked. Miss Walker reckons these to be about 150. Then

[1] 'No examination, so far as I know, has been made of the aims and accuracy of the collation underlying this or other Folio texts' (Miss Walker, *Problems*, p. 22). Miss Walker handsomely acknowledges Greg's help in her calculations (p. 23), but some credit should also go to A. W. Pollard's *Richard II*, 1916, and to Dover Wilson's C.U.P. editions of Shakespeare (e.g. *Love's Labour's Lost*, 1923, p. 189).

there are the errors of Q3, which F made no attempt to correct. When printing from Q6, F altered a reading in every three or four lines; therefore in the 500 lines or so it printed from Q3 it should have made perhaps another 150 alterations. Miss Walker concludes that, after we have corrected F by comparison with Q1, there may remain something like 300 errors uncorrected.

Greg added several warnings, the last of which seems to me particularly important: 'it is safe to say that the majority of the errors uncorrected in F, since they make sense, must always remain undetected.'[1]

Less pessimistic than Greg, Miss Walker has tried to locate, and correct, the 'common errors' in QF texts that 'make sense'. She called for a loosening of editorial restraints—and, in her own editions, emended many QF readings for the first time. As a few reviewers quickly observed,[2] the results were disquieting. Some of the newly-rejected QF readings deserved a better fate: they could be defended and should have been left alone. In what follows I shall try to strengthen the case for the defence, confining myself to a single edition, the C.U.P. *Othello*, in order to underline the far-reaching repercussions of the corrective method.[3]

I. *Metrical Irregularity*. If we are on the look-out for common errors in Q and F, metrical irregularity may be a useful clue. At least, Miss Walker thought so, and emended accordingly.

(a)   And when she seemed to shake and fear your looks,
        She loved them most.
            Othello.   And so she did.
            Iago.   *Why then*,
        She that so young could give out such a seeming,
                (III.3.209–11; QF: *Why go too then*)

(b)   O, 'tis the spite of hell, the fiend's arch-mock,
        To lip a wanton in a secure couch,
        And to suppose her chaste! No, let me know;
        And knowing what I am, *know what shall be*.
                (IV.1.70–3; QF: *I know what she shall be*)

[1] Greg, *F.F.*, pp. 198–9. Miss Walker recognised that often QF errors will defy detection (*Problems*, pp. 60, 158), but misjudged the extent of our helplessness.
[2] Cf. especially Alexander (*R.E.S.*, 1958, IX, 190 ff.), and Brockbank (*R.E.S.*, 1961, XII, 80–2).
[3] Modernised quotations, and line-references, are taken from the C.U.P. *Othello* throughout this section.

I would agree that in certain circumstances imperfect metre may point to corruption—when supported by other evidence. But on its own it seems quite inadequate as evidence, simply because so many plays of the period share this irregularity. For safety's sake I illustrate not from a printed text but a manuscript, a particularly apt one, the 'Shakespearian' portion of *Sir Thomas More*. One speech alone contains long lines such as

> to quallyfy a rebell, youle put downe straingers (l. 119)
> shoold gyve you harber go you to ffraunc or flanders
> to any Iarman province, spane or portigall (ll. 127–8)
> owed not nor made not you, nor that the elamentes (l. 136)[1]

The dramatist also had a weakness for starting and finishing some verse speeches with short lines hanging loose from the metrical pattern: 'Comaund them to a stilnes' (l. 52), 'good masters heare me speake' (l. 57), 'woold feed on on another' (l. 87), 'yf you so seek ⟨yt⟩' (l. 147), and possibly one in mid-speech, 'what rebell captaine' (l. 114, but this cannot be pressed, in view of the preceding deletions).[2] When a speech breaks off the metre also suffers (ll. 95–6):

> | | and twere no error yf I told you all |
> | | you wer in armes gainst g⟨od⟩ |
> | all | marry god forbid that |
> | moo | nay certainly you ar |

Such irregularities are familiar, of course, in Shakespeare's printed texts.

I return to the QF 'errors' emended by Miss Walker. Does metrical irregularity alone condemn them? If so, they can claim the same right to stand as the long lines in *Sir Thomas More*. Or are they suspect on other grounds as well? Of (*b*) Miss Walker said:

> The Q.F. reading seems nonsense: if he knows he is a cuckold, he knows what she is and has been. What the words should mean is 'knowing I am cuckolded, know what follows' (i.e. what measures to take), thus adding point to Othello's 'O, thou art wise'.

I cannot accept that QF make nonsense. Two interpretations seem

---

[1] Here and below I expand contractions, suppress a deletion, and re-space a line from *More* for the sake of clarity. The quotations are taken from Greg's transcript in Alexander's *Shakespeare*, 1951.

[2] A. C. Bradley noted Shakespeare's partiality for ending scenes with part-lines of verse (*A Miscellany*, 1931, chap. 11). Cf. Alexander on the metrical irregularities of *Othello*, *loc. cit.*

feasible, the first a perfectly obvious one: 'No, let me know (that she has been unchaste); and, knowing myself to be the man I am (i.e. a man of action), I know what she shall be (i.e. she shall be murdered).' The lines could also continue the biblical allusions of the scene, especially after 'the spite of hell, the fiend's arch-mock': 'No, give me knowledge (i.e. rather than contented ignorance); and then, knowing myself for what I am (i.e. fallen, imperfect), I know that sooner or later she too will be unchaste.'

Regarding (a) Miss Walker said:

> The extrametrical words are too familiar and, what is worse, break the thread of the argument. Iago is not dismissing the point Othello has made (which 'go to' implies) but, on the contrary, following it up.

Too familiar? Is it not typical of the vulgar side of Iago that he becomes familiar whenever he has won a slight ascendancy over another? Thus he tells Emilia *and Desdemona*, 'you are pictures out of doors ... and hussies in your beds' (II.1.109–12), and presses distasteful sexual images upon a reluctant Cassio (II.3.13 ff.). And does 'go to' imply dismissal? The first entry in *O.E.D.* gives it the meaning 'Come on!'—precisely what is wanted: he is jollying Othello along, and follows up the half-admission of 'And so she did' with 'Why, come on, then—what are we arguing about?'

Emendation seems to me unjustified in (a) and (b), particularly in (a), since lines split between two or more speakers not infrequently over-shoot their ten syllables.

II. *Repetition*. Copyists and compositors sometimes anticipate or re-collect a word in neighbouring lines and substitute it for the word in their text. The plural 's' can likewise be assimilated to adjacent words. Editors have therefore always looked upon repetition, verbal or literal, as an invitation to emend.

(c)   Hold, ho! Lieutenant—sir—Montano—gentlemen—
Have you forgot all sense of place and duty?
The general speaks to you; hold, hold, for shame!
(II.3.162–4; QF: *Hold, the*)

(d)   'Tis even so;
For let our finger ache, and it indues
Our other healthful *members* to a sense
Of pain.
(III.4.149–52; QF: *members, Euen*)

(e)   O, good my lord, yonder's foul *murder* done!
                    (V.2.109; QF: *murders*)

Unfortunately some writers, especially fast ones, tend to repeat words just as much as copyists, so that we can never be sure whether an attractive emendation restores or improves the original.[1] In the best printed texts of Shakespeare this is a familiar phenomenon, as in the 147 lines of *Sir Thomas More*—and, of course, in the theatre repetition of the spoken word would pass almost unnoticed. I feel, therefore, that unless there are other signs of corruption, we are bound to assume that Shakespeare himself wrote the repeated word in some cases, and therefore to beware of overhasty emendation. The mere stylistic awkwardness of QF inclines me to follow Miss Walker in the emendation of, for example, II.3.223, II.3.302, V.1.124. But I am not convinced by others.

(c) ' "Hold" at the beginning of the line breaks the thread of the sense', we are told. True; but why not, in the excitement of the scuffle? No one fails to grasp the sense.

(d) 'It looks as if "euen" had been caught from l. 149.' Possibly: but it could just as well be Shakespeare's oversight as a compositor's.

(e) 'Emilia's plural in l. 173 is idiomatic but less so here where it looks like a case of assimilation to "yonder's".' Yet one could argue that Emilia has heard that Cassio is 'almost slain, and Roderigo dead' (V.1.114), therefore that to speak of two murders instead of one was justifiable pessimism.

For similar reasons I would refuse to abandon QF at I.3.58, II.3.150, III.4.42 and some other places where Miss Walker emends. Not only because corruption is not proved but also because so often it is quite impossible to decide which of the two occurrences of a word to impugn. A famous crux from *Othello* will drive home the difficulty.

(f)   Neuer Iago. Like to the Ponticke Sea,
           Whose Icie Current, and compulsiue course,
           Neu'r *keepes* retyring ebbe, but *keepes* due on
           To the Proponticke, and the Hellespont:
           Euen so my bloody thoughts, with violent pace
           Shall neu'r looke backe, neu'r ebbe to humble Loue, . . .
                    (III.3.455–60, F)

Q omits the passage, and the editors almost without exception emend F's first *keepes* to *feels*, the reading of Q2. 'Clearly one of F.'s errors of

---

[1] For Shakespeare's repetitions cf. p. 77.

anticipation', Miss Walker explained. Can we be certain, however, that it is anticipation and not recollection? A little-known commemorative poem by Thomas Powell, *Vertues due*, 1603, contains the lines

> Her resolution was *Proponticke* right,
> And forward stem'd against the Moones retreat.[1]

As in *Othello* the Propontic becomes an image of resolution. It looks as if there may be a connection, and for my purposes it scarcely matters which version came first,[2] since 'Ne'er keeps retiring ebb but *stems* due on' wins support from Powell either way, as source or as echo. The bare possibility of *stems*—I claim no more for it than that—should then discourage the confident alteration of 'Neu'r *keepes* retyring ebbe': F as it stands probably has one error in the line, but modern editions following Q2 may well have two.

III. *Bad Grammar*. Modern editors still 'emend', as they call it, usages in Shakespeare permissible in his day, simply because they do not conform to modern standard English. Thus, despite Abbott's assurance that the third person plural of the verb ending in -s was 'extremely common in the Folio',[3] we find it registered as a QF 'common error' by Miss Walker and therefore repeatedly expunged.

> (*g*)   he's embarked,
> With such loud reason to the Cyprus wars,
> Which even now *stand* in act, that, for their souls,
>   (I.1.150–2; QF: *stands*)

Miss Walker commented: 'Although "wars" was often singular in meaning (O.E.D. 1 *c*), we accept the usual emendation here, and also at 1.3.234, 3.3.67, 352.'[4] Against this it should be said that not only *Othello* but several other plays of Shakespeare treat 'wars' as a singular: 'I . . . vndertake / This present warres against the Ottamites', 'Farewell

[1] Sig. B$_6$^{a}. Reprinted in Charles Edmonds' *A Lamport Garland* (Roxburghe Club), 1881.

[2] Dover Wilson thought that *Othello* 'can hardly be later than early 1603, and may even belong to 1602' (C.U.P. ed., p. xv). Powell also seems to echo the play in his *A Welch Bayte*, 1603: 'Before this newes was stale came a taile of fresh sammon to countermand it with other certaine newes of a something nothing, and a priest that was neither dead nor aliue, but suspended betwixt both' (sig. C$_2$^{b}). Cf. *Othello*, III.3.160: 'Who steals my purse steals trash—'tis something, nothing'. Shakespeare used the verb 'stem' in *Othello* I.3.37, which makes it possible that he used it again in a similar context in III.3.457.

[3] E. A. Abbott, *A Shakespearian Grammar*, ed. 1884, section 333.

[4] *Othello*, ed. Alice Walker, p. 145.

the plumed troope, and the big warres: / That makes ambition vertue' (*Othello*, Q, I.3.234, III.3.351; F agrees); 'The warres hath so kept you vnder . . .', 'Oh 'tis braue warres', 'Warres is no strife' (*All's Well*, I.1.183, II.1.25, II.3.284); 'Wars hath not wasted it' (*Richard II*, Q1, II.1.252), 'is there not wars?' (*2 Henry IV*, Q1, I.2.69), 'Hector, then 'tis warres' (*Troilus*, F and Q, V.3.49). Sometimes, it seems, Shakespeare took 'wars' to mean 'warfare'—as in a deleted line in *Sir Thomas More*: 'to kneele to be forgyven / is safer warrs, then euer you can make'. We cannot reasonably classify all these occurrences as errors: while, therefore, an editor may *modernise* 'the Cyprus wars, / Which even now *stand* in act', this is not, strictly speaking, an *emendation*, a recovery of Shakespeare's original. Similarly, other instances of 'bad grammar' should not go down automatically in the list of 'common errors'.

IV. *Verbal Balance*. Their insistence on verbal or stylistic balance, by far the most dangerous weapon of the new correctors, forces a large-scale retreat to the position of the eighteenth century—and therefore deserves the most scrupulous attention. Is it really necessary to alter so many singulars into plurals, and *vice versa*, in order to secure agreement with antecedents, nouns in apposition and the like?

(h)
                     O my sweet,
    I prattle out of fashion, and I dote
    In mine own *comfort*.
        (II.1.203–5; QF: *comforts*)

(i)
                   Exchange me for a goat,
    When I shall turn the business of my soul
    To such exsufflicate and blown *surmise*
    Matching thy inference.
        (III.3.182–5; QF: *surmises*)

(j)
    If my offence be of such mortal kind
    That nor my service past nor present *sorrow*,
    Nor purposed merit in futurity,
    Can ransom me into his love again,
        (III.4.119–22; QF: *sorrowes*)

The change to *comfort* (h) is inspired by a reading sixteen lines earlier ('My soul hath her content so absolute / That not another *comfort* like to this / Succeeds in unknown fate.'). Of *surmise* (i) Miss Walker writes, 'This should match in number with inference', and for (j) no justification is printed, though presumably the same argument holds. Here I can only meet one assertion with another. I do not believe for a moment that Shakespeare's mind worked so neatly, so fussily, that he felt bound to balance and echo words in the manner suggested. After all, he tolerated much larger 'inconsistencies' in his plays (cf. p. 39), and like most poets vastly enjoyed taking risks with words. Sometimes, indeed, one can defend QF from the context: plural *sorrowes* in (*j*) comes as a relief after a clutter of nouns in the singular.[1]

Scepticism about nouns having to 'match in number' increases when other QF readings are married off and executed as briskly.

> (*k*)   In troth, I think I should; and undo't when I had *done't*.
>   (IV.3.72–3, prose; Q: *done it*; F: *done*)

If *done't* on the analogy of *undo't*, we have to ask whether it is not equally likely that Shakespeare wrote *it* both times. But, even if this difficulty could be shelved (cf. *keepes—keepes*, p. 157), I imagine that Shakespeare would be just as supremely indifferent to exact balance as in *Sir Thomas More*, where he wrote (presumably monosyllabic) *babes* (l. 63) but continued his elaborate comparison with (disyllabic) *babyes* (l. 75).

Sometimes, moreover, we cannot determine swiftly and painlessly with what a word ought to balance.

> (*l*)   Our bodies are gardens, to the which our wills are gardeners;
>   so that if we will plant nettles or sow lettuce, set hyssop and
>   weed up *tine*, supply it with one gender of herbs or distract
>   it with many . . . the power and corrigible authority of this
>   lies in our wills . . . But we have reason to cool our raging
>   motions, our carnal stings, our unbitted lusts: whereof I take
>   this, that you call love, to be a *set* or scion.
>   (I.3.320–32; QF: *Time*; *Sect*)

Does it put an end to the matter to say, with Miss Walker, that ' "set" (= scion) is wanted to carry on the garden metaphor'? Within the garden metaphor Shakespeare distinguished *genders* or kinds, classes, of herbs: and *sect* may well revert to this line of thought, rather than tamely paraphrase *scion*, since *sect* could also mean 'a class or kind'.[2]

---

[1] Other emendations in the C.U.P. *Othello* on the principle of 'balance of numbers', all of which I would disallow, occur at I.1.129, II.3.134–5, IV.1.87, V.2.109, and possibly III.3.408.

[2] Usually a class or kind of person (*O.E.D.*, sb. 1). There may also be a half-concealed joke at the expense of those who make love a religion, taking love as a religious 'sect'.

That is, just as nettles etc. are classes of herb so 'love' is a class of lust: the comparison helps to degrade love, and *sect* seems to be firmly mortised into the speech. A similar reinterpretation of Shakespeare's 'balance' was proposed by Miss Jean Robertson in defence of QF *Time* (= thyme) against Miss Walker's *tine* (= tare). Miss Walker parted company with QF because 'the emendation gives the necessary anti-thesis . . . "thyme", an aromatic herb like hyssop, confuses the argu-ment'. The symmetry of the passage, replied Miss Robertson, is built on a chiasmus:

plant Nettels, or sowe Lettice: Set Hisope, and weede vp Time

'In the first limb folly is followed by wisdom; in the second wisdom by folly. To preserve the symmetry we must read "thyme".'[1]

All things considered, anyone committed to a policy of emendation may very well introduce more errors than corrections, unless a more circumspect policy is evolved than in the C.U.P. *Othello*. None of Miss Walker's principles of emendation seems adequate on its own—though I would follow her where any two of them apply simultaneously.

(*m*)   And therefore little shall I grace my cause
          In speaking for myself. Yet, by your *patience*,
                    (I.3.88–9; QF: *gracious patience*)

(*n*)   Do you perceive in all this *company*
          Where most you owe obedience?
          Desdemona.   My noble father,
                    (I.3.179–80; QF: *noble company*)

(*o*)   With fresh suspicions? No: to be once in doubt
          Is once resolved. Exchange me for a goat,
                    (III.3.181–2; Q: *Is once to be*; F: *Is to be*)

In each of these cases a word or phrase in an hypermetrical line echoes the same word or phrase from a neighbouring line: here we still cannot be *certain* of corruption, yet we cannot safely turn down Miss Walker's plea for emendation. On the other hand, over and above the four principles of correction already outlined there are many scattered emendations in Miss Walker's *Othello* which seem totally unnecessary and demonstrate all too clearly the excesses of the new school.

[1] Quoted in Alexander's review of Miss Walker's *Othello* (R.E.S., 1958, IX, 188–93), where some ideas used in this chapter are anticipated.

(p) Cassio. A knave teach me my duty! I'll beat the knave
Into a twiggen bottle.
        Roderigo.   Beat me!
        Cassio.   Dost prate, rogue? [striking Roderigo]
        Montano. Nay, good lieutenant; pray sir, hold your hand.
        Cassio. Let go, sir, or I'll knock you o'er the mazard.
        Montano. Come, come, you're drunk.
        Cassio. Drunk!   [they fight
    (Iago. Away, I say; go out and cry a mutiny.
            (II.3.147–53; QF: Doest thou prate; Let me goe)

(q)   Put money in thy purse; follow thou these wars; defeat thy
    favour with an usurped beard.
            (I.3.339–40; Q: these; F: thou the)

According to Miss Walker 'speed and metre seem to be wanted' in (p).
If speed, surely 'Dost thou prate, rogue', being less of a tongue-twister
than 'Dost prate, rogue', should survive. I am not convinced, however,
that the 'metre' carries much weight, for lines 147–50, sandwiched
between prose passages, look like prose too and, as Miss Walker admits,
'many editors print as prose'. The metre being in doubt, we are
scarcely justified in tampering with 'Dost thou prate, rogue' and 'Let
me go'. To bolster thou these (q) Miss Walker alleges:

F. suggests trimming to suit the compositor's convenience; 'follow
the wars' merely = 'enlist'. A reference to the particular Cyprus wars
is wanted.

The F line is much more generously spaced than others in the same
speech, however: 'these' could easily have been squeezed in instead of
'the'. A reference to the particular Cyprus wars? I cannot believe that
anyone would fail to take the point as F stands: either F or Q or both
could be right here, and emendation therefore seems unwise.

*　　*　　*

Recent editors of Othello, says Miss Walker, 'are unanimous in rejecting about 170 F. readings against about 500 of Q.' On the evidence
of Richard III and Lear, in which roughly one in ten or one in nine Q
errors escaped correction in F,

we must expect to find about fifty-five errors common to Q. and F.
[in Othello]; and the number will be nearer eighty if Q.'s errors are
(as most editors have supposed them to be) in the region of 700.[1]

---

[1] Othello, 1957, p. 133.

Such figures certainly encourage correction in *Othello*, at first glance. Should the possibility arise, however, that Q and F represent divergent authorial strains the unanimous rejection of 500 Q readings becomes irrelevant, since first thoughts, likely to be inferior variants often enough, would have to be subtracted from the 500. Moreover, what right have we to talk of 'the Folio collator',[1] as though only one man was engaged on the job? Yet even supposing there was only one collator, will his standard of accuracy have remained constant from play to play or from page to page, irrespective of legibility of copy, pressure of work, fatigue, etc.?[2] In order to make plausible the high incidence of 'common errors' in *Othello* conjecture is reared upon conjecture.

As students of the probability of error the new correctors would have done well to survey their conclusions pessimistically from the vantage point of their own special knowledge. No one disputes that there will be 'common errors' in the Q and F texts of such a play as *Othello*[3]: as Greg recognised, however, most of them 'must always remain undetected'. Miss Walker triumphed where many predecessors failed in detecting several: yet she set about the loosening of editorial restraints altogether too hopefully. It is as true today as it was in the age of Francis Bacon that 'rash diligence hath done great prejudice' to the 'true correction and edition of authors . . . And therefore as it hath been wisely noted, the most corrected copies are commonly the least correct' (*The Advancement of Learning*).

★   ★   ★

Correcting Shakespeare has been a pastime since the eighteenth century, and one rule of the game, forgotten all too often, is in special need of reiteration. 'I am willing to comply with any meaning that can be extorted from the present text, rather than change it', Dr Johnson maintained.[4] The more modern attitude, fostered by Coleridge and the Romantics, who believed that 'Caesar can do no wrong', supposes that whenever Shakespeare admits of improvement he could not have written the words in the substantive texts. This absurdity enables the

---

[1] Miss Walker, *Problems*, p. 57 etc.

[2] Cf. Greg on a not dissimilar point, 'the error of supposing that every transcription introduces approximately the same number of variants' (*The Calculus of Variants* (Oxford 1927), p. 59).

[3] Whether the F compositor printed from corrected Q as copy, or from a manuscript and 'occasionally consulted' Q, common errors could arise.

[4] Johnson's *Shakespeare*, 1765, on *Cymbeline*, I.6.9.

would-be editor to 'restore' Shakespeare without the inconvenience of demonstrating the impossibility of a reading accepted for centuries. Against the Romantics, however, we may quote Ben Jonson, who disliked the idolatry of Shakespeare and knew that this particular Caesar could 'do wrong': 'Many times hee fell into those things, could not escape laughter . . .'

It is, *pace* Coleridge, the easiest thing in the world to 'improve' Shakespeare. Some of the best improvements have been unconscious, the result of a lapse of memory in quotation, which suggests that great opportunities await anyone with a fully conscious talent. One could regard Hazlitt's misquotation of *Cymbeline* III.3.37 as 'better than Shakespeare'. Hazlitt[1] created the marvellous line, 'wind and rain beat dark November down' in place of F's

> When we shall heare
> The *Raine and winde beate darke December? How*
> In this our pinching Caue, shall we discourse
> The freezing houres away?

Even Shakespeare's best plays contain thoroughly bad lines which must be his, so that we can hardly boggle at allowing him some inferior words: lines such as 'Too much of water hast thou, poor Ophelia' (*Hamlet*, IV.7.186), and 'He says he will return incontinent. / He hath commanded me to go to bed' (*Othello*, IV.3.11–12).

Editorial meddling can give us words and lines 'better than Shakespeare'—for the simple reason that a mature poet will not always load every rift with ore. The drama in particular requires 'neutral lines' to set off 'strong lines', *diminuendo* as well as *crescendo*, and therefore local improvements are feasible, though the speech, scene or play as a whole may suffer.

> Legitimate Edgar, I must haue your land,
> Our Fathers loue, is to the Bastard Edmond,
> As to th' legitimate: fine word: Legitimate.
> Well, my Legittimate, if this Letter speed,
> And my inuention thriue, Edmond the base
> Shall to' th' Legitimate: I grow, I prosper:
> Now Gods, stand vp for Bastards.
>   (*King Lear*, I.2.16–22, F)

[1] See Stanley Jones, 'An Unidentified Shakespearean Allusion in Hazlitt' (*English Studies*, 1964, XLV, 126 ff.).

Q prints as prose ('Edmund the base shall tooth' legitimate:'). Almost without exception the editors have bowed to an eighteenth-century substitute, 'Edmund the base / *Shall top* th' legitimate', on the assumption that 'Shall to' could only mean 'Shall fight against'. Yet QF make sense, if we allow for the illegibility of the Q copy, and the fact that 'to' and 'too' were not always distinguished in spelling[1]: 'if this letter speed, and my invention thrive, Edmund the base shall too. The legitimate! I grow, I prosper—'. After the exclamations 'Legitimate!' and 'my legitimate' (ll. 18, 19), another disgusted 'th' legitimate!' (l. 21) cannot be misunderstood, and the context supplies the verb: 'Edmund the base shall (speed, thrive, grow, prosper) too!'[2] Here, I think, *top* gives a stronger line than QF, yet emendation is not strictly necessary: the editors had no cause to let their invention thrive.

The Eclectic Text

Only one year after Miss Walker's New Cambridge *Othello*, 1957, there appeared the New Arden edition of the play, in which M. R. Ridley expounded an entirely different editorial procedure. Like Greg he believed that the Folio transmits some of Shakespeare's second thoughts.

> I think that in Q1, amplified by the reinstatement of the cuts, we have as near an approximation as we are likely to get to the play as Shakespeare first wrote it, with nothing between us and him but the blunders of honest but not always skilful transcriber and compositor. On the other hand, I think that in F we have probably a good deal of Shakespeare's second thoughts, but also, almost certainly, a good deal of divergence from the original for which he was not responsible.

I follow Greg and Ridley in accepting that the Q and F of *Othello* offer two authorial strains, but draw away sharply from the conclusion of Ridley's valuable section on 'The Textual Problem'. Because of the difficulty of deciding on the provenance of F alternatives ('with each individual instance of divergence we are left to guess-work selection of

---

[1] 'It is also clear that the [Quarto] copy was very badly written and often baffled the compositor' (Greg, *F.F.*, p. 379). For to-too compare the Shakespearian pages of *More*: 'plodding tooth portes' (l. 76), 'com to short of your great trespas' (l. 124).

[2] Cf. Mercutio's repeated exclamations of disgust, 'A plague a both your houses' (three times), followed by 'Your houses!' (*Romeo*, III.1.88–105).

the source, Shakespeare, the actors, memorial contamination, editorial sophistication'), he gives Q the status of a 'preferred text'.

On the analogy of Keats's revised ending for *The Eve of St. Agnes* and Wordsworth's 1850 version of *The Prelude* Ridley argued that 'second thoughts are not always improvements', and that therefore we are not bound to admit them to our modern texts, so that 'it is much more helpful to the reader to give him Q1, cured of obvious errors, and let him make up his own mind which of the divergences of F he will admit to the final text that he makes for himself'.[1] This is to take too modest a view of the duties of an editor, for if he cannot produce a 'final text' how shall the reader? Moreover, the comparison with *The Eve of St. Agnes* and *The Prelude* is misleading, since both poems were altered some considerable time after their original composition, when the general quality of their authors' work was falling off: a Shakespearian fair copy, on the other hand, would be very much a contemporary of the foul papers. Even at a date so close to the first creative impulse a great poet may interpolate changes for the worse, of course (cf. p. 73), yet this possibility does not save the editor from the irksome responsibility of producing a synthetic text.

Perhaps more corrupting agents intervened in the production of the *Othello* F than in the case of Q, but this scarcely empowers us to say, with Ridley, that 'with F we do not know where we are, whereas with Q1 we do'.[2] For one thing, even if F went through more hands, a 'corrector' seems to have changed some of Q's errors in preparing the F text, and to some extent redressed the balance. For another—*do* we know where we are with Q? Did Ridley know about Q's copyists and compositors—and do we know all we want to about them today?[3] Supposing F gives Shakespeare's revised readings and appears to be a 'better' text, as even Ridley grants, F and not Q should serve as the basis of a modern text—if such a basis is really required.

Of late the use of a 'copy-text' has come under fire, since even in the most advantageous circumstances the author's accidentals (spelling, punctuation, etc.) would be modified by one or more compositors.[4] Drop the idea of taking either Q or F as 'copy-text', however, and there are still many who would argue that if one is the 'better text' we

[1] *Othello* (New Arden), pp. xliii–xliv. In his *King Lear* (New Temple) Ridley adopted a similar policy (p. xii).
[2] Ridley, *Othello*, p. xliv.   [3] Cf. Note A, p. 112.
[4] Cf. Bowers, *Editing*, chap. III. Cf. also with the general drift of this section Greg's 'The Rationale of Copy-Text' (*S.B.*, 1950), III, 19–36.

should always accept its readings where the variants are indifferent.[1] This 'mechanical' rule would spare one a great deal of trouble—if only it could be detached from a miscalculation upon which Greg has remarked.

> to say that one text contains twice as many errors as another tells us next to nothing about their relative accuracy, unless we also know the frequency of variation ... Even if there were on an average one *variant* in every blank-verse line (of about eight words), the texts would still have respectively 96 and 92 per cent of the *words* correct, and their relative accuracy would not be in the ratio of 2:1 but of 24:23, which is after all pretty close.[2]

The relative accuracy of those of Shakespeare's plays most packed with variants is much closer than we are sometimes invited to think. If editors reject 170 readings from *Othello* F and 500 from Q, and if the 170 and 500 were all errors (which, I have suggested (p. 163), they need not be), we could scarcely describe F as anything but a 'very slightly better text'. To follow F's indifferent variants as a matter of course is therefore to take a miscalculated risk.

Convenient though it is to distinguish 'indifferent' variants from more important ones, I believe that editors retreat far too often behind a word which can as aptly describe the beholder as the thing observed. Many, indeed, assume that the variation of my-mine, spoke-spake, in-on, or singular-plural, is 'indifferent' *per se* without reference to context, an absurdity easily exploded in some passages where euphony or the need for repetition raises one such variant above its fellow. These are evasions of full eclecticism without much to recommend them even when both substantive texts go back to one arch-text. But when we have to reckon with two arch-texts, in *Othello*, say, or *Troilus*, the case for eclecticism grows stronger still—if the two are contemporaries, foul papers and fair copy, or two fair copies. For if we think of the second text not as a 'revision' of the first but as a transcript incorporating afterthoughts to which the author attached no great importance, and if we cure ourselves of the notion of a finalised text (cf. pp. 2, 192), we are

---

[1] E.g. G. I. Duthie in his two editions of *Lear*, 1949, p. 120, and 1960, p. 136. For a discussion of 'indifferent variants' in reprints containing both authorial corrections and compositors' errors cf. Arthur Friedman, 'The Problem of Indifferent Readings in the Eighteenth Century, with a Solution from *The Deserted Village*' (S.B., 1960, vol. XIII).

[2] *Ed. Problem*, p. xxx, ftn.

at liberty to select from either as we please.[1] Doubtless the later version will often improve on the earlier, and will sometimes fall below it in both conscious and unconscious substitutions: no difficulty then arises. But how shall we grapple with the remaining 'indifferent' variants which presumably lie concealed among the mass of Shakespeare's QF variants?

Not, I have urged, with the aid of 'mechanical' rules such as 'prefer the better (or earlier, or later) text', unless one is far and away the better. No: the editor must screw his courage to the sticking place and choose between each pair of variants. In short, he must discard the labour-saving idea of 'indifferent' variants, recognising at the same time that to attempt a feat left undone by Shakespeare, to finalise an unfinalised text, will create a version that never existed in the author's hand. At first this will seem a wrong-headed ambition. Reflect, however, that an editorial tradition of long standing (proceeding, however, from different assumptions) lends its authority to our search for the best possible synthetic text, and the suggestion loses most of its daring. It could be applied, of course, to any play that rests on two substantive texts of roughly equal reliability, whether the question of second thoughts arises or not: even if he holds that the two texts of *Othello* go back to the same arch-text the editor must not be allowed to duck down behind either Q or F 'on principle', whenever there is half a chance of pleading indifference in the variants.

An editor tackling 'indifferent' variants will often find reasons for selecting one rather than the other once he begins to look. Not always: and his reasons will be tenuous at times, amounting, perhaps, to no more than a personal preference. As long as he understands that eclecticism always throws him back in the last resort upon 'personal preference', even when deciding between 'substantive' variants in cases where pages can be written in support of either one (e.g. *solid—sullied*

---

[1] 'The aim of a critical edition should be to present the text . . . in the form in which we may suppose that it would have stood in a fair copy, made by the author himself, of the work as he finally intended it' (Greg, *Ed. Problem*, p. x, following McKerrow). This, the accepted 'rule', presupposes a finalised text and therefore requires modification, especially as it affects indifferent variants. Bowers, I think, went too far in the opposite direction in urging that with plays like *Troilus*, based on two arch-texts, 'the only truly established text, in any pure sense, must be the documentary corrected state of each as a separate entity' ('Established Texts and Definitive Editions', *P.Q.*, 1962, XLI, 17): Bowers here puts the 'revision' of *Troilus* in the same class with the revision of *Every Man in his Humour* and of *The Prelude*.

(*sallied*) in *Hamlet*), the idea of exercising an essentially unreasoned choice will become less abhorrent. An honest editor will admit that reason fails him quite often, and therefore a fully eclectic-synthetic text will not disturb him unduly.

Some 'rules' cause disquiet when applied to two-text plays, whether we have to reckon with one arch-text or with two. Others, including the most highly respected, become questionable more particularly when brought to bear on plays deriving from two authorial versions. Should we 'prefer the harder reading' in *Troilus and Cressida*? As I have mentioned, poets sometimes tone down a word in order to give the appropriate emphasis to a more important word[1]: this happened in some of the extracts quoted in chapter V, in the second version of *Every Man In His Humour*, and elsewhere. Some weaker readings in the *Troilus and Cressida* Quarto will be post-authorial corruptions, but not necessarily all. The 'rules' deployed against corrupt texts will, as I have already indicated at some length,[2] mislead the editor of a two-text play the variants of which include an unknown quantity of first shots and afterthoughts.

The 'Optimism' of the New Bibliography

In his British Academy Lecture of 1923 A. W. Pollard described himself as 'an incurable optimist'. This was not a charming irrelevance for, though he made no such claim, Pollard's optimism must have counted as one of the chief assets of the New Bibliography during his lifetime. It set the tone, it offered an inspiration. Greg, rightly, found space in his survey of the achievements of the half-century to praise 'the soundness of Pollard's optimism',[3] and no one will deny that in Pollard's own work, and in the work of his immediate associates, it had an influence almost wholly for the good.

Pollard's optimism centred on the subject of textual transmission: unlike his predecessors he believed that Shakespeare's own manuscripts formed the 'copy' for the good quartos. After 1923 this optimism was carried by other bibliographers into textual criticism, and over-indulged. An enormous body of new facts relating to Shakespeare's text was made available, bringing with it many new uncertainties. We welcomed the facts and, all too often, shut our minds against the uncertainties: healthy optimism degenerated into wishful thinking. It is

[1] Cf. p. 74.   [2] Cf. pp. 64–77.
[3] *F.F.*, pp. 96–7.

as well to recognise that though we have learnt much from the closer study of Shakespeare's text, we have wasted our time if we have not also learnt caution. In particular, we have concentrated too exclusively on printed books, and neglected authorial manuscripts. If the two texts of a play like *Troilus and Cressida* contain first and second shots, as is generally admitted, a glance at authorial substitutions in holograph manuscripts will warn us to proceed with extreme caution, and to announce that scores of variants leave us completely in the dark.

Quite naturally it is daunting for the modern editor to raise his eyes to this new prospect of darkness, and his quickest escape-route from it will be found in compositor studies and other 'scientific' methods. These again draw upon facts and uncertainties mortised together, and therefore it should be emphasised that the optimists are at their most dangerous precisely when they offer the world new 'bibliographical facts'. Dover Wilson assigned *Hamlet* Q2 to a single novice compositor, but later J. R. Brown found evidence for two men. Hinman and others have challenged Miss Walker's compositor determination of many texts, and I believe that in giving the whole of the *Othello* Quarto to one compositor Hinman and Miss Walker are both wrong. Bowers declared that he 'could prove on physical evidence not subject to opinion' that Shakespeare wrote 'sullied flesh' and not 'solid flesh' in *Hamlet*, yet opinion has refused to yield.[1] Extraordinarily helpful as the New Bibliography has been, its 'facts' are not always as securely established, nor as easily interpreted, as we may be invited to think.

'Optimistic' editors skim airily over too many unknowables in their corrective and eclectic labours, especially when dealing with plays probably resting on two arch-texts: not least, in their reliance upon bibliography, their certainty that they can detect error, and their rules for restoring the lost original. A realistic attitude to the unknowables forces us, I think, to veer away from Pollard towards pessimism or, at any rate, scepticism.

The pessimistic editor will remember the unknowables in his play's history—and also those in his own judgment. Consequently he will tamper as little as possible with his substantive texts, preferring to retain a doubtful reading rather than to emend, and recognising his inevitable

---

[1] Cf. J. R. Brown, 'The Compositors of *Hamlet* Q2 . . .' (*S.B.*, 1955, VII, 17 ff.); Charlton Hinman, *The Printing and Proof-Reading of the First Folio of Shakespeare*, I, 205, 211 etc.; Bowers, *Textual & Literary Criticism*, p. 2; and also T. H. Hill, 'Spelling and the Bibliographer' (*The Library*, Fifth Series, 1963, XVIII, 1 ff.).

limitations in finalising a play based on two arch-texts. For he will tremble at the thought of the base Indian (or Judean) who threw a pearl away, holding it an editor's worst offence to campaign against any reading that might be Shakespeare's.

Appendix A (Cf. page 12)

THE DRAMATIST'S 'RIGHTS' IN HIS PLAY

How many dramatists had a hand in the publication of their own plays? F. P. Wilson summarised the accepted view:

> The dramatist sold his rights in his play when he sold it to the theatre. If, like Shakespeare, he was also a sharer in his theatre, then he owned a share in his play, but he owned it as sharer not as dramatist. A writer like Ben Jonson, however, who set the example of seeing his plays through the press suitably furnished with dedications, must have made an agreement with the theatre that his plays should be published; otherwise, it is incredible that his plays should have been printed one after another so soon after their first performance.[1]

He added (p. 97) that beside Jonson, 'Marston, Webster and some other dramatists' took care to see their plays published. How many 'other dramatists' were there, and to what extent could their practice compel us to modify Wilson's general picture?

Even in the highest circles misapprehensions about this subject are not unheard of. Greg thought that prefatory matter from the dramatist 'guaranteed' authorised publication in such plays as Armin's *Two Maids of Moreclacke* 1609, Middleton and Dekker's *Roaring Girl*, 1611, etc., and Bowers that a dramatist who signed a dedication 'doubtless furnished the printer with the manuscript'. Against such optimism I would pit another statement by Bowers: 'a dramatist could still write an introduction even though he had not provided the manuscript'.[2] Armin's *Two Maids*, published by the playwright against the wishes, as it seems, of the players, would not be 'authorised' in F. P. Wilson's

---

[1] *Retrospect*, p. 84. The views attributed to F. P. Wilson in this appendix are, of course, his summaries of scholarly opinion *circa* 1940; Arthur Brown's remain very similar in 1964 ('The Printing of Books', in *Sh. Survey 17*, 1964). I am much indebted throughout this appendix to Greg's *Bibliography of the English Printed Drama*, and to Miss Albright's *Dramatic Publication in England*. All the evidence I cite concerning play-publication derives from the title-pages and prefatory matter of the plays in question, unless I state the contrary.

[2] Greg, *F.F.*, p. 40; Bowers, ed. *Dekker*, III, 253, 5. Cf. Albright, *op. cit.*, p. 205, where it is assumed that dramatists who provided dedications etc. 'oversaw' the publication of their plays.

terms, and Middleton's epistle for *Roaring Girl* proves only that the printer contacted him (or *vice versa*) before the book appeared, not that he supplied—or approved of—the text. So many writers of this time complain that they learned of the printing of their book only when it reached the press 'accidentally' that *some* of them, one feels, must be telling the truth[1]: yet, though they did not furnish the text, and perhaps never set eyes on it in the printing-house, they provided epistles. My attitude to unspecific epistles, viz. such as make no claims about the text, therefore inclines to scepticism: an author's epistle *per se* tells us very little, I think, about the provenance or even about the soundness of the text.

No doubt the notion of an outright sale of plays to the actors was influenced by modern studies of Elizabethan 'copyright': an author lost control over his book once a printer got hold of it, and therefore the dramatist's helplessness *vis-à-vis* the players seemed to follow. The assumption that the dramatist was even required to hand over his foul papers to the players, only recently challenged by Bowers (cf. p. 20), affords one indication that we have perhaps taken the degradation of the professional writer too much for granted. Be that as it may, we can conjecture, in the absence of any concrete evidence, that the 'rights' of the author of a play would not cause trouble before capitalism revolutionised the theatrical world. By the 1580's, and certainly by the 1590's, some safeguards for the interested parties will have been evolved—though not necessarily defined.

What little evidence we possess dates, unfortunately, from a later period, and represents only one party—the actors. Sir Edmund Chambers and Miss Albright, whose books were written at the same time, independently draw upon roughly the same records, which, it should be noted, establish only that the dramatic companies disliked having their plays printed and not any widely recognised legal 'rights'.[2]

1. The Admiral's men in 1600 paid 40/- to stay the printing of one of their plays. 'Blocking' entries of plays from 1598 onwards also testify that the players resisted publication.

2. The articles of association of the King's Revels company of 1608 debarred its members from printing the group's plays.

[1] E.g. Heywood in *The Golden Age*, *The Four Prentices*, *The English Traveller*, and respecting other early plays in *The Rape of Lucrece*; Middleton, *The Family of Love*; Marston, *The Fawn* ('it cannot auoide publishing', as Marston wrote).
[2] Chambers, *Eliz. Stage*, III.183 ff; Albright, *Publication*, p. 238 ff. Miss Albright's book, though published in 1927, was completed in 1923.

3. The reference to the 'grand possessors' in *Troilus and Cressida*, 1609, seems to indicate publication against the wishes of the actors.

4. Heywood confessed in *The English Traveller*, 1633, that 'some Actors . . . thinke it against their peculiar profit to haue them [plays] come in Print'.

5. Brome's contract of 1635 to supply the Salisbury Court theatre with three plays a year prohibited publication without consent.

6. Letters from the Lord Chamberlain to the stationers in 1637 and, probably, in 1619, forbade publication without the players' consent.

According to Chambers the articles of association of 1608 (No. 2, above) 'may perhaps be taken as typical'. Miss Albright thought Brome's contract (No. 5) very probably 'a fair example of the method of employing a popular playwright'.[1] It is worth recalling, however, that in the very year of the articles of association Heywood denounced in his *Lucrece* the unauthorised publication of plays, which were then leaking to the printers: more stringent precautions might be thought necessary at this time. The 1635 contract shows which way the wind was blowing, but cannot really throw much light on the years 1594–1609, the years when Shakespeare might have passed on plays to the printers.

While the actors may have been unwilling to publish, there are always two sides to a bargain: would not some at least of the playwrights have wished to publish? This other side has been neglected. We are told that Jonson 'must have made an agreement with the theatre that his plays should be published'. Why only Jonson? A good deal of evidence survives to show that, whatever the *rights* the dramatists sold to the players, they certainly retained an *interest* in their works, which they sometimes insisted upon until the players gave way, and sometimes asserted in defiance of the grand possessors.

I. Some dramatists claim to have taken the initiative in the publication of their plays, in a few cases so casually that the possibility of infringing the rights of the players does not seem to occur to them.

1. Webster, *The White Devil*, 1612: 'In publishing this Tragedy, I do but challenge to my selfe that liberty, which other men haue tane before mee . . . since it was acted, in so dull a time of Winter, presented in so open and blacke a Theater, that it wanted . . . a full and vnderstanding Auditory . . .'

2. Daborne, *A Christian Turn'd Turk*, 1612: 'I haue, so farre as my

---

[1] Chambers, *op. cit.*, I, 379; Albright, *op. cit.*, p. 220.

weake power extended, procured the publishing this oppressed and much martird *Tragedy* . . .'

3. Massinger, *The Bondman*, 1624:

> The author, in a Christian pity, takes
> Care of your good, and prints it for your sakes.
>
> (Verses by W.B., ed. Gifford)

Compare also Marston, *The Malcontent*, 1604; Marston, *The Fawn*, 1606; Day, *Humour Out Of Breath*, 1608; Armin, *The Two Maids of Moreclacke*, 1609; Heywood, *The Brazen Age*, 1613; R. A. Gent., *The Valiant Welshman*, 1615; Brome, *The Antipodes*, 1640.

In the case of Sharpham's *The Fleer*, 1607, as in that of George Wilkins' plays (cf. p. 178, below), we must at least suspect the author of aiding and abetting surreptitious publication. First entered in the S.R. on 13 May, 1606, by J. Trundell and J. Busby ('PROVIDED that they are not to printe yt tell they bringe good aucthoritie and licence'), *The Fleer* was transferred to J. Busby and A. Johnson on 21 November, 1606, yet published in 1607 as 'Printed and are to be solde by F.B. in Paules-Church-yard, at the signe of the Flower de Lnce [*sic*] and the Crowne'. Greg observed that 'the modesty of both printer and bookseller points to its having been surreptitious'.[1] Inside the quarto there is a note from the stationer explaining that the author gave him 'an Epistle or Apological praeamble', which he has lost: it looks as if Sharpham came to terms with F.B. while the play was blocked by the Children of the Revels, who performed it, or supplied F.B. with a manuscript to anticipate publication through the regular channels.

Miss Albright mentions several plays published by the authors to anticipate a pirated text: Heywood's *The Rape of Lucrece*, 1608, Chapman's *All Fools*, 1605, and Marston's *The Malcontent*, 1604, seem her safest examples.[2] To these may be added I.C.'s *The Two Merry Milkmaids*, 1620, in which the printer's address to the reader declares that the author had the same motive: 'had not false Copies trauail'd abroad (euen to surbating) this had kept in; for so farre the Author was from seeking fame in the publishing, that hee could haue wisht it bound about with the Ring.'

Probably Miss Albright is also right in crediting the dramatists with the publication of plays that ran into trouble with the authorities, though this cannot always be proved. She lists Daniel's *Philotas*, 1605,

---

[1] *Bibliography*, I, 387.   [2] *Publication*, p. 210 ff.

Machin and Markham's *Dumb Knight*, 1608, and *Eastward Hoe, Sejanus, Byron*.[1]

The dramatists seem also to have promoted the dissemination of manuscript copies of plays in some—perhaps very few—cases. Middleton not only retrieved the manuscript play *The Witch* from the King's Men to dedicate it to Thomas Holmes, but wrote out a 'private transcript' of *A Game at Chesse*, helped to write out another, inserted verses in a third which indicate that the volume was a New Year's gift (presumably from the author) to Mr William Hammond, provided an autograph title-page for a fourth and probably corrected a fifth.[2] I do not propose to make too much of a play with an unusual stage-history, but it is worth asking: what *right* had Middleton to continue to concern himself with his plays?

II. Many plays came out as a vindication of the author's art, or with a complaint against the actors, who shortened or altered the text; or simply with the promise of the full, as distinct from the acted, version. When an author's epistle follows we may be the more confident, in doubtful cases, that he helped to bring about publication.

    1. Jonson, *Every Man out of his Humour*, 1600: 'As it was first composed by the Author B.I. Containing more than hath been Publickely Spoken or Acted...'

    2. Barnes, *The Devil's Charter*, 1607: 'As it was plaide before the Kings Maiestie, vpon Candlemasse night last: by his Maiesties Seruants. But more exactly reuewed, corrected, and augmented since by the Author, for the more pleasure and profit of the Reader...' (Author's dedication follows on $A_1{}^b$).

    3. Webster, *The Duchess of Malfi*, 1623: 'As it was Presented... By the Kings Maiesties Seruants. The perfect and exact Coppy, with diuerse things Printed, that the length of the Play would not beare in the Presentment.' (Author's dedication follows on A_3.)

    4. Fletcher's *The Faithful Shepherdess*, c. 1610, belongs to this group, for the tributes of Beaumont, Jonson, Chapman, as well as Fletcher's 'To the Reader', underline that the author here defends himself against misunderstanding. *The White Devil, A Christian Turn'd Turk* and *The Antipodes* (cf. group I) also reached the press to heal the author's wounded self-esteem.

---

  [1] *Publication*, pp. 213–14.
  [2] See R. C. Bald's edition, *A Game at Chesse*, pp. 26 ff., xi, and Bald's two articles, cited p. 51, n. 1.

III. Some dramatists proof-read their plays or supplied marginal notes for the reader. This suggests more solicitude about publication than a mere epistle.

Percy Simpson lists as proof-readers Jonson, Marston, Massinger.[1] To these may be added Webster and Dekker.[2] Marginal notes for the reader's benefit occur in plays by Jonson, Webster, Daniel, Chapman etc., the most famous being probably Webster's in *The Duchess of Malfi*: 'The Author disclaimes this Ditty to be his' (III.4).

IV. One kind of evidence pointing to the author's help in the publication of plays has been almost entirely overlooked.[3] The Latin tags or mottos quoted on many title-pages came in the large majority of cases from the authors, as, apparently, did biblical quotations in theological works. (A little later, in *An Apology for Smectymnuus*, 1642, Milton took it for granted that an author was often the 'emblazoner of his title-page', and in the *Pro Se Defensio*, 1655, that he controlled the wording 'in the very title-page'.) We can be sure that Jonson supplied his own; and the fact that they coincide almost invariably with an author's epistle, or other addition to the text, corroborates.

Often there is no doubt that the author chose the tags—simply because the same one appears on several of his books, though these were printed by and for different men. Greene used 'Omne tulit punctum qui miscuit utile dulci' almost as a second signature in his prose pamphlets, and Brome 'Hic totus volo rideat Libellus' on a number of plays put out by different printers. During Shakespeare's lifetime, however, plays were not as a rule thought sufficiently important to be dignified with Latin inscriptions, common as these became later,[4] and we may suppose that only very few dramatic manuscripts would carry them before printing was contemplated. Some of Greene's did, for his posthumously published *James the Fourth*, 1598 (S.R. 1594) proclaims

[1] *Proof-Reading in the Sixteenth, Seventeenth and Eighteenth Centuries*, 1935, pp. 11–13.

[2] See J. R. Brown, 'The Printing of John Webster's Plays' (*S.B.*, VI, 127, 130; VIII, 117, 120). Bowers (ed. *Dekker*, I, 301) takes the errata-list on A₄ᵇ of *Satiromastix*, 1602, to be by Dekker, as also the corrections for the second edition of *I Honest Whore* (*ibid.*, II, 5).

[3] Cf. however J. G. McManaway, 'Latin Title-Page Mottoes as a Clue to Dramatic Authorship' (in *The Library*, Fourth Series, 1946, vol. XXVI).

[4] Jonson seems to have started the fashion in 1600. Between 1590 and 1600 the only publicly acted plays with a title-page motto are Lodge's *Wounds of Civil War*, 1594, which, however, also has a Latin subscription at the end, so that very likely *both* stood in the manuscript; and Greene's *James the Fourth*, 1598.

on the title-page, 'Omne tulit punctum', and the explicit of *Friar Bacon*, 1594, almost certainly came from his pen ('Finis Frier Bacon, made by Robert Greene, Maister of Arts. Omne tulit punctum qui miscuit vtile dulci.')—but Greene's partiality for his tag makes him a special case. Manuscript plays surviving from the period very rarely flaunt a motto, and therefore we must deduce that normally the author selected his tag for publication and handed it in to the printer with his prefatory matter.[1]

Very occasionally it happens that the Latin motto does not coincide with prefatory matter by the author. Excluding closet plays, 'entertainments', plays performed by amateurs etc. we are left with only four plays from the professional repertories falling into this category between 1600 and 1612. Three of them were printed by Edward Allde,[2] who may have supplied them himself, or requested them: the fourth exhibits another extraordinary feature which makes it practically certain that the author interfered behind the scenes.

George Wilkins' *The Miseries of Enforced Marriage*, 1607, was printed (by William Jaggard) for George Vincent 'As it is now playd by his Maiesties Seruants'—with the motto 'Qui Alios, (seipsum) docet'. Another play in which Wilkins collaborated came out in the same year,

---

[1] The few manuscript plays with title-page mottos (e.g. *Dick of Devonshire, Love's Changeling's Change, The Parliament of Bees*) date from a period when printed books had established the fashion for such mottos, viz. from after 1610. In some of Marston's plays the Latin mottos occur not on the title-page but in the margin of the first page of dialogue: these may have stood in his MSS. before printing was contemplated, but, as Marston definitely oversaw the printing of some of his plays we cannot dogmatise about the provenance of his mottos. The explicit in printed plays must often derive from the manuscript, and conceivably the author's explicit might be used as a title-page motto without his knowledge. With the exception of Jonson's, however, the explicits of the period are almost always distinguishable from mottos as variations of the 'Laus Deo' formula: cf. Yarington, *Two Lamentable Tragedies*, 1601; *The Puritan*, 1607; *What You Will*, 1607, or the MS. play *Juno's Pastoral*. The only exceptions I have observed are *Friar Bacon*, 1594, Lodge's *Wounds of Civil War*, 1594, and Nashe's *Summer's Last Will and Testament* (probably not a publicly acted play: cf. McKerrow, *Nashe*, IV, 419), and Jonson's plays. Despite its textual history I cannot believe that the explicit of *Doctor Faustus* came from anyone but the dramatist—Greg, however, ascribed it to the printer (*Marlowe's 'Doctor Faustus'* (Oxford 1950), p. 403).

[2] *Blurt Master-Constable*, 1602, *The Tragedy of Tiberius*, 1607, *The Turk*, 1610. Allde also printed many plays without mottos, so that it is possible that he found those in these three plays in his MSS., or that the authors provided mottos but nothing more for these plays. After 1612 the desire to dress up play-texts grew, and some more printers may have taken it upon themselves to supply mottos: cf. *The Knight of the Burning Pestle*, 1613, *The Honest Lawyer*, 1616.

The Travels of the Three English Brothers, printed (by George Eld) for John Wright 'As it is now play'd by her Maiesties Seruants'. Of these two plays *The Miseries* could not have been written before 1604 but might be two or three years younger (it is based on a pamphlet of 1604), and *The Travels*, entered in the S.R. on 29 June, 1607, follows a source, by A. Nixon, which was entered in the S.R. on the 8th June preceding. Without any hesitation we can therefore accept the title-page assurances that the two plays still held the boards at the time of publication. And yet not only would publication before the end of the 'run' be most unusual[1]—the wording 'As it is now played' is, so far as I can discover, quite without parallel on a new play between 1590 and 1616, the regular form being always in the past ('As it hath been acted' or 'As it was played' etc.)[2] When we recall that in the following year Wilkins brought out *The Painful Adventures of Pericles Prince of Tyre*, a prose narrative 'Being The true History of the Play of *Pericles*, as it was lately presented', that at the same time a S.R. entry was made to block the play (20 May, 1608), and that the next year saw a bad quarto of the play thrust into the world—a picture begins to take shape.

Jaggard, the printer of *The Miseries*, on only one other occasion issued a play with a Latin motto, N. Field's *A Woman is a Weathercock*, 1612, a play provided with an epistle and address signed by the author and with verses by Chapman to his 'Loued Sonne' Field: like other mottos accompanied by epistles etc. this one of 1612 must be the author's. On the title-pages of his non-dramatic books Jaggard sometimes went in for a motto—with such books as usually required them, as for example legal treatises (George Saltern's *Of the Antient Lawes of Great Britaine*, 1605, Thomas Ridley's *A View of the Civile and Ecclesiasticall Law*, 1607)—though his tendency up till 1607 was to omit them. As for George Vincent, the publisher of *The Miseries*, he floated only four

[1] Cf. p. 188.
[2] The 1635 editions of *Catiline* and *The Knight of the Burning Pestle*, both by N.O. for I.S., adopt the formula 'As it is now Acted', as does the second edition of *The Scornful Lady*, 1625 ('As it was now lately Acted'), and its successors: but these were all reprints, and therefore could be put out when it suited the publishers. Only one play, apart from the two by Wilkins, carried the formula in the first edition, and that one was about twelve years old when first issued: *Love's Metamorphosis*, 1601, 'First played by the Children of Paules, and now by the Children of the Chappell'. (All the plays cited here in the category 'As it is now played' were already tracked down by Miss Albright, *op. cit.*, p. 258.) The title-page of Wilkins' *Three Miseries of Barbary* (*c.* 1606), incidentally, promises 'a relation of the death of Mahamet the late Emperour: and a briefe report of *the now present Wars* . . .' (my italics).

new books between 1602 and 1611 and none of them has a motto—so that it seems a near-certainty that neither printer nor publisher but Wilkins himself chose the motto for the play.[1] I suggest that Wilkins took the play to the printer without permission from the players, attached his name, which would not identify him as the man who sold the copy, but did not dare to write any preliminary matter, for this would have made his guilt much more apparent. He must have advised the use of the 'As it is now played' blurb, and, I believe, could not resist the flourish of a Latin motto, never imagining that it might serve as a clue. I strongly suspect that Wilkins threw together the prose *Pericles* (which on the title-page and in the Argument he entreats the reader to accept as the equivalent of the play, a most extraordinary proceeding) against the wishes of the company, perhaps because he felt he had a right in the play (as part-author?)[2] and yet was forbidden to publish.

V. Dramatists' epistles and dedications, though they signpost some sort of connivance in publication, are not easy to interpret. As I have said, they do not necessarily prove the author's responsibility for the printed version, nor the players' consent. When, however, an author repeatedly supplies epistles (e.g. Chapman from 1608), or repeatedly protests that the text came 'accidentally' to the press (e.g. Heywood), we may suspect that he sometimes helped to push through the sale.

One curiosity regarding the prefatory matter in plays deserves special mention. Very few early plays carried a proper dedication— very few, that is, in comparison with other pamphlets by the same authors. Dekker supplied an address to the reader for several early plays (*The Shoemakers' Holiday*, 1600, *Satiromastix*, 1602, *The Whore of Babylon*, 1607) and Middleton one for Middleton and Dekker's *The Roaring Girl*, 1611, but up to this date Dekker failed to send a single one into the world armed with a dedication: nevertheless, of the many prose

---

[1] For Jaggard's and Vincent's books cf. Paul G. Morrison's *Index of Printers, Publishers and Booksellers in . . . S.T.C.*, (Charlottesville 1950). Jaggard printed without a motto such deserving books as *The Historie of Iustine*, 1606, and Topsell's *Historie of Foure-Footed Beas es*, 1607, and *Historie of Serpents*, 1608. The author's epistle in this last book perhaps explains Jaggard's remissness in supplying mottos. Jaggard, according to Topsell, 'wanting the true knowledge of the Latine tongue', failed to correct Latin misprints in *The Historie of Foure-Footed Beastes*: it is unlikely, therefore, that Jaggard would add Latin tags of his own free will—and we may suppose that those few of his books which boast a motto were given it by the author rather than by the printer. *The Miseries* was printed from foul papers: cf. G. H. Blayney, *J.E.G.P.*, 1957, LVI, 23–41.

[2] Cf. Appendix B.

pamphlets ascribed to him in the *Short-Title Catalogue* nine out of six-teen were addressed to patrons before 1612. There must be a reason for this discrepancy. And a reason is hinted at by Francis Burton, the publisher of *The Tragedy of Tiberius*, 1607, who can recall 'but a singular President' for the dedication of a play:

> the reason wherefore so many Plaies haue formerly beene published without Inscriptions vnto particular Patrons (contrary to Custome in diuulging other Bookes) although perhaps I could nerely guesse yet because I would willingly offend none, I will now conceale.

Some dramatists pretended to look upon a play as a trifle, unworthy of a dedication,[1] but I do not think that Burton had in mind such mock-modesty: rather, he seems to suggest some sort of underhand practice.

A writer as unhappily insolvent as Dekker would not willingly forgo the forty shillings which were the usual gratuity for a dedication. Why did he, and Marston and Middleton and so many more lose their opportunities at this time even though they were consulted about the printing?[2] Why did Dekker, who managed to insert four separate dedications in *Foure Birds of Noahs Arke*, 1609, put none into his first half dozen plays, though these were much more substantial literary monuments? I think that it is possible that we see here some signs of a struggle between the dramatists and their employers. If my deductions from the title-page of *The Miseries of Enforced Marriage* are not mistaken George Wilkins stood up for himself—as did Dekker in Bowers's view.

> Dekker seems often to have been eager to print his popular plays, doubtless because he needed the extra profit, and soon after the writing of *Westward Ho* we find Henry Rocket entering for his copy in the Stationers' Register on 2 March 1605. When the licence was made conditional upon the securing of further authority, which I interpret here to mean the company's permission, and this authority was not forthcoming, the entry was vacated and the quarto was not printed until the Hodgets edition of 1607. This date coincided with the dissolution of the Children of Paul's, at which time various other of their plays were released for printing.[3]

Bowers's reading of the 1605 S.R. entry must remain a conjecture, yet

---

[1] Chapman, *The Widow's Tears*, 1612; Massinger, *The Unnatural Combat*, 1639.

[2] N. Field, *A Woman is a Weathercock*, 1612, tells us that a dedication brought forty shillings (A_3^a). Marston dedicated *Antonio and Mellida*, 1602, to 'No-body' and *The Malcontent*, 1604, to Jonson—from neither of whom he would collect forty shillings.   [3] Bowers, *Editing*, p. 17.

it finds some support in the publication-histories of other early Dekker plays. *Satiromastix* was entered in the S.R. on 11 November, 1601, 'vppon condicon that yt be lycensed to be printed', and could not be more than half a year old then and perhaps not so much[1]; likewise *I Honest Whore*, entered in the S.R. on 9 November, 1604, reached print early, as it dates from that year (Bowers thinks the copy would be delivered to the players 'before mid-1604'[2]). *Old Fortunatus* was entered in the S.R. on 20 February, 1600, yet Dekker received payments for work on the play in November and December, 1599; *Patient Grissill* was entered on 28 March, 1600, ten days after Henslowe paid forty shillings 'to staye the printing', yet Dekker, Chettle and Haughton were being paid for the play from October to 29 December, 1599; and *The Shoemakers' Holiday* appeared in 1600 (without S.R. entry), Dekker being paid for it on 15 July, 1599. Clearly someone took energetic measures to get Dekker's plays into print: so many different publishers were involved that we are led to the conclusion that the driving force was Dekker himself.

*   *   *

'No doubt', wrote Greg, who apparently subscribed to the notion that a dramatist sold all his rights when he sold his play, 'there was a vague feeling abroad that an author, or at any rate the possessor, of a work had an equitable right to the same'.[3] This feeling, in so far as it affected authors generally, found expression more often than Greg implied (he related it to the Lord Chamberlain's letter to the Stationers of 1637) but is not easy to pin down. I believe there is some evidence for it in the epistles etc. collected by Kirschbaum to prove his rather different thesis that 'Publication without the author's knowledge or consent was not considered at large, in Shakespeare's time, as in any way reprehensible'.[4] *Legally* the author had no redress against un-authorised publication, yet *morally* the marauding publishers admitted themselves to be in the wrong—why else their apologies? Confining myself to Kirschbaum's examples, which, I repeat, were selected to support the opposite case, I note the following.

1. The publisher to the author, in a surreptitiously printed book of

---

[1] See Chambers, *Eliz. Stage*, III, 293.   [2] *Dekker*, ed. Bowers, II, 3.
[3] Greg, *F.F.*, p. 69. Cf. Milton in *Eikonoklastes*: 'human right . . . commands, that every author should have the property of his own work reserved to him after death, as well as living' (*Prose Works*, ed. Bohn, 1848, I, 329).
[4] Kirschbaum, *Stationers*, p. 147.

1605: 'I haue put my selfe in the way of your *reproofe*; and am become a *theefe* of this nature, to *steale* no more from you then I will againe giue to you ... My *fault* is, I haue done that which would haue beene done ...'

2. The publisher to the reader, *Tottel's Miscellany*, 1557: 'It resteth nowe (gentle reder) that thou *thinke it not euill doon*, to publish ... those workes which the vngentle horders vp of such treasure haue heretofore enuied thee ...'

3. The publisher in his dedication, of an unauthorised book, 1600: 'To couer this *presumption*, I haue made your Ladiships partners in the patronage because, I am sure, howsoeuer hee shall dislike the publishing; yet it shall please him that your Ladiships' names are honored ...'[1]

Unauthorised publishers so regularly apologise for their *boldness* and *presumption* that Kirschbaum will have to stretch the meaning of the word if he really believes that their ventures were not 'reprehensible'. The writers of the day without unnecessary circumlocution stigmatised such publishers and their agents as thieves and scoundrels.

1. Bacon, of his *Essays*, printed on his behalf to forestall piracy: 'Louing and beloued Brother, I doe now like some that haue an Orcharde ill neighbored, that gather their fruit before it is ripe, to preuent *stealing* ...'

2. Sir Lewis Lewkenor, 1595: 'The former treatise ... was by a fellow, that had *stolne* a coppy thereof, *foysted to the print*, in hope of benefit ...'

3. Daniel, 1604: '*Madame. In respect of the vnmannerly presumption of an indiscreet Printer*, who without warrant hath divulged the late shewe at Court ...'[2]

And of course there are many other unambiguous indictments of the presumptuous publisher not cited by Kirschbaum. My favourite one is the charmingly resigned complaint of Thomas Playfere in the 1597 edition of *The Meane in Mourning*.

thys Sermon hath beene twise printed already without my procure-ment or priuitie any manner of way. Yea, to my very great greefe and trouble ... what others, eyther by reporting or printing woulde make of it, that was not my faulte, that was not in mee eyther to helpe or to hinder. Therefore *I haue not gone vnto any Magistrate to complaine, but though it bee one of the greatest iniuries that euer was*

---

[1] Kirschbaum, *Stationers*, pp. 106, 109, 121: cf. pp. 103, 344. My italics.
[2] Kirschbaum, *op. cit.*, pp. 128, 142, 140: cf. pp. 138, 396. My italics.

offered mee, yet because I know not what secret purpose the Lord had in laying this affliction vpon me, I doe most willingly pardon it.
[My italics]

The most famous statement of all on the subject is equally direct: 'you were abus'd with diuerse stolne, and surreptitious copies, maimed, and deformed by the frauds and stealthes of iniurious impostors'. With these words Heminge and Condell flayed unauthorised publishers no less than thieves of copy.

It is sometimes said that Wither, who feuded with the stationers because they opposed his patent, was prejudiced and a bad witness.[1] Whenever his own immediate interests are involved one senses in Wither's style an emotionalism that makes one sceptical: but his remarks on an author's rights seem to me of the highest evidential value, especially as they coincide with those of other professional writers. He insists, for example, that authors invest their scholarship in their books and therefore, 'hauing their *proper rightes* incroched vpon' by the stationers, must seek what redress they can: a book which I have written 'is naturally myne own'. He asserts that stationers will publish 'any written Coppy' that comes into their power if 'likely to be vendible, whether the Author be willing or no'.[2]

Kirschbaum's book is crammed with useful information but in this particular he has, I am confident, misread his own evidence. The stationers, one may grant, supported the publisher of surreptitiously acquired books, as long as no other stationer's 'copyright' suffered: but the literary world at large was not amused. To argue, as does Kirschbaum, that publication without consent was not thought reprehensible is to turn a deaf ear to the fulminations of the authors and to disregard the facts of human nature.

The author's equitable right in his own work, hinted at in a few records of the stationers themselves,[3] could apply to dramatic productions as to others. 'In publishing this Tragedy, I do but challenge to my selfe that liberty, which other men haue tane before mee', announced Webster (cf. p. 174). And the dramatic author's *right* to oversee the

[1] 'Wither was a man with a grievance and his evidence is certainly open to cross-examination' (Greg, *F.F.*, p. 71).
[2] George Wither, *The Schollers Purgatory* (c. 1625), ed. 1872 (Spenser Society), pp. 35, 36, 129, and 13, 101. My italics.
[3] W. W. Greg, *Some Aspects and Problems of London Publishing Between 1550 and 1650* (Oxford 1956), p. 16.

publication of his own writings seems, again, to be conceded in
Heminge and Condell's dedication and address to the readers in 1623.
Shakespeare, they lament, did not enjoy 'the fate, common with some,
to be exequutor to his owne writings'—not because he sold all his
rights in his plays to his company but simply because he died too soon.
Again—

> It had bene a thing, we confesse, worthie to haue bene wished, that
> the Author himselfe had liu'd to haue set forth, and ouerseen his
> owne writings; But since it hath bin ordain'd otherwise, and he by
> death departed from that *right*, we pray you do not envie his Friends,
> the office of their care, and paine, to haue collected & publish'd
> them . . . [My italics]

Shakespeare's *right* to set forth and oversee *his owne writings* derives not
from his being a sharer but from his just claims as *the Author*. We are
not told, of course, that the author could publish his plays whenever
he liked—but, on the other hand, Heminge and Condell stop short of
divorcing the author completely from his play once he sold it to the
theatre.

An aside by Sir Edmund Chambers based on statistics confirms that
such a complete divorce never took place.

> So far as the professional companies are concerned, the repertories
> which have probably been best preserved, owing to the fact that the
> poets were in a position to influence publication, are those of the
> boys.[1]

Dramatists pressed the publication of their plays whenever they could:
they did not surrender their 'rights' as a matter of course.

★   ★   ★

I have suggested that other dramatists besides Jonson, of those writing
for the adult companies, influenced publication. So far I have confined
the argument to title-pages, prefatory matter, and the concept of the
author's equitable right. The economics of authorship deserve some
consideration as well.

The fact that Brome's contract of 1635 required a stipulation against
printing without consent indicates, I think, that no generally binding
laws upon this subject existed: and it follows that, when sufficiently
established, the dramatists could negotiate their own terms. Evidently

---

[1] *Eliz. Stage*, III, 182.

Jonson did so. Very gradually, as we know, the lot of the playwright improved, and with it his power to bargain. Greg observed that at the close of the sixteenth century 'Chapman appears ... to have commanded prices rather above the average' (compared, that is, with Henslowe's other retainers); that around 1599 the prices of plays 'begin to fluctuate considerably'; that a decade later 'prices had risen greatly. A third-rate poet like Daborne, evidently deep in Henslowe's toils, gets £10 to £20 a play, and is constantly asserting in his correspondence that he can get £25 elsewhere.'[1] Henslowe's attempts to secure the exclusive services of some dramatists (Porter in February, 1599, and probably Chettle in March, 1602), and his new phrase in purchasing plays, 'paid *for the use of the company*' (thrice in October, 1599), seem to confirm that the exploitation of the dramatists could no longer be taken for granted. I have the impression too from Greene's *Francesco's Fortunes*, 1590, and *Groat's Worth of Wit*, 1592, that a popular writer could demand any sum he liked from the players, and in that case 'the only Shake-scene in a country' inherited the Fortunatus' purse of the author whose fame he 'eclipsed'.[2] To confirm this impression we need search no further than a familiar passage in *Hamlet* where, alluding to the war of the theatres, Rosencrantz says: 'There was for a while no money bid for argument, unless the poet and the player went to cuffs in the question' (II.2.350 ff.).[3] That the bidding of money here refers to a process of bargaining and not to a simple 'take-it-or leave-it' offer from the actors emerges clearly from the speech placed beside Rosencrantz's as comment and amplification:

> It is not very strange; for my uncle is King of Denmark, and those that would make mows at him while my father lived give twenty, forty, fifty, a hundred ducats apiece for his picture in little.

What I wish to bring into question is the notion of a fixed and unalterable relationship between dramatists and players, which includes the widely-accepted subsidiary that 'A dramatist sold his play outright

---

[1] *Henslowe's Diary*, II, 126, 127, and cf. p. 142.

[2] Greene wrote in 1590: '*happie were those Actors* in short time that could get any of his workes, he grewe so exquisite in that facultie' (*Francesco's Fortunes*, B₃ᵇ), and Nashe's echo of 1592 clarifies the implications of the words I have italicised: 'In a night & a day would he [Greene] haue yarkt vp a Pamphlet as well as in seauen yeare, and *glad was that Printer that might bee so blest to pay him deare* for the very dregs of his wit' (*Nashe*, I, 287).

[3] Cf. *The Alchemist*: 'You shall ha' your ordinaries bid for him, / As play-houses for a poet' (*Jonson*, V, 353).

to the theatre'.[1] The dramatists, I submit, despite the pitiful story chronicled in Henslowe's diary, fended for themselves, and at least one died a rich man. They asked for more money when they could. They received their 'benefits' on the third day, though some managed to carry off the second, and one, of the few whose contracts escaped the dark backward and abysm, insisted on the first.[2] Shakespeare, in a controlling position in his company and unrivalled in public esteem as a dramatist, must have been able to dictate his own conditions. He might even have refused to sell his plays to his fellows and hired them out instead: we have it on the best authority that such 'renting' could and did take place.

> We know for certain that a small number of the plays performed by the Admiral's men from 1594 onwards were the personal property of Edward Alleyn and others of Martin Slaughter, for we find these men selling the books in question to the company at a later date . . . there is some reason to suppose that a few pieces may have been in Henslowe's hands . . .[3]

The allusion in the quarto of *Troilus and Cressida* to 'the grand possessors' makes it unlikely that Shakespeare hired out his plays: but others did. This should be a warning to us not to generalise too sweepingly about the sale of plays. If the prospect of not securing a third-rate dramatist's new work could inspire nervousness in the actors,[4] no company would have been foolhardy enough to put up an implacable resistance if Shakespeare chose to reserve printing-rights. Let us remember, too, that sharers frequently quarrelled and split up, and that a dramatist who committed himself to the exclusive service of one company would probably do so for a period of years (Brome signed for three years) and then would get his contract revised: thus an opportunity to demand more favourable terms would recur from time to time.

As I see it, the following picture emerges during Shakespeare's years in London. Often a play would be sold outright to the theatre—but others apart from Jonson will have made reservations about printing from about 1599 onwards. After the failure or partial failure of a play

---

[1] F. P. Wilson, *Retrospect*, p. 84.

[2] See Chambers, *Eliz. Stage*, I, 373 n. 4, and G. E. Bentley, *The Jacobean and Caroline Stage* (Oxford 1941 etc.), I, 295.

[3] Greg, *Henslowe's Diary*, II, 119; cf. also Albright, *op. cit.*, pp. 222, 224.

[4] N. Field, on behalf of his company, to Henslowe, 1613: 'wee would not loose it, wee haue so assured a hope of it, and, on my knowledge Mr. Dauborne may haue his request of another Companie . . .' (*Henslowe Papers*, p. 84).

on the stage the dramatist may have regarded it as derelict, i.e. of no further use to the players, and consequently resumed his 'equitable right' and taken it to the printer. He might or might not contact the players before this step (Daborne did, apparently, for *A Christian Turn'd Turk*, Webster probably not for *The White Devil*)—depending, conceivably, on whether he believed the failure to be his own fault or that of the players, and on his possessing a copy of the text. When a play ended its 'run', that is, no longer appeared even sporadically, the author might also, I think, decide to glean a second harvest and take it to the printers. All this suggests that a war was going on between at least some of the dramatists and the players. By and large the authors respected the inviolability of the 'run': even Jonson almost always allowed a year or so to pass before printing, though common sense and Thomas Middleton gave the assurance that it was best to get a play 'published when the general voice of the people had seald it for good, and the newnesse of it made it much more desired'.[1] Naturally only a few of those who defied the players would shout the fact from a title-page or an epistle. On the other hand—this is important for Shakespeare —the dramatists who published 'with consent' would not necessarily supply an epistle or dedication before 1605 (the date of the authorised *Hamlet*, the last play barring *Troilus* the publication of which Shakespeare could have initiated) because, as Francis Burton acknowledged in 1607, plays were then 'published without Inscriptions'.

I date the more aggressive attitude of the dramatists 'about 1599' for various reasons. Jonson, already renowned in 1598, began only in 1600 to publish his own plays, and Dekker seems to have started on the same road in the same year—the sale of several of these plays dating from 1599. Greg tells us that around 1599 the prices of plays began to fluctuate considerably, and there are signs that a new type of agreement ('for the use of the company': cf. p. 186 above) was now sometimes negoti-

---

[1] Middleton, *The Family of Love*, 1608. Miss Albright thought that 'Jonson . . . seemed to have no difficulty in getting his plays into print as soon as he liked' (*op. cit.*, p. 234), but, if so, why did he delay so regularly? 'Ménage observed that in the Paris of his youth (*c.* 1630) plays seldom got into print until a year after their first performance' F. P. Wilson reminds us (*Retrospect*, p. 88), and in London too a 'protected life' of this length would have been desirable. (Cf. also Miss Albright, pp. 260, 249 ff., 240, for the gap between production and publication.) Some plays were held up, of course, by the printer (*The Knight of the Burning Pestle* for two years; cf. also Chambers, *Eliz. Stage*, III, 184, n. 2) but a man like Jonson who kept in touch with the printer to proof-read would scarcely have tolerated many long delays.

ated. As a boost for the dramatists the issue late in 1598 of Meres's *Palladis Tamia* must have been decisive, for the names of 'popular' writers were for the first time laid before the world as a subject of interest, while play title-pages printed the authors' names increasingly from about 1598–9,[1] and the personal element in the War of the Theatres (*c.* 1599–1601), a publicity stunt rather than a genuine war, reinforced the well-known author's claims when treating with the players.

That the dramatists took the law into their own hands was, of course, stated quite explicitly by Heywood: 'some haue vsed a double sale of their labours, first to the Stage, and after to the presse' (*The Rape of Lucrece*, 1608).

*   *   *

A secondary purpose of this Appendix is to question the prevalent view that 'Shakespeare took no care to see that his plays were published'.[2] There are no signs of authorial proof-reading in the quartos; no epistles, dedications etc. by the author adorn them; and some are badly printed. What, then, can be said to the contrary? So many perfectly proper publications were not proof-read by their writers that I attach no great importance to this negative evidence: and the absence of authorial prefatory matter falls into the same category of negative evidence, indeed, an informed contemporary witnesses to the effect that dedications with plays were the exception rather than the rule. As for the quality of the printing, the greatest disappointment for Shakespeare must have been the *Hamlet* of 1604–5, and it may be not without significance that, apart from the special case of *Troilus and Cressida*, 1609, the stream of good texts came to an abrupt end in 1605 (suggesting, perhaps, that a badly produced good quarto annoyed the author very little less than a bad quarto).

Some have held that the dramatist had no right to concern himself with publication: to this I retort that many dramatists did so concern themselves, if only to the tune of a dedication, once such interference grew into a custom. (A custom, say the lawyers, can become a right: *consuetudo pro lege servatur.*) Furthermore, the Shakespearian good

---

[1] Shakespeare's name figured on the title-pages of Q1 of *Love's Labour's Lost*, 1598, of Q2 of *Richard II*, 1598, of Q2 of *Richard III*, 1598, and seems to have become generally known either in 1598 or in 1599.

[2] F. P. Wilson, *Retrospect*, p. 97. Cf. also above, p. 12.

quartos brought out to replace bad ones demand our special attention (*Romeo, Hamlet*, and probably Q1 of *Love's Labour's Lost*). Why were so few bad texts by other dramatists superseded in this way?[1] Could it be because their writers lacked influence? That the writer as well as the players instigated these replacements seems to be admitted by Shakespeare's fellows in their complaint that bad texts redounded to 'the iniury and disgrace of the Authors'.[2] By the merest chance we hear that Shakespeare was 'much offended' by the unauthorised publication of *The Passionate Pilgrim*: I cannot imagine that, despite the modern myth of his complete indifference to the printing of his plays, the bad quartos could have failed to offend him as much, or rather more. Did he not rate reputation as the immortal part of a man? Would he have felt less bitter than Achilles when he found that his fame was 'shrewdly gored' . . . by a scarecrow press? A bad text did less damage to the players, the soundness of whose commodity would re-emerge when next they put on their production, than to the author, whose literary reputation might suffer permanently.

I am running close to a paradox in offering a Shakespeare sensitive about the bad quartos and yet giving no visible signs of interest in the good quartos. The replacement of bad ones by good ones, however, surely points to the author rather than to the actors: and if he chose not to proof-read or dedicate the second quartos of *Romeo* or *Hamlet* we must conclude that the other good quartos might have reached their printers from him or through his mediation, since the chief reason against Shakespeare's personal solicitude for these good texts is again nothing more than the absence of proof-reading and dedications etc. I would repeat, too, that Shakespeare's position in his company was such that the issue of his good quartos must have had his approval at the very least (cf. p. 12): their mere publication seems to me a visible sign of Shakespeare's interest in these 'good' texts.

What, then, can we guess about Shakespeare's general attitude to publication? Miss Albright provides a clue in her Preface: '*publication* has been used in its technical sense to include the public performance, as well as the printing and selling, of plays'. Later she discusses the 'apology usually made by a dramatist publishing his works', namely,

---

[1] Kirschbaum (*Stationers*, p. 4) writes: 'Good quartos of *Doctor Faustus* and *Philaster* replaced the bad texts in 1616 and 1622 respectively. The other non-Shakespeare bad quartos were never followed by good texts.' The 1616 *Doctor Faustus*, however, was not a good quarto of the same sort as Shakespeare's.

[2] Cf. p.12, n. 2.

'that the play was written for the stage and therefore loses something through the lack of scene and voice and action'. (Marston, the most emphatic spokesman of this viewpoint, declared on more than one occasion that '*Comedies* are writ to be spoken, not read: Remember the life of these things consists in action . . .')[1] The theatre gave the primary form of publication, and quarto play-books were aimed at the theatre-goer as a 'follow-up', hence the careful directions on the title-page as to company, play-house and favourite parts. Shakespeare proved his worth in the theatre, and therefore could afford to be careless about the 'second publication' (Beaumont's phrase, referring to the first edition of *The Faithful Shepherdess*), which in any case could be regarded only as a faint shadow of the real thing. The reader familiar with the play would not be baffled by untidy stage directions and variations in the names in speech prefixes: he bought his quarto for the poetry and that, except in a very few disappointing texts, he was given in a form as near the stage-version as made no difference.

Shakespeare's failure to supervise the printing of his plays no longer amazes us as it did our forbears. Mr J. B. Priestley described recently the tremendous creative effort that goes into the staging of a play after one has completed the manuscript, and confessed that for the dramatist the printed play comes as something of an anti-climax thereafter[2]: from Marston to the present day it is the same story. And we can excuse Shakespeare as well by remembering that, despite the meticulous proof-reading of Ben Jonson and some others, his indifference to the correctness of textual details is in keeping with his age and in no sense exceptional. After all, Spenser's indifference to the consistency of his narrative in *The Faerie Queene* comes to much the same thing: inadvertently he switches Redcross and Guyon (III.2.4), or separates Arthur and Guyon and a little later depicts them as travelling-companions (II.11.3, III.1.1), and so on.[3] Authors who proof-read their own work frequently did so very carelessly, and even when correcting a 'bad' text with a view to using it as printer's copy, and therefore conscious of the existence of errors, might allow hundreds of further errors to slip into their 'authorised' version—as, apparently, in the case of

---

[1] Marston, *The Fawn*, Q2: cf. also Q1, and *The Malcontent*, and Miss Albright, *op. cit.*, p. 207 ff.

[2] At the Tenth International Shakespeare Conference, Stratford-upon-Avon, 1961.

[3] Cf. Janet Spens, *Spenser's Faerie Queene An Interpretation*, 1934, Josephine W. Bennett, *The Evolution of 'The Faerie Queene'* (Chicago 1942).

Browne's *Religio Medici*.[1] I find Dr Johnson's indifference to the gross inaccuracies to which Boswell drew his attention in *The Lives of the Poets* much more extraordinary than Shakespeare's to minor textual blemishes.

Greg held that it is 'foolish to suppose that Shakespeare was indifferent to the fate of his own works':

> The mere length of some of his plays, of *Hamlet*, of *Richard III*, of *Coriolanus* for example, must have made it difficult to produce them in their entirety on the stage, and suggests that he had an alternative mode of publication in view.[2]

For the reasons indicated, I am tempted to modify F. P. Wilson's conclusion, 'there is no evidence or likelihood that he oversaw the printing of any of the quartos'—to read: 'There is little positive evidence but some likelihood that he initiated the printing of his good quartos.' A small change, but the editorial consequences are far from small. For if I am right it follows that Shakespeare did not care if an untidy draft such as *Love's Labour's Lost* Q1 was put on the market, and the possibility of alternative readings or 'second thoughts' grows in proportion with his indifference to a truly finalised text.

[1] Cf. *Religio Medici*, ed. J.-J. Denonain (Cambridge 1955), p. x.
[2] Greg, *F.F.*, p. 2.

Appendix B (Cf. page 180)

GEORGE WILKINS AND PERICLES

THOSE who have discussed the play *Pericles* and Wilkins's claims as part-author have, I believe, without exception failed to notice one early work of Wilkins not entirely irrelevant to the subject.[1] Five books bearing his name are usually quoted as yielding 'parallels' and 'stylistic evidence': *Three Miseries of Barbary* (c. 1606), *The Miseries of Enforced Marriage* (1607), the novel called *The Painful Adventures of Pericles* (1608), and two collaborations, *Jests To Make You Merry* (1607, with Dekker), and *The Travels of the Three English Brothers* (1607, with Day and W. Rowley). The hitherto neglected work is as long as the other five together: *The Historie of Iustine* ('Containing a Narration of Kingdomes, from the beginning of the Assyrian Monarchy, vnto the raigne of the Emperour Augustus . . . by that famous Historiographer Iustine, and now againe newly translated into English, by G.W. . . . 1606.') According to *O.E.D.* this 'G.W.' is G. Woodcocke,[2] but the *Short-Title Catalogue* and *Cambridge Bibliography of English Literature* expand G.W. as G. W[ilkins]. I have no idea upon what these identifications are based—possibly seventeenth-century owners wrote 'G. Woodcocke' and 'G. Wilkins' into their copies—but the ascription to Wilkins can be accepted as certain.

H. Dugdale Sykes long ago drew attention to a 'parallel' in Wilkins's novel *Pericles* to Sidney's *Arcadia*—which, as Sykes observed on another page, also turns up in the source of *Enforced Marriage*, an anonymously published pamphlet of 1605 entitled *Two Most Vnnaturall and Bloodie Murthers.*[3]

shee did resemble you: though as farre short of your perfection, as her selfe dying, was of her flourishing . . .[4]

They went forward to the triumph, in which noble exercise they

---

[1] Some of the points raised in this appendix were however passed on to F. D. Hoeniger, who used them in his New Arden edition of *Pericles*, 1963, p. lx.

[2] *O.E.D.*, Supplement.

[3] Sykes, *Sidelights on Shakespeare* (Stratford-upon-Avon 1919), pp. 96–8, 143 ff.

[4] *Arcadia*, 1590, Bk. 2, chap. 23 (Sykes, p. 176).

came almost all, as short of *Pericles* perfections, as a body dying, of a life flourishing.[1]

he was so altered in disposition from that which he was, and so short from the perfection which he had, as a body dying is of a life florishing . . .[2]

The same words occur in G.W.'s dedication of *Iustine*:

my deuotion accounted the many I might make choise of, as short of your perfections, as a body dyeng, is of a life flourishing.

Before I recognised the repetition in the last passage the ascription of *Iustine* to Wilkins already seemed plausible to me. The dedication begins and ends very much as in the *Pericles* novel:

RIght worthie Sir, *Artaxerxes* sir-named *Long-hand*, the fift king of Persia, vsed to haue the Chronicles . . . read before him euerie night . . .

. . . deuising to whom I might specially dedicate the same as an euerlasting monument erected to his *name* . . . *I submitted me to your censure* . . . (*Iustine*; my italics)

Right woorthy Sir, Opinion, that in these daies wil make wise men fooles, and the most fooles . . . seeme wise, hath made me euer feare to throw my selfe vpon the racke of Censure . . .

. . . [I] promise [to] . . . inheighten your *Name* and Memorie . . . my boldnesse now *submitting it selfe to your censure* . . .
(*Pericles*; my italics)

The ending ('submitting to your censure') was a commonplace, but the opening words together with the involved sentence that follows, commencing with a noun (Artaxerxes, Opinion), would alert most readers if aware that the initials of the authors of the two books were the same. More telling than these coincidences, I thought, were some stylistic habits of Wilkins not listed in Sykes's essay. In the *Pericles* novel he repeatedly begins sentences, and clauses after a colon or semi-colon, with 'which' or 'by which', 'to which', 'of which' etc.; and he uses participial constructions far more than is normal in the same positions. Less significant, but still indicative, he has a partiality for starting

---

[1] *The Painfull Aduentures of Pericles*, ed. K. Muir (Liverpool 1953), p. 38. All page references below are to this edition.
[2] *Two Most Vnnaturall and Bloodie Murthers*, ed. J. P. Collier, 1863, p. 6.

sentences with 'this' or 'by this', 'to this' etc.; with 'thus'; with 'in brief', and other similar locutions. Examples of the two principal features ('which' and 'participial' openings) crop up on almost every page, as on p. 50: 'Which name of Traytor being againe redoubled, *Pericles* then ... boldely replyed ...'; 'Which noblenesse of his, the king inwardly commending ... he answered ...'; 'Which wordes were no sooner vttered, but *Thaysa* ...'

The same striking mannerisms are found in G.W.'s *Iustine*. This of course proves nothing conclusively, since G.W. followed his Latin original, and other hurriedly written pamphlets of the period exhibit the characteristic tricks of Wilkins. The decisive clue for Wilkins's authorship of *Iustine* is his weakness for 'as short of ... perfections, as a body dying is of a life flourishing'. Sykes, unaware of its reappearance in *Iustine*, thought this turn of phrase, together with some lesser 'parallels', sufficient evidence to argue for Wilkins's authorship of *Two Murthers*—which would have to be granted if it could be proved that Wilkins definitely borrowed other things from *Arcadia*. (Shakespeare's co-author of the play *Pericles* certainly did,[1] and this lends some support to the view that Wilkins was the co-author: but among Wilkins's signed works no second indisputable borrowing from *Arcadia* has so far been traced.) Wilkins's other stylistic tricks are of interest, however, in so far as they may throw light on the authorship of the play *Pericles*— where 'which' openings, for example, occur in considerable numbers.[2]

> *Cleon.* The which when any shall not gratifie,
> Or pay you with vnthankfulnesse in thought,
> Be it our Wiues, our Children, or our selues,
> The Curse of heauen and men succeed their euils:
> Till when, the which (I hope) shall neare be seene:
> Your Grace is welcome to our Towne and vs.
> *Peri.* Which welcome wee'le accept, feast here awhile,

$$(I.4.101-7)$$

The text of the play being bad many heavy stops have naturally

---

[1] As Steevens showed: cf. Sykes, *op. cit.*, p. 174.

[2] Not all the mannerisms I have listed occur in all of Wilkins's signed works. They are most common in the novel *Pericles* and in *Iustine* and *Three Miseries of Barbary*. They give some help, I believe, in separating Wilkins's share from Dekker's in *Jests To Make You Merry*. In *Enforced Marriage* they are found in less profusion, much as in the non-Shakespearian parts of the play *Pericles*: quite obviously some of them would have a smaller chance of survival in a play.

vanished: a modernised text therefore helps to give a clearer picture of the unknown author's partiality for 'which' openings.

> Which by my knowledge found, the sinful father
> Seem'd not to strike, but smooth. But thou know'st this,
> 'Tis time to fear when tyrants seem to kiss.
> Which fear so grew in me I hither fled . . .
> When all, for mine, if I may call offence,
> Must feel war's blow, who spares not innocence;
> Which love to all, of which thyself art one,
> Who now reprov'dst me for't—
>
> (I.2.77–95, Alexander)[1]

Objections have been raised against Sykes's stylistic evidence in favour of Wilkins's part-authorship of *Pericles*—on the ground that the stylistic peculiarities cited by Sykes were mostly quite commonplace.[2] The evidence now added deserves the same label, and yet, I think, strengthens the case for Wilkins. For, as Greg observed of the commonplace letterforms occurring in both Shakespeare's signatures and Hand D of *More*, 'multiple agreement acquires considerable significance, even though the individual forms may be common'. Even if all Wilkins's stylistic idiosyncrasies can be paralleled, does any single work of the period offer as many correspondences as the non-Shakespearian portions of *Pericles*?

Wilkins's authorship of *Iustine* is important not only in that it confirms certain stylistic tendencies equally marked in the novel *Pericles*. In *Iustine* we have a narrative dealing with the same historical period as the unhistorical *Pericles* (Antiochus the Great figures largely in *Iustine* and in the play), we have the same geographical centre (the eastern Mediterranean), the same literary atmosphere (the history specialises in tales of violence, shipwreck, incests, brothels, sudden reversals, etc.), and some names not found in the *Apollonius* sources of the story (i.e. Twine's and Gower's versions), names such as Pericles and Lysimachus. What is more, the addition of *Iustine* to the body of his writings brings out Wilkins's special interest in Mediterranean histories: *Three Miseries of Barbary*, *The Travels of Three English Brothers*, *Pericles* (the novel) and *Iustine* all being located in the same area, it becomes more likely that

---

[1] The 'which' test confirms the usual division of the play into two parts, Acts I–II by another, Acts III–V by Shakespeare; Gower's speeches go with Acts I–II. This 'test' should not, of course, be taken too seriously.

[2] See Baldwin Maxwell's valuable chapter on *A Yorkshire Tragedy* in *Studies in the Shakespeare Apocrypha* (New York 1956), p. 193 ff.

Pericles the play originated with Wilkins too—rather than that he finished a draft by Shakespeare.[1]

Wilkins's *Iustine* also confirms an impression created by his other works, that he was an essentially parasitic writer. His two plays, *Travels* and *Miseries*, often follow their sources very closely, the novel *Pericles* transcribes some paragraphs from Twine almost *verbatim* (cf. Muir's notes), and *Jests To Make You Merry* like many another jest-book draws upon its predecessors (e.g. on *Pasquils Iests*, 1604). In *Iustine* too he preferred to follow another (Arthur Golding's translation as well as the Latin original) rather than to trust to his invention: and whoever plotted the play *Pericles* likewise decided to make do with the very episodes of Twine's novel (or of Wilkins's novel, if that antedated the play), even though this narrative structure imposed a strain on the dramatic form.

If the translator of *Iustine* was the only begetter of the play *Pericles*, as I think—Shakespeare either re-writing a new dramatist's less successful scenes, or finishing where Wilkins left off—this forces us to reconsider the possibility of a lost foreign source. Chambers already felt that 'there may have been some unrecorded channel of transmission'[2]—largely because one or two names in the play occur in earlier versions of the Apollonius story but not in the two principal sources of the play (Twine and Gower). The case for a lost source is much stronger than Chambers imagined, however, especially as presented in a book not indexed by him, S. Singer's *Apollonius von Tyrus Untersuchungen über das Fortleben des antiken Romans in spätern Zeiten* (Halle a.S., 1895). As Singer showed, the play and several German-Scandinavian versions correspond in significant details not found in Twine and Gower.

1. Antiochus decides to spare Pericles on account of his beauty (Singer, p. 40):

> Yet hope, succeeding from so faire a tree
> As your faire selfe, doth tune vs otherwise;
> Fourtie dayes longer we doe respite you,
> (*Pericles*, I.1.114–16)

ick dy ytzundes dat Höuet scholde lathen affschlahn / öuerst vmme dyner schönen gestalt willen / so wil ick dy dree Dage Respyt

---

[1] Cf. J. C. Maxwell, *Pericles* (C.U.P. edition), 1956, pp. xxii–xxiii. Possibly John Day also had a small share in the writing of the play: cf. F. D. Hoeniger's article in *Sh. Q.*, 1960, vol. XI.

[2] E. K. Chambers, *W. Sh.*, I, 527–8; cf. Hoeniger, *Pericles*, pp. xvii–xviii.

geuen / dat du dy bether bedencken mögest. ('Hamborch' *Appollonius*, B₃ᵇ–B₄ᵃ)[1]

thou hast deserued to be beheaded. Howbeit I will shew thee this courtesie, as to giue thee thirtie daies respite to bethinke thy selfe of this matter. (Twine, B₃ᵃ)[2]

> But loke well thou nought despise
> Thyn owne life: for of my grace
> Of thirtie daies full a space
> I graunte the to ben aduised.   (Gower)

2. In Twine and some other versions Apollonius tells the fishermen of Pentapolis his name, but in the play and 'Hamborch' *Appollonius* he speaks evasively, concealing his identity (Singer, p. 8):

> What I haue been, I haue forgot to know;
> But what I am, want teaches me to thinke on:
>   (*Pericles* II.1.71–2)

Ick bin nicht mehr deyenne / de ick was / my hefft dat Meer myne Güder / Ehre vnde Heerlicheit vp einmahl tho lyke genamen. ('Hamborch' *Appollonius*, C₄)

3. Singer also mentioned some other minor coincidences (cf. pp. 51–2), but overlooked what seems to me the most obvious one. In the play and 'Hamborch' version Marina knows, when Lysimachus visits her in the brothel, that he is the governor (king), and therefore appeals to him, as one 'born to honour', to demonstrate his higher qualities and spare her. (The names Marina and Lysimachus occur only in the play, of course.) Gower suppressed the episode altogether, Twine kept 'Marina' in ignorance of the disguised 'Lysimachus's' status and so altered her appeal. The *Pericles* novel here corresponds to the play (which it does not in 1 and 2 above).

I heare say you're of honourable parts, and are the Gouernour of this place ... If you were borne to honour, shew it now ... (*Pericles*, IV.6.79–91)

If as you say (my Lorde) you are the Gouernour ... If the eminence

---

[1] *Appollonius. Eine Schöne vnde Kortwylige Historia* ('Hamborch Im Iahre 1601.'). Other German-Scandinavian versions correspond closely to this one in all points raised below.

[2] *The Patterne of painefull Aduentures* ('Gathered into English by Laurence Twine') (c. 1594). All quotations are from this edition.

of your place came vnto you by discent, and the royalty of your blood, let not your life prooue your birth a bastard . . . (*Pericles novel*, p. 89)

Du bist ein Köninck / vnde schölen alle Dögede in dy lüchten / so bidde ick dy / du willest dörch de Döget der Sterckheit dynen bösen lüsten wedderstahn. ('Hamborch' *Appollonius*, $F_5{}^b$)

Similarities in the 'Hamborch' *Appollonius* to Twine also suggest a lost version of the story. In my first extract (p. 197) 'Respyt . . . dat du dy bether bedencken mögest' is identical with Twine's 'respite to be-thinke thy selfe'. If a lost ancestor existed—the story was a favourite in medieval and early modern times and went through scores of shapes in manuscript and print—it would probably be in Latin, especially if it influenced both German-Scandinavian and English congeners. It is possible, of course, that the author of *Pericles* knew one of the German-Scandinavian texts and that Twine's few echoes amount to no more than coincidence. In either case, use of a lost Latin text or use of a German-Scandinavian version, Wilkins's claims to the authorship of *Pericles* grow with the knowledge that he was active as a translator.

Appendix C (*Cf. page* 13)

THE CAPTIVES: FOUL PAPERS OR COPY?

GREG classed the manuscript of Heywood's *Captives* as foul papers;
Bowers had misgivings (cf. p. 13, n. 4). The Malone Society editor,
Arthur Brown, echoed Greg's views in 1953—Bowers's had not then
appeared—and added: 'It is uncertain, but unlikely, that there was ever
a rougher draft behind it' [i.e. behind the extant text] (p. xii). Since
believers in Shakespeare's 'unblotted papers' point to Heywood's play
as their best example of 'free composition' it is worthwhile examining
it with some care, the more so as our general theorising about foul
papers and intermediate fair copies (cf. Notes A and B, pp. 17, 19)
also turns on this text.

Changes made *currente calamo* put it beyond question that the author
himself wrote the manuscript we possess. Here and there he improvised
as he went along—as other fast writers have done in copying out their
own work. Sometimes he also anticipated or repeated a word or phrase
from a neighbouring line:

(*a*)　　　　　　and off these peevishe harlotryes at home,
　　　　　　　　make a mch greater [marry syr], market,
　　　　Mildewe. marry syr
　　　　　　　　that weare a tale' woorth listninge.

(*b*)　　　a remarke able raskall, a damnable [raskall, and]
　　　　　deceaver and a most substantiall Cinner,

(*c*)　　　Raphael I am cald
　　　　　A marchant in [my Lodginge] Marcellis and my' Lodging⟨e⟩
　　　　　Is at the parrott in the Markett-place.

(*d*)　　　and eather lend[vs] som Comffort to our greiffes,
　　　　　or send vs hence dispayringe and ashamd,

(*e*)　　　no man better, [suer] now it will go on my syde
　　　　　this is my owne mayster suer hee' canott bee so vnatrall[1]

---

[1] Pp. 11, 23, 23, 31, 83, in the Malone Society's edition, 1953, from which I
quote throughout this note.

Any fast writer could, of course, carry several lines in his head before committing one to paper. The deletions in my five quotations, however, share one unusual feature. They all connect with a neighbouring word literally, or follow or precede a word connecting with another word in this way: mar(ry)—mar(ket), (remark)able—(damn)able, Mar(cellis) —Mar(kett), (l)end—(s)end, (bet)ter—(mays)ter. This suggests the possibility of eye-skip, though a mental jump in the act of writing is not out of question. And eye-skip seems the likeliest explanation of the following:

> (*f*) Enter godfr who es that that offers violens to these gates.
>   frey   that never yet offended. what want you
>   Scrib: that wch the earth [what want you]
>   dothe fforbidd none but freely yeilds to all,[1]

Fortunately it is possible to compare *Captives* with another Heywood holograph which was definitely copied and not a first draft. His *Escapes of Jupiter*, bound up in the same collection of plays with *Captives* (British Museum, Egerton 1994), consists of various scenes from his own *Golden Age* and *Silver Age*: whether or not it is based on slightly different versions of the *Ages* from those printed, which Greg thought unlikely, it follows and cannot precede the *Ages* since, as Greg showed,[2] in writing out *Escapes* Heywood frequently copied from *Ages* only to strike out what he had transcribed and paraphrase or change.

Escapes has never been printed—Greg published only a few extracts —and therefore the relevance of this text to the discussion of *Captives*, and its great importance as an example of authorial 'instability', have not been properly appreciated. Suffice it to say that there are many examples of eye-skip in passages that follow the *Ages verbatim*. Perhaps because of his atrocious handwriting Heywood tended to jump from one line to another, often to a word at the same point in the line: to make this clear I reproduce the lineation of the manuscript (the first quotation below in each pair).

> 1.   By all my honours; more; by all the sweetes
>   I hope ffor in [my] your loves fruition   (F. 75[b])

---

[1] P. 42. The Malone Society editor notes that *what want you* in l. 2 was 'apparently added later'. I imagine that the words stood in an earlier MS. between lines 2 and 3, and that Heywood, or someone dictating to him, associated them with the wrong line because working too hurriedly.

[2] 'The Escapes of Jupiter. An Autograph Play of Thomas Heywood's' (in *Palaestra*, vol. 148, 1925).

By all my honours, and by all the sweets
I hope for in your loues fruition   (*Golden Age*, D₃ᵃ)

2.   report off your rare bewty wᵗʰ the loue
and zeale I beare to a sequestred lyffe
[welcome La⟨.⟩] compeld mee to this habit
Diana welcom Lady   (F. 77ᵃ)

Report of your rare beauty, with my loue
And zeale I still beare to a virgins life,
Haue drawne me to your seruice.
Diana. Welcome Lady.   (*G. Age*, E₁)

3.   who shall [the] bee then Cald Bacchus [by] Bimater
Hee shall bee the ffyrst planter off the vine
And ffor that Cawse bee [Cald] ⌐stild⌐ the god off grape⟨.⟩
(F. 86ᵇ)

His name Il'e *Bachus* call, and being growne,
Stile him, *The God of Grapes*;   (*Silver Age*, K₁ᵃ)

4.   Let none [lyk] the secrets off the gods Inquire
least they lyke her by heavenly flames expire   (F. 86ᵇ)

Let none the secrets of the Gods inquire,
Lest they (like her) be strooke with heauenly fire.
(*S. Age*, K₁ᵃ)

5. Alas poor Amphitrio [that] I pitty ⌐thee⌐ that art to
bee made a Cuckold, against thy wyves will   (F. 89ᵃ)

Alas poore *Amphitrio* I pitty thee that art to be made cuckold
against thy wiues will   (*S. Age*, D₁ᵃ)

6. marry I serue my Lord Amphitrio, To this place
I am goinge, and Com to [deliver] speake wᵗʰ my Lady
now what art thou [the] wiser? Nay Iff thou beest a
a [*sic*] good ffellowe lett mee pass to deliuer my message (F. 89ᵃ)

Hither I go, I serue my Maister, and come to speak with my Lady,
what art thou the wiser? nay, if thou beest a good fellow let me
passe by thee.   (*S. Age*, D₁ᵇ)

7.   as hee
hath gott my [shape,] name so hee hath gott my
shape   (F. 90ᵃ)

as he hath got my name, hee hath got my shape
(*S. Age*, D₂ᵇ)

8.   I am nowe Comminge
    looke too't I will so tickle thee and thy cownterfett
    [Comminge] companions theire   (F. 93ᵇ)[1]

    I am now comming, looke to't, I'le tickle you with
    your counterfeit companions there   (S. Age, E₃ᵇ)

Heywood himself noticed his slips in the above examples and corrected
them: but he also missed some and left others.

9. heeres a Coyle Indeede to keepe ffyare and Toe asuder
    I woonder the kinge should keepe his doughter so
    Close when for ought I can see shee hath no mind to
    bee abroad   (F. 79ᵃ)

    Heer's a coyle to keep fire and tow a sunder. I wonder the King
    should shut his daughter vp so close: for any thing I see, she hath
    no minde to a man.   (Golden Age, H₁ᵃ)

It looks as if Heywood caught 'keepe' from the previous line in Escapes,
and therefore dropped 'vp' rather than change 'keepe' to 'shut'.

To return to Captives. Not only does its text suffer from what looks
like eye-skip, a malady incident to copies rather than to first drafts and
one to which its author succumbed in copying parts of Escapes—it also
harbours in some profusion three further types of error common in
copies and comparatively rare in first drafts: the omission of essential
words, mishearing and mislineation.

1. Omissions. These are easily checked in the footnotes of the Malone
Society edition, whence it will appear that they run right through the
text. On F.59ᵇ four words, without which the dialogue collapses, had
to be interlined. Here are two in adjacent lines:

        Comodityes in all coasts woorthy coyne
        christian or heathen, by whome In distresses.
        I coold have raysd a ffortune, man vndoon
        that I should loose you thus.

Both 'have' (l. 3) and 'loose' (l. 4) were interlined with carets.

In Escapes similar omissions are found: 'they say, an ⌐owld¬ woman is
better for that then salt peter' (F.79ᵃ; cf. Golden Age, H₁ᵃ: 'they say an
old woman is better for that then Salt-peter'); 'Iff shee bee a ⌐right
woman¬ shee will only stooddy to loose that' (F.79ᵇ; cf. Golden Age, H₂ᵇ:
'if shee bee a right woman, shee will haue a minde onely to loose that').

---

[1] Heywood first wrote 'Comminge', then tried to alter to 'Companions' by
writing 'p' over the second 'm', then deleted the word.

2. *Mishearing.*

(*a*)   speake off that
         wch nwe concernes vs most where may wee [might] meete.

(*b*)   shee might have sayde
         ffor saffeguard off his [next] necke.

(*c*)   and I off that
         by reason off a late could I have gott
         [and] ⌈am⌉ at this Instant gulty[1]:

Some examples of mishearing remained uncorrected in the manuscript:
'the rocks will shelter's, vs' (l. 918), 'that ought to bee in lyffe and
government / to oothers and example' (l. 2061, *and* for *an*), 'and thus
saccoutred. wth his beaver vpp' (l. 2565).

3. *Mislineation.*

(*a*)   lett mee possesse myne owne, these' are my slaves
                    [these are] my vtensills my moove ables: and bought,
                    wth myne owne private ⌈coyne⌉ [Coyne to wch I]
         Sarlab.   to wch I am witnes.

         Mildew,   and by' the heyre I'l dragge them as myne owne
                    weart ffrom the' holly alter

         Palest: succor [Helpe,]

         Scrib: Helpe,[2]

(*b*)   Is theire no lawe in ffrance,
         Ashbur   yes syr to punish [these]
                    these chastityes seducers:

         Mildew: giue mee ffyar
                    I will not leave off all this monastery

---

[1] Pp. 49, 71, 96. In (*b*) 'next' might, however, be eye-skip, for the text continues: 'Myde my sceanes doon / the next act lyes amongst them'. Other possible
examples: 'and [whethe] wth no tarde pace. where shall I hyde mee, / [or]
whether ⌈shall I⌉ ffly' (l. 1080; possibly eye-skip); your-our (l. 1294); purchase-
purses (l. 2001); Case-cease (l. 2033); though-thou (l. 2285); liberty-lyvery
(l. 2521).

[2] P. 61. The Malone Society editor comments on the third line: '*coyne*] interlined above *Coyne* with caret after deletion, probably accidental, of *Coyne* with
to wch I'.

(c)   sett sayle ffor fflorens:

ffactor,   please you S^r [I'l stew]
                    I'l steward all that busines,:

Thoms   I'l meane tyme[1]

Mishearing and mislineation can be found close together:

(d)   ffor whome [wher] ⌜weare⌝ you a ffishinge.

Mildew,   marry for Maydes.
                    woold I knewe howe to catche them, but my gutts.
                    howe they are sweld wth Sea-brine.

Sarlab: tis good phisicke [to]
        to   cure thee off the mangy,
Mildewe,   wretched man[2]

Eye-skip, omission, mishearing, mislineation: some dispute is possible about a few of my examples, which could fall into more than one
category, but I think it will be conceded that these four kinds of corruption leave unmistakable traces throughout *Captives*—traces that
immediately suggest a copyist (that is, the author as copyist) rather than
'free composition'. Why then did Greg define the text as foul papers?

Partly, perhaps, because he did not comb the manuscript in order to
check on the types of error I have listed; and partly because these errors
taken singly are not necessarily suspicious. Each type could conceivably
occur in a first draft, e.g. an author may 'hear'—and mishear—the
words he writes; as he puts down 'market' his pen may write 'marry',
a word he has just used or is about to use; he may even write nonsense,
through omission, especially if he composes swiftly. But I know of no
authenticated first draft riddled by *four* such familiar 'copyist's errors'.

Another consideration that no doubt influenced Greg is that 'correction is much less frequent [in *Escapes*] than in *The Captives*'.[3]
Escapes being in the main a copy one may therefore assume that
Captives required more correction because not a copy. It is possible,
however, that the exceptional cleanness of *Escapes* results from its being
a copy of a copy, i.e. that Heywood was not composing freely in those

---

[1] Pp. 62, 104. In both (b) and (c) Heywood wrote words required by the verse
pattern in the following line.

[2] P. 47. The verse pattern necessitated the change with 'to'. Other examples of
mislineation occur in ll. 821, 3181.

[3] *Op. cit.*, p. 213.

passages which depart from *Ages*, but had already drafted *Escapes* in its present form before transcribing the only surviving text. This seems to be borne out by my sixth extract, where Heywood anticipates 'deliver' by two lines though 'deliver' is not used at that point in *Silver Age*.

Unambiguous signs of free composition are sprinkled through *Captives*, as I have admitted, and, to a lesser extent, through *Escapes*. The simplest explanation of all the facts will emerge, I think, from a comparison of Heywood with Shelley and other very fast writers. Shelley habitually scribbled down his first ideas for a poem in a very rough state, and sometimes several 'foul' drafts intervened between the first and final one; and even his fair copy becomes foul every so often as alternative readings pressed into his mind. Each manuscript after the first therefore contains portions in transcript and other portions where, dissatisfied, Shelley began composing afresh.[1] Deviations in *Escapes* from *Golden Age* and *Silver Age* prove that Heywood also changed earlier versions of his works very readily; and therefore the remarkable cleanness of *Captives*, coupled with the profusion of copyist's errors, argues strongly against Greg's definition of the text as foul papers. *Captives* seems to me very like some of Shelley's intermediate or nearly-finished texts, a transcript 'fouled' by frequent bursts of free composition.

[1] Cf. Neville Rogers, *Shelley at Work*, especially chap. 12.

Index

(*This is a selective index, and not every reference to an author or book or play is included. Works of known authorship are listed under the author's name: only Shakespeare's and Greg's are entered separately*)